Emotional Labour in Criminal Justice and Criminology

This book is the first volume to explore criminal justice work and criminological research through the lens of emotional labour. A concept first coined 30 years ago, emotional labour research seeks to explore the ways in which people manage their emotions in order to achieve the aims of their organisations, and understand the impact of this type of work on workers and service users.

The chapters in this edited collection explore work in a wide range of criminal justice institutions as well as the penal voluntary sector. In addition to literature review chapters which consolidate what we already know, this book includes case study chapters which extend our knowledge of how emotional labour is performed in specific contexts, and in relation to certain types of work. *Emotional Labour in Criminal Justice and Criminology* covers topics such as prisoners who die from natural causes in prison, to the work of independent domestic violence advisors and the use of emotion by death penalty lawyers in the US.

An accessible and compelling read, this book presents ground-breaking qualitative and quantitative research which will be critical to criminologists, criminal justice practitioners, students of criminology and academics in the fields of social policy and public service.

Jake Phillips is a Reader in Criminology at Sheffield Hallam University. His research is primarily focused on the intersection between policy and practice in the field of probation and community sanctions. In recent years, he has conducted research on the emotional labour of probation practice, people who die whilst under probation supervision and the impact of inspection and regulation on probation policy and practice.

Chalen Westaby is a Senior Lecturer in Law at Sheffield Hallam University. She has published primarily in the field of emotional labour. Her empirical qualitative research has focused on legal professionals, law students and most recently, probation officers and criminological researchers. She has also undertaken research into emotion in the legal profession, particularly focusing on empathy and its role within professional practice.

Andrew Fowler is a Senior Lecturer in Criminology at Sheffield Hallam University. As a former probation officer and practice tutor assessor, he also teaches on the Professional Qualification in Probation and the undergraduate criminology programme. He has published work centring on emotional labour in probation practice. Andrew is currently undertaking research into the Skills for Effective Engagement Development Supervision model (SEEDS) for Her Majesty's Prison and Probation Service (HMPPS).

Jaime Waters is a Senior Lecturer in Criminology and Fellow of the Sheffield Institute for Policy Studies at Sheffield Hallam University. Her main research interests include illegal drug use, gambling and emotional labour. She is co-author of *Illegal Drug Use through the Lifecourse* and *Mixed Methods in Criminology* (both with Routledge), and editor of the special issue 'Entering the field of criminological research' in the *British Journal of Community Justice*.

The Editors of *Emotional Labour in Criminal Justice and Criminology* are to be congratulated for bringing together an important and innovative collection of essays that will give all researchers conducting empirical studies in criminology pause for thought about their own emotional labour, as well as that performed by professionals in the criminal justice sector. Foregrounding culture, context and conflict, this book is a must-read for anyone interested in the ethical and emotional dimensions of qualitative methodologies and criminal justice.

— Yvonne Jewkes, Professor of Criminology,
University of Bath

Emotional Labour in Criminal Justice and Criminology brings the topic of emotion work to a range of professions across the criminal justice spectrum. Focussed and in-depth studies deepen our understanding of the multi-faceted experiences, displays and management of emotion in criminal justice work. The book provides criminal justice practitioners, scholars and policy makers with rigorous empirical evidence on the inter-personal and organisational contexts of emotional labour.

— Sharyn Roach Anleu, Matthew Flinders
Distinguished Professor,
Flinders University

Routledge Frontiers of Criminal Justice

For more information about this series, please visit: www.routledge.com/
Routledge-Frontiers-of-Criminal-Justice/book-series/RFCJ

Emotional Labour in Criminal Justice and Criminology

Edited by
Jake Phillips, Chalen Westaby,
Andrew Fowler and Jaime Waters

Routledge
Taylor & Francis Group

LONDON AND NEW YORK

First published 2021
by Routledge
2 Park Square, Milton Park, Abingdon, Oxon OX14 4RN

and by Routledge
52 Vanderbilt Avenue, New York, NY 10017

Routledge is an imprint of the Taylor & Francis Group, an informa business

British Library Cataloguing-in-Publication Data
A catalogue record for this book is available from the British Library

Library of Congress Cataloging-in-Publication Data
Names: Phillips, Jake, editor.
Title: Emotional labour in criminal justice and criminology / edited by Jake Phillips, Chalen Westaby, Andrew Fowler and Jaime Waters.
Description: Abingdon, Oxon ; New York, NY : Routledge, 2020. | Includes bibliographical references and index. |
Identifiers: LCCN 2020007311 | ISBN 9780367152017 (hbk) | ISBN 9780429055669 (ebk)
Subjects: LCSH: Criminal justice, Administration of—Psychological aspects. | Criminology. | Crime—Sociological aspects.
Classification: LCC HV7419 .E52 2020 | DDC 331.7/61364—dc23
LC record available at https://lccn.loc.gov/2020007311

ISBN: 978-0-367-15201-7 (hbk)
ISBN: 978-0-429-05566-9 (ebk)

Typeset in Bembo
by codeMantra

Contents

Illustrations

Figure

Tables

Contributors

Ian T. Adams is a PhD candidate in Political Science at the University of Utah, where he also completed a Master of Public Administration. His research interests include emotional labour, police and improving survey research among law enforcement. Prior to his academic career, Ian served in law enforcement for over 12 years. His dissertation research investigates the perceived intensity of monitoring among public employees, with a primary interest in body-worn cameras. Ian is a 2018 American Society of Public Administration Founders' Fellow, and a 2020 doctoral fellow of the Academy of Criminal Justice Sciences.

Alex Black is a Lecturer in Criminology in the Department of Law and Criminology at Sheffield Hallam University. Alex is a criminologist with an interest in policing and the management of public space. Her recent work has focused on frontline responses to domestic violence, police understandings of cybercrime and the implementation of powers under the Anti-Social Behaviour, Crime and Policing Act 2014.

Lisa Marie Borrelli is a Postdoctoral Researcher in the National Competence Centre for Research (NCCR) – on the move, at the HES-SO Valais-Wallis, Switzerland. She completed her PhD at the Institute of Sociology, University of Bern. Her doctoral dissertation looked at ambivalent laws and emotions of street-level bureaucrats working on irregular migration in the Schengen Area. She conducted ethnographic fieldwork with police and migration authorities in Italy, Switzerland, Germany and Sweden and has further conducted ethnographic research in Lithuania and Latvia. She has also been a visiting researcher at the Centre for Migration Law at Radboud University, Nijmegen, and a visiting graduate student at the Centre for the Study of International Migration at UCLA with the support of the Swiss National Science Foundation Doc.Mobility Grant (172228).

Iain Britton is a Senior Researcher at the Institute for Public Safety, Crime and Justice, University of Northampton, UK. He works with the police and other public safety organisations to encourage the engagement of volunteers and to help and support evidence-based innovation and improvement of volunteering programmes. His research interests focus on police and public safety volunteering, both in the UK and internationally.

Anders Bruhn is a Professor in Social Work and an Assistant Professor in Sociology at Örebro University. His main research areas are work life, organisations and professional groups.

Marian Duggan is a Senior Lecturer in Criminology at the University of Kent. Her research focuses on recognising and responding to gendered experiences of sexual, domestic and hate crime victimisation. Marian is the Chair of the British Society of Criminology's Women Crime and Criminal Justice Network and a long-serving Trustee for the Rising Sun Domestic Violence and Abuse Charity.

Anthony Ellis is a Lecturer in Sociology and Criminology at the University of Salford, UK. His research interests include violence, criminological and social theory. Anthony's current research addresses the recent recorded increases in incidents of serious violence in parts of England and Wales.

Lisa Flower is a Senior Lecturer and Researcher in Sociology and Criminology at the Department of Sociology at Lund University. Her research interests include the emotion work of defence lawyers and the unwritten rules of courtroom interactions. She is currently working on a project exploring how criminal trials and legal professionals are depicted and responded to in online news updates with particular focus on emotions and gender representations.

Andrew Fowler is a Senior Lecturer in Criminology at Sheffield Hallam University. As a former probation officer and practice tutor assessor, he also teaches on the Professional Qualification in Probation and the undergraduate criminology programme. He has published work centring on emotional labour in probation practice. Andrew is currently undertaking research into the Skills for Effective Engagement Development Supervision model (SEEDS) for Her Majesty's Prison and Probation Service (HMPPS).

Sarah Goodrum is currently the Chair of the Criminology and Criminal Justice department at the University of Northern Colorado. Dr Goodrum has more than 16 years of experience conducting research on victimisation, intimate partner abuse and the criminal justice system. She is affiliated with the Center for the Study and Prevention of Violence in the Institute of Behavioral Science at the University of Colorado Boulder, where she served as a Research Associate for two years. In 2016, she coauthored and testified before the Colorado legislature's SB15-214: Committee on School Safety and Youth in Crisis, a project that examines violence in school settings.

Matthew John-William Greife is an Instructor at Colorado State University and a criminal defence attorney practicing at the state and federal levels in Colorado and California. Matthew primarily researches social control and legal processes. His current focus is on understanding what legal and extra-legal variables predict sentencing outcomes for corporations prosecuted for violating environmental laws. Matthew is also interested in understanding how the socialisation of lawyers and other criminal justice actors influences broader legal processes.

Laura Knight is the Director of the Institute for Public Safety, Crime and Justice, University of Northampton, UK. Her research areas of interest include policing, organisational development, volunteering in public safety and driving evidence-based policy and practice. Her latest research has addressed frontline experiences, leadership in violence prevention and understanding the value and impact of volunteering in policing.

Karen Lumsden is an Assistant Professor in Criminology in the School of Sociology and Social Policy at the University of Nottingham. Karen's recent work has focused on police-academic partnerships, constructions of evidence-based policing, and risk and emotional labour in police organisational cultures. She also has expertise in, and has published widely on, interpersonal cybercrime and online abuse and qualitative research methods – specifically reflexivity.

Sharon H. Mastracci is a Professor and the Director of the Programs of Public Service at the University of Utah. She has researched emotional labour in public service for most of her academic career and is currently exploring various facets of use of force and violence in law enforcement and corrections, the emotional labour demanded of these agents of state control, and the fallout of these demands. She hopes to eventually study the effects on workers of working in the Huntsville, Texas death house, the most active execution chamber in the US.

Sarah Nixon is a Lecturer in Criminology at the University of Gloucestershire. She has researched peer work and desistance in prisoners, probationers and former probationers. Other research interests include the role of prison officers, prison officer occupational culture and issues around gender and sexuality in prison officers. Prior to an academic career, she was a prison officer in a category 'B' local.

Per Åke Nylander is a Senior Lecturer and Reader in Social Work at Örebro University – lectures in Social Work and Criminology programs. His research concerns prison officer work, drug treatment in prisons and children with imprisoned parents.

Jake Phillips is a Reader in Criminology at Sheffield Hallam University. His research is primarily focused on the intersection between policy and practice in the field of probation and community sanctions. In recent years, he has conducted research on the emotional labour of probation practice, people who die whilst under probation supervision and the impact of inspection and regulation on probation policy and practice.

Mark Pogrebin is a Professor at the University of Colorado at Denver. Professor Pogrebin is one of the nation's premier scholars in the area of prisons, probation and policing. For over 30 years, Professor Pogrebin's research has advanced the fields of sociology and criminology while informing public policy. Professor Pogrebin's most recent research uncovered the stresses parolees face after leaving prison – namely the difficulties in finding employment and how un- and under-employment is a primary cause of parole revocations.

Kaitlyn Quinn is a PhD candidate in the Department of Sociology at the University of Toronto, Canada. Her dissertation research investigates the penal voluntary sector in Canada with a focus on criminalised women. She is also a Research Associate at the University of Nottingham, UK, in the School of Sociology and Social Policy.

Anne Robinson worked as a Probation Officer, mainly in youth justice and managed a youth offending team before joining Sheffield Hallam University in 2005. She currently leads the programme for probation officer training there. Amongst other works, she is the author of *Foundations for Youth Justice: Positive Approaches to Practice* and co-editor of *Moving on From Crime and Substance Use: Transforming Identities* (both with Policy Press).

Carol Robinson is a Lecturer in Criminology at the University of York. Her latest research uses ethnographic methods to explore the impact on prison regimes, cultures and relationships of the increasing numbers of prisoners dying of natural causes. She previously worked as a prison chaplain.

Andrea Subryan is a Senior Lecturer in the Department of Management at Sheffield Hallam University. She is an active researcher in the fields of emotion work and emotional labour. Her PhD research explores the dynamics of display rule conflict among family law practitioners. Andrea has presented her research at conferences and has conference publications. Her research interests are primarily focused on the influence of power and conflict when practising emotional labour.

Philippa Tomczak is a Senior Research Fellow in Criminology at the University of Nottingham. She researches prison suicide, prison regulation and the penal voluntary sector. She co-ordinates CRIMVOL: the international criminal justice voluntary sector research network.

Jaime Waters is a Senior Lecturer in Criminology and Fellow of the Sheffield Institute for Policy Studies at Sheffield Hallam University. Her main research interests include illegal drug use, gambling and emotional labour. She is co-author of *Illegal Drug Use through the Lifecourse* and *Mixed Methods in Criminology* (both with Routledge), and editor of the special issue 'Entering the field of criminological research' in the *British Journal of Community Justice*.

Chalen Westaby is a Senior Lecturer in Law at Sheffield Hallam University. She has published primarily in the field of emotional labour. Her empirical qualitative research has focused on legal professionals, law students and most recently probation officers and criminological researchers. She has also undertaken research into emotion in the legal profession with particular emphasis on empathy and its role within professional practice.

Foreword

In law enforcement and corrections, managing feelings is part of the job. Emotion matters, just as cognitive and technical skills matter. All are skills that must be applied in order to be effective on the job, to care about the work and to return tomorrow to do more of it. As sophisticated as data analytics are, as much as information and communication technology shapes how officers communicate, emotion is the very human element that is as important now as it has ever been.

Too often, we delude ourselves into thinking that emotion is secondary to cognition. Language is filled with words that describe cognitive functions, making job descriptions that focus on cognitive demands easy to write. That which is overlooked is the central element in criminal justice work. Police and corrections officials are well aware of the emotive demands in their jobs, but they struggle to talk about it because language does not contain words refined enough to describe it. Now comes this excellent book that reveals the emotive in criminal justice and criminology.

Policing and criminal justice work as an emotive citizen-state encounter

Policing and criminal justice work is a form of encounter between citizen and state that requires a combination of emotional intelligence and emotional labour – a complex combination of other-awareness, emotive self-regulation and emotional labour that is both self-focused and other-focused.

Emotion humanises the citizen–state encounter. It is the source of job satisfaction and meaningfulness for practitioners, and it produces feelings of trust (or distrust) on the part of citizens.

The citizen–state encounter is a two-way street. The feelings that citizens have about the criminal justice system result in large part from their emotive experience in interactions with the people who deliver services. Trust and engagement do not arise from hostile encounters. Confidence, belonging-ness, safety, security and respect do not result from threats and cold formalism. The emotive component is the human touch, and it is an essential component in this work. In fact, the emotive component in criminal justice work is its connective tissue. For citizens to comply, they must respect the law and the officials who enforce it.

It is not spreadsheets and policies that cause people to love police or hate them; it is feelings. Citizens want criminal justice staff to have cool heads and warm hearts, to be able to deal with whatever crisis is at hand and to do it with compassion, empathy and confidence. These are all emotive character-istics. At the same time, when the police, for example, are face-to-face with hostile crowds, the emotive demands on them are huge. They must mask their feelings of anger, or fear, and respond with a calmness and confidence that disguises how they actually feel. This is not confined to the police but is applicable to all those working in the criminal justice system.

The relationship between citizens and law enforcement must engender trust or at least a sense of fairness. Empathy and rapport are necessary for a satisfactory transaction to take place, as is the emotive display of confidence and self-assurance that officials must don when confronted with a hostile public. The work extends to the public information officer who must display compassion and confidence while explaining unspeakable tragedy at press briefings.

Emotional labour

For too long, occupations have excluded the emotive dimension from job de-scriptions and the list of requisite knowledge, skills and abilities. It is time to take the affective turn – to acknowledge the emotive dimension – and build it into job requirements. Such inclusion would more honestly represent the nature of the work.

To acknowledge the full gamut of skills that are required improves the likelihood that emotionally intense jobs, such as policing and the other roles analysed in this book, are recognised for their difficulty. Including the emo-tive component in job analyses makes job descriptions more accurate and paves the way for recruiting staff who have the skills to perform the job. It also provides guidance in how to tailor training and development.

Emotive competencies for police officers include the ability to maintain fo-cus in the midst of chaos, to be calm, and to appear confident. The same goes for others in the criminal justice system. They must be able to size up a situ-ation and adapt to whatever exigencies arise. They must be able to suppress how they are feeling in order to express whatever emotion is appropriate for the moment. This is emotional labour. The job cannot be done well without it. Whether the encounter is one of personnel exercising power or providing supportive services, emotive skills are at its heart.

Like the hand in the crowd that waves frantically to be acknowledged, the emotive component in criminal justice has much to reveal. A deeper, richer, comprehension of it will smooth the square corners of the field, rounding out our understanding of why procedures produce the desired result in some encounters and not in others and why logic prevails in some interventions and not others. Affect is the communication that shapes and seals feelings of trust, safety and security. It is also the communication that engenders anger, defiance, resistance and revolt.

For there to be justice in criminal justice, citizens must *feel* good about those who enforce the law. *Feeling* is not a word used by number-crunchers, but it is used by citizens. Absent its incorporation into criminal justice practice, the basis for how citizens judge law enforcement comes up short. The skills of the best workers are overlooked. And so, I commend this book to you. It breaks new ground in criminal justice and criminology, and builds awareness of how emotional labour is central to the work.

In conclusion, it is time to move beyond Cartesian dualism – the belief that mind and body are separate – and the belief that cognition is to be elevated in importance while emotion is unworthy of mention. Emotive competencies are as important as, if not more important than, cognitive and technical competencies in policing. Emotive skills, especially the ability to regulate one's own emotions, make the difference between those who are perceived to be empathic and those who come across as cold and uncaring. Those who are skilled at regulating their own emotions – holding their fear in check, masking their anger, subduing their joy – are better at performing it, and they are less likely to suffer burnout.

Mary E. Guy (Orcid.org/0000-0001-9193-8798) is an expert on emotionally intense jobs and what it takes to perform them well. She has published three books on the subject and has spoken to audiences around the world about the importance of emotional labour. She is a Fellow of the National Academy of Public Administration, past President of the American Society for Public Administration, and a faculty member in the School of Public Affairs at the University of Colorado Denver.

Acknowledgements

A project of this kind is always the product of the work of many people – probably too many to mention by name. However, the book would never have come to fruition were it not for the hard work of all the contributors, and so we are incredibly thankful to all of them. We would also like to thank the participants in all of the research covered in this book: if it wasn't for people's willingness to talk about the emotional labour in their work, our knowledge would be much shallower as a result. Thanks also to the team at Routledge for their guidance and perseverance in getting the book over the line – thanks in particular to Tom Sutton and Jess Phillips.

Finally, we are academics but also parents, spouses and partners, and so we extend our thanks to our respective families for the support and belief that we could do this!

—The Editors

Acknowledgements

Part One

Chapter 1

Introduction

Why study emotional labour in criminal justice and criminology

Jake Phillips, Chalen Westaby,
Andrew Fowler and Jaime Waters

Introduction

Emotional labour, a term coined by Hochschild (1983) in her seminal work *A Managed Heart: Commercialization of Human Feeling*, alerts us to the ways in which people are required to manage and display their emotions in order to achieve the goals of the organisation that they work for. Although initially developed in the context of the private sector and with a focus on how emotions can be appropriated and deployed for the purpose of profit, more recent academic attention has focused on the ways in which professionals and those working in public services use emotional labour as part of their work. This body of knowledge has explored the reasons for using emotional labour in public services, its impact in terms of effective governance as well as on the consequences of that emotional labour on employees. Emotional labour brings to the fore the relational element of public service with a focus on trust and the role of the 'encounter' between state and citizen. In this chapter, we begin by providing an overview of what emotional labour is in order to lay some definitional groundwork for subsequent chapters. We then discuss why emotional labour is particularly pertinent to the field of criminal justice and criminology and finish by providing an overview of the structure of the book.

The concept of emotional labour

Emotional labour is 'the management of a way of feeling to create a publicly observable facial and bodily display...which is for a wage' (Hochschild, 1983: 7fn). The fact that emotions are being managed for a wage is central to Hochschild's definition of emotional labour because it illustrates the way in which human feelings are increasingly being commodified by organisations. However, as we see in this volume, this definition has been stretched in recent years to include work that is done for other non-pecuniary benefits. Workers engaging in emotional labour are expected to control their own, and others, feelings. This requires effort, planning, time and knowledge (Morris & Feldman, 1996; Skilbeck & Payne, 2003).

As is readily recognised with physical work, emotional labour can be hard work. Hochschild (1983) provides three criteria which must be fulfilled in order for a worker to engage in emotional labour:

> First...face-to face or voice-to voice contact with the public. Secondly, they require the worker to produce an emotional state in another person...Third, they allow the employer, through training and supervision, to exercise a degree of control over the emotional activities of the employees. (1983: 147)

The first criterion means that workers must interact directly with people as part of their job for emotional labour to be possible. When emotion management moves into the public domain emotions become commodified and so emotional labour primarily occurs in 'frontline' or customer-facing roles. That said, jobs can demand emotional labour between employees within an organisation. For example, the secretary may need a pleasant disposition towards the attorneys they assist and, doing so, must perform emotional labour (Hochschild, 1983: 148).

The second criterion required for an employee to perform emotional labour is that the worker is expected to manage *their* emotions *as well as* the emotions of the recipient of their emotional display. For example, police officers regularly have to control their own feelings, as well as the general public with whom they are required to interact, and 'who are often at their worst-injured, upset or angry' (Martin, 1999: 561). We can start to see that, given the nature of work within the field of criminal justice and criminology, where extreme emotions such as despair, anger and revulsion are commonly felt, the expectation to manage the emotional displays of both the worker and the recipient is often particularly challenging.

Although the original studies on emotional labour focused on the need for face-to-face or voice-to-voice contact as paramount to a job requiring emotional labour, in recent years, modern information technology has developed which serves to replace or enhance human services and these kinds of jobs are being seen to demand emotional labour (Froehle, 2006; Jin & Oriaku, 2013). Consequently, studies are now beginning to be conducted on the effects of automation on emotional labour and the emotional labour expectations of online customer service workers. For example, in his study of tutors based in a private European online tutoring centre, Webb (2012) discovered that while the amount of online interaction is to some extent limited, tutors still engaged in considerable emotional labour with learners. In a separate example, Ishii and Markman (2016) found that online service workers engaged in emotional labour and in particular were expected to display positive emotions to customers when they were aggressive or they demanded additional attention.

The third criterion for emotional labour is that the employer must have a certain amount of control over the emotional displays of the worker.

The focus of Hochschild's initial study was the commodification of emotion by organisations in relation to 'frontline' human service workers such as air stewards and bill collectors. This has led some to argue that professionals cannot perform emotional labour because they have a much higher degree of autonomy.

Hochschild's (1983) focus on control over worker's emotional activities through training and supervision precluded a number of job roles such as those inhabited by 'professionals'. These workers were seen differently because they are not considered to be performing whilst under the direct supervision of a superior. This narrow definition of who can do emotional labour has been challenged by a considerable body of work on the emotional labour of public service workers (Guy et al., 2008; Mastracci et al., 2012).

Whilst professionals are self-regulating – i.e. workers can use discretion and have autonomy in how they work – they are also governed by formalised codes of practice that prescribe universal standards (Harris, 2002). This unique form of standard setting has an impact on the nature of the emotional labour performed. Such workers might be described as 'privileged emotion managers', in contrast to the 'emotional proletariat' (Orzechowicz, 2008: 143 and 144, cited in MacDonald and Sirianni, 1996). Orzechowicz (2008) suggests that these types of workers conform to informal emotional labour expectations, based on codes of practices and professionals socialisation. The use of the term 'privileged emotion managers' suggests that workers who self-supervise are considered to be affluent and implies that their 'income and reputation might decrease the impressiveness of the "exploitation" and the "costs" of emotional labour, and that is perhaps why they are excluded' (Wouters, 1989: 100). That said, workers in what Wouters (1989) describes as 'the true professions', such as lawyers, social workers and therapists who are not directly supervised, can be seen to possess stronger emotional management skills than those who are closely supervised. Indeed, the changing nature of service work provided by professionals have been called upon to become more 'customer focussed' and management have attempted to directly control the professional's 'feeling rules'. It might be argued that professionals– and, for the purposes of this volume, criminal justice practitioners – are not as far away from the service workers in Hochschild's study as we might think. This is important because emotional labour is about the commodification of emotion by organisations and is thus 'sold for a wage and therefore has *exchange value*' (Hochschild, 1983: 198, 7fn).[1]

Drivers of emotional labour

How people know what emotional labour to perform is a key question posed by scholars in this field. The answer lies, to some degree, in Hochschild's concept of feeling rules; 'rules or norms according to which feelings are judged appropriate to accompanying events' (1983: 59). Some researchers prefer to use the term display rules instead of feeling rules (Ashforth & Humphrey, 1993; Morris & Feldman, 1996; Rafaeli & Sutton, 1989). This term is more attuned to emotions that are publicly displayed rather than the internal feelings of the worker (Ashforth & Humphrey, 1993). Consequently, display rules can be defined as 'behavioural expectations about which emotions ought to be expressed and which ought to be hidden' (Rafaeli & Sutton, 1989: 8), and therefore 'provide standards for the appropriate expression of emotions in the job, emphasising the publicly observable side of emotions rather than the actual feelings of employees' (Diefendorff & Richard, 2003: 284).

Feeling rules or display rules are further divided into three types: societal, organisational and occupational norms (Rafaeli & Sutton, 1987). Societal display rules play a role in shaping the performance of emotional labour as they:

> guide interpersonal behaviour in all cultures and provide general rules regarding how and what emotions should be expressed in the work environment. This is because the expression of emotion in organizational roles is influenced by the more general norms of the culture in which the organization is based. (Mann, 1997: 5; see also Ashforth & Humphrey, 1993)

Organisational feeling rules are rules or guidelines, the purpose of which is to achieve the aims and objectives laid down by the organisation (Ashforth & Humphrey, 1993). Occupational norms derive from 'occupational communities':

> who consider themselves to be engaged in the same sort of work; who identify (more or less positively) with their work; who share with one another a set of values, norms, and perspectives. (Van Maanen & Barley, 1984: 287)

These occupational cultures establish cultures which are based on codes of practice which dictate proper and improper behaviours, and develop task rituals and work codes for certain routine practices (Van Maanen & Barley, 1984). According to Ashforth and Humphrey (1993), organisational and occupational feeling rules are generally in alignment.

The performance of emotional labour

Emotional labour 'requires one to induce or suppress feelings in order to sustain the outward countenance that produces the proper state of mind in others' through the use of one of two types of acting: deep acting or surface acting (Hochschild, 1983: 7).

Surface acting

Surface acting is where a worker simulates the emotions to be displayed in order to produce a desired emotional reaction in another person. This way of performing emotional labour results in the emotion that is being displayed differing to the one(s) being felt. For example, Per-Ake Nylander et al. explore the use of surface acting by Swedish prison officers. They maintain that this type of acting is the predominant mode of performing emotional labour in security wings of prisons, with the often-expected requirement that Swedish prison officers 'wear a mask' and 'simulate behaviours they did not feel' (2011: 475). Similarly, Bhowmick and Mulla (2016) discuss surface acting as a useful strategy for Indian police officers who are required to engage in negative emotional displays such as anger and intimidation over attempting to change inner emotions which brings with it the risk of emotional alignment with those negative emotions.

Deep acting

Deep acting is where a worker engages in the emotional display either directly or indirectly through the alignment of inner feelings with emotional labour expectations. This can be achieved through either invoking those emotions through experience or through a trained imagination. In this way, the worker regulates their emotions in order to harmonise them with those expected by the organisation (Grandey et al., 2007a, b; Rafaeli & Sutton, 1987).

This type of acting has been further divided into two types of deep acting. The first, active deep acting, is akin to the description above, and requires the worker to expend effort in order to invoke the expected emotions. An example of this type of deep acting can be seen in the study of probation practitioners by Fowler et al. (2018), where one participant states that:

> no two lives are identical but…everyone's got some sort of life experience, whatever that may be…and I think that's how you, you know, you kind of click into those, those feelings and those, your own background to be able to say, well, you know it wasn't always easy for me but, you know, look at, this is how you do it…

The 'clicking into' those feelings is an active way of engaging in deep acting for this probation practitioner in order to empathise with their clients. Passive deep acting, meanwhile, is where a worker may already feel the emotion expected in a certain situation and so requires no conscious effort to align their feelings with expected emotional displays (Bono & Vey, 2005; Kruml & Geddes, 2000). For example, Bruhn et al. (2012) describe situations where Swedish prison officers engage in passive deep acting in particular wings, such as the treatment wing. Prison officers working in this wing were able to develop more personal relationships with prisoners, and therefore displayed genuine anger when prisoners did not behave appropriately. Even though there is some degree of alignment between displayed and felt emotion in these examples, it is important to note that there is still some degree of emotional suppression occurring.

Genuine emotional responses

The third way of performing emotional labour is genuine emotional responses (Ashforth & Humphrey, 1993). Here, a worker's feelings may align with the emotional expectations of an organisation leading to that worker displaying a genuine emotional response. That said, emotional labour is still required because the genuine emotional response still needs to be regulated in order to be appropriately displayed. For example, Bhowmick and Mulla (2016) provide evidence of an Indian police officer who described being physically unable to fake emotions. Authenticity was the reason he gave as to why he was only able to display genuine emotions, even if these were negative emotions such as anger.

Detachment

Finally, researchers have identified a fourth way of performing emotional labour: detachment. Detachment occurs when dealing with particularly difficult customers or clients and consists of a worker removing any kind of emotional engagement or support from that person (Sutton, 1991; Wolkomir & Powers, 2007). For example, Kadowaki describes situations where US attorneys found a client to be particularly unpleasant and thus found it impossible to perform emotional labour through deep or surface acting. In these cases, they resorted to detachment by effectively taking emotion out of the relationship in order to depersonalise it and stick to 'strictly business' (Kadowaki, 2015: 338). In this way, detachment is 'self-protective' but still requires the use of emotional labour 'to strip away niceties, suppress feelings of anger and frustration, while still meeting requirements set by organisational feeling rules' (Kadowaki, 2015: 328).

Consequences of performing emotional labour

Emotional labour is a 'double-edged sword' because its performance can have both positive and negative consequences for workers (Ashforth & Humphrey, 1993: 96; see Pugliesi, 1999). Many of the chapters in this book deal with the consequences of emotional labour, and so it is useful to go over what we already know here.

Negative consequences

The negative consequences of conforming to emotional labour expectations are particularly well documented. Workers can wholeheartedly associate with the job by engaging in active deep acting, which can cause burnout. At the other end of the continuum, a worker may consciously separate themselves from the job, and thus engage in surface acting which, in turn, can result in feelings of insincerity. Alternatively, a worker can adopt a more positive approach to their work – considering this separation and the surface acting they perform as positive – although with this comes the risk of alienation from, and scepticism towards, the acting which needs to take place as a result.

Studies have revealed that the performance of emotional labour can result in negative consequences. For example, Jeung et al. (2018) provide an overview of the health-related consequences of emotional labour and many have made the link between emotional labour and burnout (Tolich, 1993; Wharton, 1993). Other negative consequences include stress (Mann & Cowburn, 2005), role overload (Wharton & Erickson, 1993), poor self-esteem, cynicism, role alienation, self-alienation (Ashforth & Humphrey, 1993; Fineman, 1993), emotional exhaustion (Harris, 2002), emotional dissonance (Abraham, 1998) and emotional deviance (Fineman, 1993; Tolich, 1993). Mann (2007) also highlights serious medical conditions such as coronary heart disease and cancer as a potential consequence of performing emotional labour.

Positive consequences

While there has been much focus on the negative consequences, performing emotional labour can bring positives. Of particular interest to us is the idea that the findings for workers who undertake emotional labour gain more job satisfaction than workers who do not engage in emotion management (Wharton, 1993). This may be because workers who have job roles requiring emotional labour may be more inclined to perform emotion management and therefore are more drawn to such work. In their work on emotional labour in public service, Guy et al. (2008) highlight the positive effects of emotional labour in terms of it giving meaning to one's work. Other positive consequences that have been highlighted are task effectiveness (Ashforth & Humphrey, 1993; Harris, 2002); increased satisfaction, security, self-esteem (Strickland, 1993; Tolich, 1993; Wharton, 1993); decreased stress and psychological well-being (Conrad & Witte, 1994); and an increased sense of community (Shuler & Sypher, 2000).

Why study emotional labour in criminal justice?

This – albeit brief – overview of emotional labour has included some examples from emotional labour research that has been carried out in the criminal justice system. These examples provide some idea about how useful the lens of emotional labour is in terms of analysing criminal justice work and criminological research. Emotion is important because 'it is through emotion that we see the world' (Hochschild, 2013: 4). Thus, an examination of emotion and the effort required to manage emotions sheds light on the cultural constraints imposed on employees by the institution for whom they work. Emotion thus becomes a means with which to understand what organisations are seeking to achieve, and how they seek to achieve those goals through an examination of the management, display and suppression of emotion. As Crawley (2004: 414) suggests in relation to prison officers, emotional labour is key to much work in this field:

> emotions are not freely expressed. Rather, prison officers try to ensure that when they perform emotion they do so in the 'right' circumstances and settings. Consequently, prison work requires...an (often significant) engagement in emotion-work and, relatedly, the employment of specific emotion-work strategies. In short, prison officers are obliged to manage their *own* emotions as well as those of prisoners.

Guy et al. (2019) ask why 'emotional labor matters in public service'. Their argument is that 'governance, collaboration, coproduction, citizen engagement, and relational contracting' all rest on a single foundation: 'the relationship between citizens and between citizen and state'. Guy et al. (2019) make the critical point that 'for governing to be effective, citizens must *feel* good about those who govern'. This is of particular relevance to the field of criminal justice because legitimacy – a concept which encapsulates Guy et al.'s (2019) argument – is key to many facets of criminal justice work and its effectiveness. For example, Tyler's (2006) work on why people obey the law demonstrates that where people see the government and the laws it passes as legitimate, they are more likely to obey the law. As the main institution for enforcing those laws, the emotional labour deployed by the police in enforcing the law becomes critical in terms of enhancing the legitimacy of the law in the eyes of members of the public. In the context of prisons and probation, evidence suggests that where 'offenders' see their sentence and the way it is carried out as legitimate, they are more likely to comply and, in turn, stop offending (Brunton-Smith & McCarthy, 2016; McCarthy & Brunton-Smith, 2018).

Not only does emotional labour help us understand how citizens engage with criminal justice, it also speaks to other contemporary debates in criminology, specifically the ways in which policy manifests in practice. Importantly, analyses underpinned by emotional labour show that it is not the policy which makes a citizen see a system of governance as legitimate, and thus worth engaging with. Rather, it is the way in which that policy is relayed to them by an agent of the state – a police officer, probation officer, domestic violence worker – through face-to-face or voice-to-voice interaction which creates that sense of legitimacy. Thus, citizens' behaviour cannot be manipulated simply by pulling the lever of policy. Rather, the behaviour of citizens rests on co-relation and coproduction between the citizen and the state which is mediated by those who activate those policies: through the 'encounter' between civil servant and member of the public. That encounter will always involve emotion, and thus, every single one of those interactions will involve some form of emotional labour. Such an analysis is similar to that of Lipsky's (1980) notion of a street-level bureaucrat whereby individual practitioners' uses of discretion are based on their own understanding of the situation and shape the way that policy gets implemented. Emotional labour focuses our attention on the use of emotion in that context. It is the argument in this book that we need to examine those interactions and, specifically, the emotions that are managed and displayed within them to ascertain the impact of that interaction on the person with whom the state agent is working, be that member of the public, defendant, witness, victim, potential victim, prisoner or probationer.

Through the concept of feeling rules, the emotional labour requires us to think about how organisations shape emotional display through formal rules and policies as well as through the occupational cultures which exist within those organisations. The lens of emotional labour shows us how criminal justice agencies manipulate employees' emotion to achieve the goals of their job. This has potentially serious consequences for those working in the field, and so emotional labour also enables us to understand the impact of working in criminal justice settings. This is particularly pertinent in a sector in which people work with potentially dangerous people, in dangerous situations.

Emotional labour has relevance to criminal justice in other ways, too. In addition to chapters on criminal justice policy and practice, we have included chapters on the process of doing criminological research. Criminological research is used – to varying degrees – to inform policy and practice within the field of criminal justice. By examining the process of doing research through the lens of emotional labour, we can begin to see how knowledge is created and disseminated. In turn, this results in policies which will have certain effects. If we understand the process of knowledge generation, then we can begin to analyse the potential impact of that knowledge on policy, practice and the broader aims of criminal justice.

Emotional labour shifts our gaze away from a top-down understanding of policy and reinforces the idea that in order to truly understand how criminal justice functions, we need to (1) understand the processes which underpin citizens' engagement with those policies and (2) appreciate that those interactions will involve some degree of emotional labour. Thus, research in this field alerts us to the way in which emotional labour is incorporated by the penal industrial complex. Each of the chapters in this book engages with those processes in a range of contexts – both institutional and jurisdictional. As such, we hope that readers will be able to use this book to both gain an in-depth understanding of the use and role of emotional labour in specific contexts and institutions as well as gain a broader insight into how emotional labour relates to the whole field of criminal justice and discipline of criminology.

Overview of the book

This book has two main aims: (1) to bring together the existing literature on emotional labour in the field of criminal justice and criminology and (2) to extend our knowledge through presenting new empirical chapters on the use of emotional labour in criminal justice and criminology. The book is split into two parts roughly along these two aims. Thus, the chapters in Part One are, in the main, literature review chapters which seek to synthesise and highlight the main findings from extant research. In order to make each chapter useful to criminologists working in different fields, we took the decision to split these chapters, roughly, along the lines of individual criminal justice agencies.

Chapter 2, by Black and Lumsden, focuses on existing research in the police by exploring the shifting structures and expectations placed on police officers in carrying out their duties. In doing so, they suggest that efforts to reduce the strains related to the performance of emotional labour in the police would be better targeted at the structures create the stress, rather than the symptoms of those stressors. Chapter 3, by Westaby and Subryan, focuses on the role and form of emotional labour in the legal professions, a discipline which puts rationality on a pedestal and sees emotion as something which muddies judgement and clear thinking. By focusing on the rules which dictate the way that emotional labour is performed, they show that practising law requires a significant amount of emotional labour, partly down to the many different display rules to which they must conform. In Chapter 4, Phillips, Westaby and Fowler trace the history of emotion work in probation where they argue that emotions fell out of favour in probation policy in the latter part of the 20th century. They then draw on the – albeit limited – extant research in this field to show what types of emotion work probation practice involves as well as what the consequences of it are. Chapter 5 by Nylander and Bruhn provides an overview of the emotion work involved in being a prison officer. They emphasise the importance of the individual prison and its particular circumstances which shape the use of emotion as well as the impact of this on the prisoner themselves.

Chapter 6 takes us away from the formal criminal justice system and to an analysis of the emotional labour performed by workers in the penal voluntary sector. Quinn and Tomczak unpick the tensions between the traditional aims of the voluntary sector – citizen engagement, advocacy and empowerment – and the penal system which has, increasingly, made use of the voluntary sector to achieve its aims become apparent. The final chapter in Part One by Waters, Fowler, Phillips and Westaby concerns the emotional labour of doing criminological research. In this chapter, we bring together the limited research on the emotional labour of doing research, arguing that the nature of much criminological research means that emotional labour is likely to be necessary. The type of emotional labour required can be linked to what it means to do 'good' and/or 'rigorous' research and is thus highly disciplinary with emotion work being seen to 'muddy' the scientific process of analysis. On the contrary, we argue that to ignore emotion can result in damage to the research process.

Part Two takes a more empirical approach and comprises nine shorter chapters which focus on specific areas of criminal justice and criminology in order to deepen and extend our knowledge of emotional labour. Thus, Chapter 9 by Carol Robinson explores the emotional labour involved in providing end of life pastoral care to prisoners. Here we see prison officers manage emotions in a way which allows them to walk the tightrope between organisational and occupational norms and rules and the real feelings experienced when a prisoner dies. Chapter 10 by Duggan focuses on the work done by Independent Domestic Violence Advisors and the way in which they use emotion to support victims of domestic violence. Duggan argues that there is a real emotional toll for workers in this unexplored area of criminal justice. Anne Robinson's chapter focuses on youth justice: a relatively un-explored area when it comes to emotional labour. What stands out in Robinson's discussion – when compared to other criminal justice institutions – is the unique place of youth justice in the broader penal field. What shapes emotional labour in youth justice is the tension between the preventative aims and largely welfarist ethos of youth work working in a 'system' which demands the imposition of punishment on young people. Chapter 12 by Ellis picks up on the themes from Chapter 7 by offering an auto-ethnographic account of the emotions required when conducting research in 'high-risk environments'. In particular, Ellis examines the way in which his own biography shaped his use of emotion in his research and how that, in turn, resulted in particular forms of data that were collected. Chapter 13 by Flower takes us back to the law and, in particular, the courts with findings from an innovative piece of research which involved observations of the emotions displayed and deployed in Swedish courtrooms. Swedish lawyers, Flower argues, manage emotions in whole range of ways that linked to professionalism and client expectations. Adams and Mastracci, in Chapter 14, make a distinction between the emotional labour performed and experienced by different types of police officer in the US arguing that perceived organisational support is critical in terms of reducing the risk of burnout – one of the most significant adverse effects of emotional labour.

In Chapter 15, Borelli takes us to the borders of Europe in an analysis of the way in which police border guards display and manage emotions when dealing with people who are identified as being in breach of immigration rules. This chapter focuses attention on the tensions contained within single roles – dealing with crime and dealing with immigration issues – and the implications that this has for those caught up in the middle. Chapter 16 by Nixon looks at the use of emotional labour by prison listeners who, despite not being paid, receive other benefits and privileges for the work they undertake which, in the prison context, is analogous to payment. Being a prison listener, Nixon argues, and performing emotional labour, allows prisoners to step back and view their own situations differently. Britton and Knight's chapter focuses on special constables – volunteer but fully warranted police officers – in England. They highlight the structures and contexts in which they perform emotional labour and argue that much more needs to be done to both understand and support specials in their role. Chapter 17 takes us back to the US and back to the field of law with an examination of the emotion work undertaken by defence lawyers working with people on death row. This chapter picks up on the concept of emotional culture which pushes us to think more deeply about the occupational display rules which are at play in the field of law. The chapter focuses on the use anger by defence lawyers – not, as one might expect, anger towards those convicted of murder but anger directed to the death sentence itself. Linked to the previous discussion about the consequences of performing labour, the chapter highlights a potential positive effect of emotional labour – an emotion which drives them to work harder for their clients and which also opens them up to other emotions such as compassion and empathy which might not otherwise occur.

This overview of the chapters contained in this volume book has already served to highlight some key themes that run throughout: a lack of knowledge, the importance of context, circumstance and structure and how these factors shape the performance of emotional labour. In the concluding chapter, we bring these together and reflect on what we have learnt and where we need to focus attention as we move forwards. We finish this introduction by reiterating our aims for the volume: to both consolidate and extend knowledge on the performance of emotional labour in criminal justice and criminology.

Note

1 Hochschild contrasts this definition with emotion work or emotion management, which unlike emotional labour is conducted in the private context and therefore has 'use value'. Whilst emotional labour highlights the way in which emotions are done for a wage, emotion work merely connotes the work that is done.

References

Abraham, R. (1998) Emotional dissonance in organizations: Antecedents, consequences, and moderators, *Genetic, Social and General Psychology Monographs*, 124(2) 29–246.

Ashforth, B.E. & Humphrey, R.H. (1993) Emotional labor in service roles: The influence of identity, *The Academy of Management Review*, 18(1) 88–115.

Bhowmick, S. & Mulla, Z. (2016) Emotional labour of policing: Does authenticity play a role? *International Journal of Police Science & Management*, 18(1) 47–60.

Bolton, S.C. (2000) Who cares? Offering emotion work as a 'gift' in the nursing labour process, *Journal of Advanced Nursing*, 32(3) 580–586.

Bono, J.E. & Vey, M.A. (2005) Toward understanding emotional management at work: A quantitative review of emotional labor research, In Härtel, C.E.J., Zerbe, W.J., & Ashkanasy, N.M. (Eds.), *Emotions in Organizational Behavior* (Mahwah, NJ: Lawrence Erlbaum) 213–233.

Bruhn, A., Lindberg, O. & Per-Ake Nylander, O. (2012) A harsher prison climate and a cultural heritage working against it - sub cultural divisions among Swedish Prison Officers, In Ugelvik, T. & Dullum, J. (Eds.), *Penal Exceptionalism? Nordic Prison Policy and Practice?* (Abingdin: Routledge), 215 – 232.

Brunton-Smith, I. & McCarthy, D.J. (2016) Prison legitimacy and procedural fairness: A multilevel examination of prisoners in England and Wales. Justice Quarterly, 33(6) 1029–1054.

Conrad, C. & Witte, K. (1994) Is emotional expression repression or oppression? Myths of organizational affective regulation, *Annals of International Communication Association*, 17(1) 412–428.

Crawley, E.M. (2004) Emotion and performance: Prison officers and the presentation of self in prisons, *Punishment & Society*, 6(4) 411–427.

Dickson-Swift, V., James, E.L., Kippen, S. & Liamputtong, P. (2009) Researching sensitive topics: Qualitative research as emotion work, *Qualitative Research*, 9(1) 61–79.

Diefendorff, J.M. & Richard, E.M. (2003) Antecedents and consequences of emotional display rule perception, *Journal of Applied Psychology*, 88(2) 284–294.

Fineman, S. (1993) *Understanding Emotions at Work* (London: Sage Publications).

Fowler, A., Phillips, J. & Westaby, C. (2018) Understanding emotions as effective practice. The performance of emotional labour in building relationships, In Ugwudike, P., Raynor, P. & Annison, J. (Eds.) *Evidence-Based Skills in Community Justice: International Research on Supporting Rehabilitation and Desistance* (Bristol: Policy Press).

Froehle, C.M. (2006) Service, personnel, technology, and their interaction influencing customer satisfaction, *Decision Sciences*, 37 5–38.

Grandey, A. A., Cordeiro, B. L., & Michael, J. H. (2007a). Work-family supportiveness organizational perceptions: Important for the well-being of male blue-collar hourly workers? *Journal of Vocational Behavior*, 71(3), 460–478.

Grandey, A.A., Kern, J.H., & Frone, M.R. (2007b). Verbal abuse from outsiders versus insiders: Comparing frequency, impact on emotional exhaustion, and the role of emotional labor, *Journal of Occupational Health Psychology*, 12(1) 63–79.

Guy, M.E., Newman, M.A. & Mastracci, S.H. (2008) *Emotional Labour: Putting the Service into Public Service* (New York: M.E. Sharpe).

Guy, M.E., Mastracci, S., & Yang, S.-B. (Eds.). (2019). *The Palgrave Handbook of Global Perspectives on Emotional Labor in Public Service*. Basingstoke: Palgrave Macmillan.

Harris, L.C. (2002) The emotional labour of barristers: An exploration of emotional labour by status professionals, *Journal of Management Studies*, 39(4), 553–584.

Härtel, C.E.J., Hsu, A.C.F. & Boyle, M.V. (2002) A conceptual examination of the causal sequences of emotional labour, emotional dissonance and emotional exhaustion: The argument for contextual and provider characteristics, In Ashkanasy, N.M., Zerbe, W.J. & Härtel, C.E.J. (Eds.), *Managing Emotions in the Workplace* (New York: M.E. Sharpe) 251–275.

Hochschild, A.R. (1983) *The Managed Heart. Commercialization of Human Feeling* (Berkeley: University of California Press).

Hochschild, A.R. (2013) *So How's the Family?* (Berkeley: University of California Press).

Ishii, K. & Markman, K. (2016) Online customer service and emotional labour: An exploratory study, *Computers in Human Behavior*, 62 658–665.

James, N. (1989) Emotional labour: Skill and work in the social regulation of feeling, *The Sociological Review*, 37(1) 15–42.

Jeung, D.-Y., Kim, C., & Chang, S.-J. (2018). Emotional labor and burnout: A review of the literature. *Yonsei Medical Journal*, 59(2), 187–193.

Jin, Y. & Oriaku, N. (2013) E-service flexibility: Meeting new customer demands online, *Management Research Review*, 36 1123–1136.

Kadowaki, J. (2015) Maintaining professionalism: Emotional labor among lawyers as client advisors, *International Journal of the Legal Profession*, 22(3) 323–345.

Kruml, S.M. & Geddes, D. (2000) Exploring the dimensions of emotional labor. The heart of Hochschild's work, *Management Communication Quarterly*, 14(1) 8–49.

Lipsky, M. (1980) *Street-level bureaucracy: Dilemmas of the individual in public services.* New York: Russell Sage Foundation Publications.

Macdonald, C. L. & Sirianni, C. (1996) *Working in the service society.* Philadelphia: Temple University Press.

Mann, S. (1997) Emotional labour in organizations, *Leadership & Organization Development Journal*, 18(1) 4–12.

Mann, S. (2007) Expectations of emotional display in the workplace. An American/ British comparative study, *Leadership and Organization Development Journal*, 28(6) 552–570.

Mann, S. & Cowburn, J. (2005), Emotional labour and stress within mental health nursing, *Journal of Psychiatric and Mental Health*, 12 154–162.

Martin, S.E. (1999) Police for or police service? Gender and emotional labor, *The Annals of the American Academy of Political and Social Science*, 561(1) 111–126.

Mastracci, S.H., Guy, M.E. & Newman, M.A. (2012) *Emotional Labour and Crisis Response Working on the Razor's Edge* (New York: M.E. Sharpe).

McCarthy, D. & Brunton-Smith, I. (2018) The effect of penal legitimacy on prisoners' postrelease desistance. *Crime & Delinquency*, 64(7) 917–938.

Morris, A. & Feldman, D.C. (1996) The dimensions, antecedents, and consequences of emotional labour, *The Academy of Management Review*, 21(4) 986–1010.

Per-Ake Nylander, O., Lindberg, O. & Bruhn, A. (2011) Emotional labour and emotional strain among Swedish prison officers, *European Journal of Criminology*, 8(6) 469–483.

O'Brien, E. & Linehan, C. (2014) A balancing act: Emotional challenges in the HR Role, *Journal of Management Studies*, 51(8) 1257–1285.

O'Brien, E. & Linehan, C. (2018) The last taboo?: Surfacing and supporting emotional labour in HR work, *The International Journal of of Human Resource Management*, 29(4) 683–709.

Orzechowicz, D. (2008) Privileged emotion managers: The case of actors, *Social Psychology Quarterly*, 71(2) 143–156.

Phillips, J., Fowler, A. & Westaby, C. (2018) Self-disclosure in criminal justice: What form does it take and what does it achieve? *International Journal of Offender Therapy and Comparative Criminology*, 62(12) 1–20.

Pugliesi, K. (1999) The consequences of emotional labor: Effects on work stress, job satisfaction, and well-being, *Motivation and Emotion*, 23(2) 125–154.

Rafaeli, A. & Sutton, R.I. (1987) Expression of emotion as part of the work role, *The Academy of Management Review*, 12(1) 23–37.

Rafaeli, A. & Sutton, R.I. (1989) The expression of emotion in organizational life, *Research in Organizational Behavior*, 11 1–42.

Roach Anleu, S. & Mack, K. (2005) Magistrates' everyday work and emotional labour, *Journal of Law and Society*, 32(4) 590–614.

Salyers, M.P., Hood, B.J., Schwartz, K., Alexander, A.O. & Aalsma, M.C. (2015) The experience, impact, and management of professional burnout among probation officers in juvenile justice settings, *Journal of Offender Rehabilitation*, 54(3) 175–193.

Shuler, S. & Sypher, B.D. (2000) Seeking emotional labor. When managing the heart enhances the work experience, *Management Communication Quarterly*, 14(1) 50–89.

Skilbeck, J. & Payne, S. (2003) Emotional support and the role of Clinical Nurse Specialists in palliative care, *Journal of Advanced Nursing*, 43(5) 521–530.

Strickland, W.J. (1993) Institutional emotion norms and role satisfaction: Examination of a career wife population, *Sex Roles*, 26 423–439.

Sutton, R.I. (1991) Maintaining norms about expressed emotions: The case of bill collectors', *Administrative Science Quarterly*, 36 245–268.

Tolich, M.B. (1993) Alienating and liberating emotions at work. Supermarket clerk's performance, *Journal of Contemporary Ethnography*, 22(3) 361–381.

Tracy, S.J. (2005) Locking up emotion: Moving beyond dissonance for understanding emotional labor discomfort, *Communication Monograph*, 72 261–283.

Tyler, T.R. (2006) *Why People Obey the Law*. Princeton: Princeton University Press.

Van Maanen, J. & Barley, S. (1984) Occupational communities: Culture and control in organizations, *Research in Organizational Behavior*, 6 287–365.

Webb, S. (2012) Online tutoring and emotional labour in the private sector, *Journal of Workplace Learning*, 24(5) 265–388.

Westaby, C., Fowler, A. & Phillips, J. (2019) Managing emotion in probation practice: Display rules, values and the performance of emotional labour by probation practitioners in their interactions with clients, *International Journal of Law, Crime and Justice* (forthcoming).

Wharton, A.S. (1993) The affective consequences of service work: Managing emotion on the job, *Work and Occupations*, 20 205–232.

Wharton, A.S. & Erickson, R.J. (1993) Managing emotions on the job and at home: Understanding the consequences of multiple emotional roles', *The Academy of Management Review*, 18(3) 457–486.

Wolkomir, M. & Powers, J. (2007) Helping women and protecting the self: The challenges of emotional labor in an abortion clinic, *Qualitative Sociology*, 6(1) 153–169.

Wouters, C. (1989) The sociology of emotions and flight attendants: Hochschild's managed heart, *Theory, Culture & Society*, 6(1) 95–124.

Chapter 2

Emotional labour in policing

Alex Black and Karen Lumsden

Introduction

This chapter outlines the emotional labour which is part of police occupational culture and the everyday police work of officers and staff. Emotional labour is the process of regulating feelings and expressions in line with organisational goals and involves 'deep acting' and 'surface acting' (Hochschild 1979). In previous studies, scholars observed that emotional labour can be fun, exciting and rewarding in contrast to merely alienating employees (Shuler and Sypher 2008). However, in policing, the emotional labour associated with police officers' everyday interactions can also lead them to develop work personalities which are 'marked by feelings of social isolation, suspicion, cynicism and conservatism' (Hawk and Dabney 2014: 1129). As emotion workers, police officers and staff are exposed to 'emotionally demanding interpersonal interactions (such as death, illness, accidents and crimes) on a daily basis, requiring them to regulate their feelings and expressions' (Brunetto et al. 2012: 428).

In addition to the above, policing has been recognised as a stressful and emotionally heightened occupation. This stress is exacerbated in the neoliberal criminal justice and policing contexts of Anglophone countries such as the United Kingdom, as public services including the police face cuts to budgets, staffing and resources, coupled with an increased demand for services from the public in a post-austerity context. The management and display of emotions in policing is shaped by, and associated with, a host of macro, meso and micro factors. This includes the aforementioned economic and political contexts and pressures. They are also shaped by police occupational working culture/s including processes of risk mitigation and new public management principles, and a traditional masculinised and reactive policing culture which dictates appropriate 'feeling rules' for various police roles and situations (Brown 2011). Finally, emotional labour is shaped by everyday interactions (and expectations) between police and the public, police and victims of crime, and police officers and staff as they collectively employ strategies to cope with and/or resist the daily pressures of the job. Crucially, we cannot analyse emotional labour in policing without taking account of the influence of the societal context, the occupational culture, and the way that these shape the everyday practices and experiences of emotion management tactics and strategies by officers and staff (Brown 2000).

This chapter begins by reviewing literature and studies of emotional labour and emotions in policing. This includes: police occupational culture and emotional labour; interactions with the public and 'double-faced' emotion management; gender and emotional labour as 'dirty work'; stress, burnout and cognitive dissonance; and the impact of police reform on emotions and the social organisation of policing. The final part of the chapter provides a case study of emotional labour in policing by drawing on the authors' ethnographic study of a police force control room in England (Black and Lumsden 2019; Lumsden and Black 2018).

Police occupational culture and emotional labour

As Jennifer Brown (2011: 130) notes, in police occupational culture 'a pervasive set of informal norms constructs a (largely) male identity of police and masculinised ways of doing policing' which valorises the physical and eschews the emotional. Although policing does consist of a softer element, described by scholars as 'social work' (Punch 1979) or 'peacekeeping' (Banton 1964) roles, the external perception of policing tends to focus on its masculinised reactive law and order culture (Reiner 1985, 2013). Research has indicated that whilst officers spend relatively little time responding to incidents with a criminal element, they still see catching offenders as their primary justification for policing (Loftus 2010). This occupational identity also consists of the ability to manage, supress and control emotions, presenting a calm and rational front to the public. However, there are elements of police culture which offer coping devices that allow officers to exhibit emotion without losing rational status, such as humour, solidarity and support (Brown 2000; Pogrebin and Poole 1991), which we explore in the case study at the end of this chapter.

Janet Chan (2007) utilises Pierre Bourdieu's concepts of 'field' and 'habitus' to examine the relationship between police occupational culture, officers' experience of stressors and means of coping with these. *Stressors* are disruptions of the usual conditions which require readjustments by officers. This is distinguished from *stress*, which is the 'strain experienced by individuals as a result of not being able to deal with the demands of the disrupting conditions' (p. 130). Stressors are those demands placed on officers within the 'field' which can be physical, psychological, political, social, legal, organisational or symbolic. The police 'habitus' is developed to allow officers to deal with these demands – police habitus being police occupational culture. Police culture is shaped by these stressors, but also offers a framework of 'assumptions and shared values' for responding to them (p. 130). Thus the demands placed on officers have created police cultural expressions of isolation, cynicism, machoism and hardness as a strategy of coping. As Chan notes from her study of police recruits in Australia, it is the organisational changes and pressures, rather than traumatic and dangerous frontline incidents, which are most likely to lead to police stress and alter the occupational habitus.

Stressors may also be produced by any changes or uncertainties in the police 'field' which then requires incremental changes to the police occupational 'habitus' in order to generate the appropriate frame to make sense of these changes. Some of the more recent organisational changes, such as increased accountability, integrity and professionalisation of the police service, for example, have shifted the traditional forms of culture from a 'code of silence' solidarity to a more cynical 'covering your arse' self-protective behaviour (Lumsden and Black 2018). These incremental changes to the habitus as caused by the stressors in the police field may lead to permanent cynicism (Chan 2007).

Interactions with the public: police work as emotional labour

Policing is an extremely varied profession which places complex demands on individual officers. They are at once public servants, but also at the same time public protectors authorised to use necessary force (Schaible and Six 2015). In his chapter 'The Asshole', Van Maanen (1978) notes how police officers create attitudes and typologies as a means of accomplishing their job more efficiently. He identifies three types which explain how police view their occupational culture and the citizens they encounter: 'assholes', 'know nothings' and 'suspicious persons'. The 'asshole' classification in particular is susceptible to 'street justice', stigmatised and treated harshly due to their failure to meet the norms of interaction between police and citizen (1978: 5). They challenge police legitimacy and transgress moral boundaries of acceptable identities. Although he does not explicitly refer to the emotional labour and management undertaken in these interactions with the public, Van Maanen's observations make evident that the 'asshole' classification and the action taken when police officers encounter one, provide an emotional 'expressive outlet' for the daily frustrations faced by patrol officers. Through this emotional outlet, the 'asshole' allows the officer to reinforce their superior status and allows them to reaffirm the necessity of their position

> ...the discovery and subsequent action taken when the police encounter the asshole provides an expressive outlet – almost ceremonial in its predictability – for much of the frustration policing engenders. To the patrolman, one particular asshole symbolizes all those that remain 'out there' untouched, untaught and unpunished. Such emotional outbursts provide, therefore, a reaffirmation of the moral repugnance of the asshole.
>
> (Van Maanen 1978: 18)

Examples like Van Maanen's demonstrate that unlike many other public facing roles in which employees are expected to express positive emotions and suppress negative ones, police officers are expected to express a whole range of emotions depending on the context. For example, they may be expected to display anger towards a suspect whilst also providing empathy to a victim (Van Gelderen et al. 2007). Incidents may also require officers to supress emotions and exhibit emotional neutrality, especially in situations where calmness is needed in order to smooth a situation (Shuler and Sypher 2008). This complex role of an officer demands them to be both 'nicer than nice' and 'tougher than tough' (Guy et al. 2008).

In his study of policing and emotional labour in Amsterdam, Van Stokkom (2011) draws attention to the changing nature of police-public relations due to a more repressive 'broken windows' police policy of fining citizens for minor breaches of the law, leading to an increase in 'unruly' and aggressive interactions. Analysis of these interactions and citizen complaints identified two types of unprofessional treatment: displays of power and bad-mannered behaviour. The first is traced to a 'forcing' style, and the second to a 'mirroring' style of policing (Van Stokkom 2011: 240). Both of these styles of policing erode professionalism and trust. The 'forcing' style of policing indicates to the citizen that 'the police are "above" and the citizen "beneath"' (Van Stokkom 2011: 240). In contrast, 'mirroring' involves the police officer assuming the role of the other and getting 'carried away with the emotions of the citizen' (Van Stokkom 2011: 241). Forcing involves 'depersonalisation (suppressing emotions)', whereas mirroring involves 'emotional contagion (letting emotions off the leash)' (2011: 242). Van Stokkom notes that all officers are prone to mirroring from time-to-time, but usually 'only' in relation to a specific situation or context and can therefore be overcome. For Van Stokkom, police officers could be better trained to manage their emotional outbursts by developing their emotional intelligence and argumentative skills. This may also help shape the emotions of the citizen they are interacting with as officers are not only required to manage their own emotions; they are also routinely required to manage the emotions of the citizens they encounter.

Double-faced emotion management

This dual management of emotions, of both officer and citizen, is what Tracy and Tracy (1998) refer to as 'double-faced emotion management'. In their study of police emergency call centres in America, Tracy and Tracy (1998) demonstrate how 911 call takers navigated the callers' feelings of anger or fear whilst also managing their own feelings of 'irritation, disgust, [and] amusement' (p. 407) in order to obtain the necessary call outcome.

Schaible and Six (2015) highlight how policing is an ends–orientated occupation. The necessity to achieve a particular situational outcome means that the ability to display a range of emotions can be an asset for officers. Contrary to previous research which suggests that 'surface acting' is most likely to lead to negative emotional effects, the work by Schaible and Six (2015) in an American police department shows how the ability to select from a range of emotions through surface acting may actually release officers from organisational display rules which require them to perform particular emotions. They are instead free to select the emotional expression most likely to achieve the desired results.

That being said, Barkworth and Murphy's (2015) study of the Queensland Police Service in Australia found that if officer treatment of citizens generates negative emotional responses, those citizens are less likely to comply with the law (cf. Van Stokkom 2011). This expands our understanding of 'double-faced emotion management' (Tracy and Tracy 1998) to consider not only the management of emotions within the situational context but also how that procedural engagement between officer and citizen may shape *future* compliance behaviour. This literature shows that the mediating factor between treatment and compliance is *emotion*. If people perceive procedural *injustice* by an authority, the negative emotions generated from this (e.g. anger, frustration) are more likely to lead to non-compliance in the future (Murphy and Tyler 2008). In the context of police-public interactions, Barkworth and Murphy (2015) conclude that the police need to be trained to interact with the public in a manner that reduces negative emotions and ensures the highest level of compliance. This has implications for police autonomy over emotional expression and the organisational display rules that guide them.

Gender and emotional labour as 'dirty work'

Literature has also drawn attention to the gendered nature of emotional labour in policing. Martin (1999) observes that women entering policing can encounter gender-related dilemmas in coping with norms related to emotional labour. They may face accusations of being too emotional in their response or too unfeminine if not emotional enough. In interpersonal relations with other officers, they are expected to adopt the role of confidante, and be 'supportive of a man's emotional venting, but criticised for expressing similar feelings' (Martin 1999: 124). Research by Brown and Campbell (1990) demonstrated that female officers differed significantly from their male counterparts in experiencing adverse reactions to the police environment and that a major source of their stress was the discrimination and harassment they suffered from male officers (see also Brown and Fielding 1993).

Martin's above observations regarding the gendered nature of emotional labour further highlights the tendency for emotional labour to be viewed as 'dirty work' and 'out of place' in various occupational contexts. As McMurray and Ward (2014) note, those workers who manage 'dirty emotions', emotions that may be 'out of place, contextually inappropriate, burdensome or taboo', can become tainted by that work, much like those workers who undertake physically or morally dirty tasks (p. 1139). This taint is a 'socio-logical consequence of the performance of emotional labour as emotional dirty work' (p. 1140). McMurray and Ward's ethnography focused on the Samaritans (who sit at the end of telephone lines listening to the concerns and fears of anonymous callers) and identified them as agents conducting society's emotional dirty work. Similar to the Samaritans, much police work involves being the last line of defence and/or picking up the pieces of a broken public sector including filling in for social and health care services during out of hours calls, and as a result of increased demand and economic cuts (Lumsden and Black 2018). Therefore, police officers are also required to handle bur-densome and disruptive emotions, which are often written out of rational accounts of work, and 'outsourced to others who act as society's agents in the containment of emotional dirt' (McMurray and Ward 2014, p. 1123).

Stress, burnout and cognitive dissonance

Policing is one of the most stressful occupations a person can undertake (Williams et al. 2010). This is further exacerbated because it is an 'occupation that is customer-facing with high emotional labour' (Cooper et al. 2005: 413; Lumsden and Black 2018). This stress can lead to above average levels of nega-tive mental health; negative physical health; and a negative impact on personal and family life (Schaible and Six 2015). The negative aspects of police work have been amplified in the past decade as police forces in England underwent austerity cuts which included reduced budgets, staffing and resources, against a backdrop of increased public and political scrutiny (Holdaway 2017).

Literature has shown that burnout, as a consequence of surface acting, is a psychological syndrome that leads to depersonalisation, emotional exhaus-tion and a lack of personal accomplishment. Deep acting, on the other hand, contributes to feelings of personal accomplishment and job satisfaction and is said to reduce feelings of exhaustion and depersonalisation (Bhowmick and Mulla 2016). Essentially, emotional labour only becomes problematic when the individual has to express emotions that do not reflect their own self-identity or do not align with their expectation/understanding of what their occupational role should be. As the organisation places requirements on an individual to perform emotional labour, it may emerge that the organisa-tional values do not align with the individuals' values, resulting in value dis-sonance, which, when executing the requirements of their role, combine to produce emotional dissonance (Schaible and Gecas 2010). Bakker and Heu-ven (2006) studied burnout amongst police officers in the Netherlands. Their findings indicated that the emotionally varied and charged nature of po-lice work requires surface acting which produces emotional dissonance. The more these officers deplete their emotional resources through surface acting, the greater the incidences of displays of cynicism and emotional exhaustion to citizens, including negative attitudes and victim blaming.

However, a complexity arises within policing in relation to the benefits of deep acting when the required emotions are negative (i.e. anger or aggression). Police officers are often expected to display negative emotions but this can be detrimental if the officer attempts to align their genuine emotions with them. Experiencing negative emotions over the long-term can lead to problems such as anxiety or depression and thus surface acting, rather than deep acting of negative emotions, might be most beneficial (Bhowmick and Mulla 2016; Schaible and Six 2015).

Bhowmick and Mulla's (2016) study of the Indian police explored deep acting in relation to negative emotions. They were interested in understanding why deep acting leads to less burnout and whether it is because organisational display rules mostly require positive emotions, with negative emotions being those most suppressed through surface acting. The assumption here is that genuinely aligning with positive emotions (deep acting) results in better job satisfaction and personal accomplishment. Their study sought to explore burnout in relation to both positive and negative display rules. They concluded that deep acting, whether positive or negative, resulted in less burnout because both emotions were *authentically* felt by the officer. For example, anger that was authentically experienced and lead to a successful outcome increased job satisfaction.

As previously mentioned however, surface acting can allow officers to distance themselves from traumatic situations and tragic circumstances (Schaible and Six 2015). Research has specifically focused on the impact of traumatic incidents on police officers. For example, Hawk and Dabney's (2014) study of homicide detectives demonstrates how officers prioritised homicide cases based on their typification of the 'true victim'. This allowed officers to be selective in who they emotionally invested in and which cases they distanced themselves from. However, as Schaible and Six (2015) demonstrate in their study of American police officers, whilst surface acting may at times preserve the emotional exhaustion of the police officers, it creates distance between officer and citizen through the process of depersonalisation which links to increased use of coercive behaviours against citizens (i.e. demonstrating position of power/authority, making someone afraid).

Emotions and the social organisation of policing

Whilst the above research focused on the interpersonal interactions between police and the public, it is important to consider the social organisation of the police role and its impact on emotional labour. As mentioned previously, additional stressors for police officers lie in the structure of the organisation, including organisational changes to their role, time pressures, staff shortages, a lack of resources and a lack of effective communication (Bakker and Heuven 2006; Chan 2007; Stinchcomb 2007). In Toch's (2002) mixed methods study, he found that police officers' sources of job satisfaction included providing assistance to citizens, exercising interpersonal skills, getting positive feedback from the public and receiving peer group support. Sources of stress tended to be specific to the job such as responding to the death of a child or the death of a colleague whilst on duty. Research has also demonstrated that employees experience positive job satisfaction when their emotions align with the expected frames of occupational culture in terms of interactions with the public or responses to calls deemed to represent 'real police work' (see below case study; Lumsden and Black 2018).

Stinchcomb's (2007) work notes that the organisational response to police stress such as psychological services has been individualised so as to focus on those traumatic, or life or death situations which are in reality few and far between in the day-to-day routines of officers. These incidents are also, as previously mentioned (Brown 2011; Loftus 2010), the types of 'episodic stressors' that officers may find most exhilarating and actually serve to reinforce the traditional ideas of what real police work is (Lumsden and Black 2018: 262). For Stinchcomb then, it is *'organizational management practices'*, such as autonomy, discretion and empowerment, which are the most significant for police stress and subsequent burnout (emphasis in original, p. 263).

It is also important to note that policing has undergone significant changes, particularly in neoliberal contexts of Anglophone countries such as the United Kingdom. Police organisations have shifted to view the public as customers or consumers to whom they deliver a professional service (Loader 1999; Westmarland 2016). The police are held accountable for meeting both consumers' needs and also the targets imposed by governments (Westmarland 2016). There has also been a huge shift to the civilianisation of police roles and the growth of an 'extended police family', re-establishing the role of an officer and the functions they perform (Neyroud 2009). For example, civilian staff can be found performing functions of policing including call taking and dispatch, managing enquiry desks, evaluating intelligence and gathering forensic evidence. A widening police remit of protecting vulnerable people contrasts against the more traditional crime fighting assumptions of the police role, resulting in renegotiation and reframing of what constitutes police work (Lumsden and Black 2018). These changes taken together may come in to conflict in different ways with the values of individuals within the police service and *their* perception of what police officers should do. As Schaible and Gecas (2010) argue:

> Depending on which blend of perspectives an officer favors and internalizes into his or her identity, he or she may have difficulties with executing the role expectations associated with competing visions of policing.
> (p. 320)

These changes can have a significant impact on an officer's emotional labour. In Schaible and Gecas' (2010) research, they identify burnout as related to value dissonance. This refers to the incongruence between the values held by police officers about the role and function of policing, and the values officers perceive other reference groups to hold (e.g. chief officers, the public and victims) about the role and function of policing. Organisational changes may lead to surface level acceptance of new organisational values which can lead to further depersonalisation and negative emotional displays (Schaible and Gecas 2010).

Hsieh (2014) observed that when public workers' personal values matched organisational goals, there was little effect on emotional exhaustion, especially when displaying positive emotions. In Bhowmick and Mulla's (2016) study of policing, those who identified strongly with the organisation were more likely to report higher levels of personal accomplishment. High levels of organisational identification reduced burnout, even where other stressors were high (such as a high workload). This demonstrates the emotional impact that the changing police role can have on officers and their self-identity. As Chapman (2009) notes, a 'very real crisis of identity' is occurring within police organisations moving from traditional policing to a customer-focused policing (p. 486) with traditional police culture at odds with some of the new organisational values.

Emotional labour and police reform

Brunetto et al. (2012) point out that public sector reform rhetoric has focused on improving service delivery, but in practice, the driving force of change has been in achieving efficiencies – sometimes at the expense of quality service delivery. Within an environment of rationalised budgets to an increasingly vocal public demanding more services, individuals delivering services face high levels of stress (Brunetto et al. 2012). Toch (2002) explores whether there is a relationship between trends in police reform and trends in police stress by focusing on shifts towards community policing and diversification of police officers. Toch argues that these reforms do not come easily to 'a profession in which rewards (and the indices of esteem) have been heavily tied to the pursuit and arrest of malefactors' (2002: 19). Other scholars have drawn attention to the impact of new public management principles and bureaucratic processes on officer and staff wellbeing. For example, Fitzgerald et al. (2002) highlight the frustrations felt by frontline officers in the Metropolitan Police when time was taken away from public relations to instead focus on the filling-in of forms. Studies have indicated that despite initiatives to stress at work and the mental health of officers, scarce progress has been made over the last two decades (Collins and Gibbs 2003). Therefore, understanding emotional labour in policing is crucial to also address issues of staff turnover and retention.

Case study: emotional labour in a police force control room[1]

The everyday emotional labour engaged in by police officers and staff is demonstrated in our ethnographic study of call handlers and dispatchers in a police force control room in England (Black and Lumsden 2019; Lumsden and Black 2018). The emotional labour performed is understood within the wider structural and societal contexts of austerity cuts, organisational change and concerns regarding staff morale. We explored the ways in which employees engaged in deep acting and surface acting in relation to boundaries of police work and non-emergency 101 calls, the handling of emergency 999 calls and their use of humour as a collective coping strategy. We found that for these officers and staff, emotional labour was tactfully employed as a means of resisting or opposing top-down organisational requirements vis-à-vis normative emotional expectations in the face of work intensification. Call handlers and dispatchers also engaged in 'communities of coping' (Korczynski 2003) in order to mitigate the pressures of increased public demand and reduced resources, to resist managerial pressures, and to create an enjoyable aspect to their emotional labour. Below, we present some of the key findings of the study including emotional labour as boundary work, the adrenaline-fuelled response to emergency calls and humour as a collective coping strategy.

Emotional labour as boundary work

Call handlers and dispatchers engaged in 'boundary work' regarding their constructions and understandings of what police work should entail. As Styhre (2011: 25–26) notes, boundary work involves the mobilisation of various resources such as political contracts, institutions, scientific and practical evidence, forms of storytelling and anecdotes in order to exclude and delegitimate certain knowledge claims and accompanying demands for authority and to legitimise others. There was value dissonance between how call handlers and dispatchers viewed the role of policing, and how they believed the organisation, other support services and the public viewed it (Schaible and Gecas 2010). They felt that police officers were filling in for the service gaps of other organisations, such as social services. This was a source of frustration as highlighted in a conversation with one call handler who suggested that 'people have no tolerance anymore' and they 'expect us to sort out everything' (Field notes, 15 February 2017). This frustration was evidence of uncertainty regarding the boundaries of police work. As Manning (1982) notes, the control room is the 'screen or mesh' through which call handlers are able to filter out what is and is not police-relevant. This boundary was not clear-cut for these call handlers. Ben described the difficulty of responding to 'the messy stuff, the stuff in the grey area'. By this he meant calls that were not crime-oriented (i.e. chasing suspects/offenders), but non-crime, social welfare incidents. For example, typical non-crime calls that were observed included escorting an intoxicated person home, responding to non-crime domestic incidents and helping an elderly lady with poor eyesight find her house keys (Field notes, 16 December 2016).

In the context of reduced resources and heightened risk awareness, the moral duty expected of police officers was a source of increased emotional pressure. Dispatchers, for example, had to resource incidents in line with priority gradings which were related to risk assessments (Black and Lumsden, 2019). Frustration was observed when officers were deployed to incidents that were not perceived to be police work but were viewed as non-crime or social work incidents, or incidents in which the victim was already known. For example, an emergency call came in to report a domestic incident. The Injured Party (IP) was known to the police and had a history of domestic incidents:

> The dispatcher was frustrated that the resource had to be taken from another incident and sent to one that she felt was not going to have a satisfactory outcome and would inevitably happen again in the future.
> (Field notes, 22 November 2016)

The incident was recorded as a 'non-crime domestic' meaning no crime had been declared. The discussion amongst dispatchers reflected on having to attend incidents that were not specifically criminal but carried an element of risk for example non-crime domestics. The implication of being the 'last line of defence' means that responsibility always falls to the police in situations like these. As a dispatcher stated: 'if anything happens [to the victim], it's on us'. Important here is the constant reflection that the employees are engaging in around what policing is in the context of reduced resources, increased demand and a risk-conscious (and averse) environment. Trying to balance all three was a source of anxiety requiring the management of emotions in calls with the public and demonstrated their engagement in surface acting as part of the handling of calls not viewed as police work.

Adrenaline-fuelled: the emotional aspects of emergency 999 calls

Call handlers and dispatchers enjoyed taking a 999 call which entailed a major crime or incident as it was viewed as increasing adrenaline and relied on quick thinking and quick responses. Emergency 999 calls required more emotional investment from the workers, but this was viewed as energy 'well spent' in allowing for the adrenaline-related buzz of these calls. One call handler (John) explained how 'horrific' his previous shift had been – it was nonstop and had been 'hell'. They had several big incidents (a murder and an explosion) and the calls were 'crazy' (Field notes, 15 February 2017). John was still driven by the buzz of the previous day's shift even though it had been emotionally demanding. The experience of this shift as emotionally demanding demonstrates how John was also required to engage in a form of surface acting when responding to the calls – displaying a calm, collected exterior, while responding to emotionally charged and traumatic events.

Another example involved an offender who was being chased by a police officer. The officer in question called out to dispatch for backup. The dispatch officer coordinated the chase and subsequent apprehension. There was excitement and energy surrounding the call. The researcher noted that in this instance, more officers made themselves available to be dispatched than in previous incidents. The dispatcher stated that it was a police duty to offer solidarity and help one another. She was also informed that these more 'traditional' forms of policing (i.e. catching offenders) were preferable to social welfare incidents or 'domestics' (Field notes, 14 December 2016). The response to emergency 999 calls by call handlers and dispatchers entailed deep acting in which they would regulate their internal feelings and expend emotional energy when it matched what they believed to be the role of the police. This was especially so when there was a satisfactory outcome, evidencing the ends-orientated nature of policing (Schaible and Six 2015).

The above examples sit in contrast to 999 emergency calls which did not meet the frame or expectations of the call handler, such as in one instance when the call taker could not ascertain the location of the caller (Field notes, 15 February 2017). The call handler expressed frustration and annoyance at the inability of the caller to provide the necessary information. The call handler tried to remain calm whilst impressing upon the caller that they needed more specific information and became increasingly frustrated, thus wrangling with both emotional displays. These examples show how emotional labour can be both alienating and liberating (Shuler and Sypher 2008) particularly in relation to whether or not the calls follow the expected frame for the practice of emotional labour.

Neutrality was an additional form of emotion labour acting as a vehicle to guide the interaction between caller and call taker to reach the necessary goal of the conversation. This occurred in addition to the deep acting the call taker was already engaged in and meant that emotions may need to be managed at a later time if feelings are to re-surface during or after their shift. As one call taker explained: '…it does affect you afterwards, and they checked she was ok, but then you have to get straight onto the next call as it is never-ending…' (Field notes, 17 January 2017).

Humour as a coping strategy: 'on a scale of 1 to 10, how Kanye are you feeling today?'

During quieter periods, call handlers and dispatchers would engage in emotional labour in the form of humorous and jovial conversations, laughing and relieving the stresses and tensions of the job. Often these jokes would be about a particular call or incident. Whilst they might seem to be in bad taste, the intention appeared to be light relief rather than anything more malicious. These moments allowed for collective ways of coping with the stresses of the job, which were often very individualising and alienating. It reflects

Korczynski's (2003) work on 'communities of coping' as way of preventing negative emotions by using those very sources of frustration as a mechanism of humour. There was demonstrable caution and hesitation amongst the staff about making humorous comments that related to callers. However, in these moments, the strategies of managing workers' emotional expressions were subverted. Resistance to the strategies of managerialism was also witnessed in relation to workplace stress. For example:

> Towards the end of the evening an A4 piece of paper came over to the dispatch officers titled: 'Kanye to Kanye'. On it was a question 'How Kanye are you feeling today?' and then there was a scale of 1 to 10, with each stage corresponding to a picture of Kanye West's head. The heads were all different from smiley down to the picture of him when he had been hospitalised because of a rumoured psychotic break down a few days prior as reported in the press. I asked about this and I was told it was a tool to measure the dispatch staff's motivation/stress levels for the shift. It was obviously intended to be facetious at the same time as showing concern for staff morale. The dispatch officers said on that shift that they were '3 Kanye' i.e. not very happy. They shouted it out as if they were talking to the whole room and people were laughing. They passed it on to the table next to us and then it got passed around the room.
>
> (Field notes, 16 December 2016)

Humour is used collectively to parody managerial techniques of stress and emotion management (Shuler and Sypher 2008). In law enforcement environments it has been found to reduce stress by allowing the expression of alternative emotions that would otherwise be supressed (Garner 1997; Pogrebin and Poole 1991). Staff acknowledged the high levels of stress within the control room. The ability to acknowledge and publicly manage the stresses of the job was a form of emotion work that acted as catharsis for the staff (Tracy and Tracy 1998). Therefore, examples such as this highlight the positive and communal aspects of emotional labour in police occupational culture, as a means of coping with the pressures of the job.

Conclusion

This chapter provided an overview of literature on emotional labour in policing. It also presented a case study of emotional labour in a force control room in England which highlights how both societal and organisational stressors impact on the expression of emotions and their management by officers and staff. Crucially, better understanding of emotional labour may help to enhance professional police performance (Barkworth and Murphy 2015). In police organisations, the importance of understanding and expressing emotions is not well-recognised and discussing emotion is usually discouraged

(Van Stokkom 2011). Policing has been recognised as a stressful and emotionally heightened occupation, and attempts to address this have mainly focused on welfare supports and employee programmes of assistance. However, these may be addressing the strains rather than the overall stressors that police experience (Collins and Gibbs 2003). The chapter highlighted how emotional labour in policing is gendered and can often be understood as 'dirty work'. In this sense, police officers and staff are often required to handle difficult emotions which are often written out of rational accounts of work, or are in contexts in which the incidents being dealt with are not seen as 'police work'. These attitudes are also partly due to the stubborn prevailing constructions and representations of policing as a traditionally masculine and reactive role, focused on maintaining 'law and order' and catching criminals. Finally, the chapter has demonstrated that police officers are expected to express a whole range of emotions due to the variety of incidents encountered; and this includes both positive and/or negative emotions as demanded by the situation. However, as emotion workers, police officers and staff are also adept at utilising surface acting and deep acting, and in creating and maintaining collective 'communities of coping'; for instance, through the use of humour in their day-to-day operational duties.

Note

1 Some excerpts from this section were previously published in: Lumsden, K. and Black, A. (2018) 'Austerity policing, emotional labour and the boundaries of police work: An ethnography of a police force control room in England.' *British Journal of Criminology*, 58(3): 606–623. http://dx.doi.org/10.1093/bjc/azx045. The authors have permission to use these.

References

Bakker, A.B. and Heuven, E. (2006) 'Emotional dissonance, burnout, and in-role performance amongst nurses and police officers.' *International Journal of Stress Management*, 13(4): 423–440.

Barkworth, J.M. and Murphy, K. (2015) 'Procedural justice policing and citizen compliance behaviour: The importance of emotion.' *Psychology, Crime & Law*, 21(3): 254–273.

Banton, M. (1964) *The Policeman in the Community*. London: Tavistock.

Bhowmick, S. and Mulla, Z. (2016) 'Emotional labour of policing: Does authenticity play a role?' *International Journal of Police Science and Management*, 18(1): 47–60.

Black, A. and Lumsden, K. (2019) 'Dispositives of risk(work) and precautionary policing in a police force control room in England: An ethnography of call handlers, dispatchers and officers' responses to domestic incidents.' *Policing & Society*. iFirst. doi:10.1080/10439463.2019.1568428.

Brown, J.M. (2000) 'Occupational culture as a factor in the stress experiences of police officers.' In: F. Leishman, B. Loveday and S. Savage (eds.) *Core Issues in Policing*, 2nd edition. London: Addison-Wesley, pp. 249–260.

Brown, J.M. (2011) 'Stress and policing: A retrospective reflection and contemporary updating.' In: T. Devonport (ed.) *Managing Stress: From Theory to Application.* Hauppage, NY: Nova Science Publishers, pp. 127–160.

Brown, J.M. and Campbell, E.A. (1990) 'Sources of occupational stress in the police.' *Work and Stress,* 4: 305–318.

Brown, J. and Fielding, J. (1993) 'Qualitative difference in men and women police officers' experience of occupational stress.' *Work and Stress,* 7: 327–340.

Brunetto, Y., Teo, S.T.T., Shacklock, K. and Farr-Wharton, R. (2012) 'Emotional intelligence, job satisfaction, well-being and engagement: Explaining organisational commitment and turnover intentions in policing.' *Human Resource Management Journal,* 22(4): 428–411.

Chan, J.B. (2007) 'Police stress and occupational culture.' In: M. O'Neill, M. Marks and A.M. Singh (eds.) *Police Occupational Culture: New Debates and Directions.* Oxford: JAI Press Inc., pp. 129–152.

Chapman, D. (2009) 'Emotional labour in the context of policing in victoria: A preliminary analysis.' *International Journal of Police Science and Management,* 11(4): 476–492.

Collins, P.A. and Gibbs, A.C.C. (2003) 'Stress in police: A study of the origin, prevalence and severity of stress related symptoms in a county police force.' *Occupational Medicine,* 53: 256–264.

Cooper, C., Cartwright, S. and Robertson, S. (2005) 'Work environments, stress, and productivity: An examination using ASSET.' *International Journal of Stress Management,* 12(4): 409–423.

Fitzgerald, M., Hough, M., Joseph, I. and Qureshi, T. (2002) *Policing for London.* Cullompton: Willan Publishing.

Garner, G. (1997) 'Humor in policing: Its relationship to the bonding process.' *Journal of Police and Criminal Psychology,* 12(1): 48–60.

Guy, M.E., Newman, M.A., and Mastracci, S.H. (2008) *Emotional Labor.* London: Routledge.

Hawk, S.L. and Dabney, D.A. (2014) 'Are all cases treated equal? Using Goffman's frame analysis to understand how homicide detectives orient to their work.' *British Journal of Criminology,* 54: 1129–1147.

Hochschild, A.R. (1979) 'Emotion work, feeling rules, and social structure.' *American Journal of Sociology,* 85(3): 551–575.

Holdaway, S. (2017) 'The re-professionalization of the police in England and Wales.' *Criminology & Criminal Justice,* 17(5): 588–604.

Hsieh, C.W. (2014) 'Burnout among public service workers: The role of emotional labor requirements and job resources.' *Review of Public Personnel Administration,* 34(4): 379–402.

Korczynski, M. (2003) 'Communities of coping: Collective emotional labour in service work.' *Organization,* 10(1): 55–79.

Loader, I. (1999) 'Consumer culture and the commodification of policing and security.' *Sociology,* 33(2): 373–392.

Loftus, B. (2010) 'Police occupational culture: Classic themes, altered times.' *Policing & Society,* 20(1): 1–20.

Lumsden, K. and Black, A. (2018) 'Austerity policing, emotional labour and the boundaries of police work: An ethnography of a police force control room in England.' *British Journal of Criminology,* 58(3): 606–623.

Manning, P.K. (1982) 'Producing drama: Symbolic communication and the police.' *Symbolic Interaction*, 5(2): 223–242.

Martin, S.E. (1999) 'Police force or police service? Gender and emotional labor.' *The Annals of the American Academy of Political and Social Science*, 561: 111–126.

McMurray, R. and Ward, J. (2014) '"Why would you want to do that?": Defining emotional dirty work.' *Human Relations*, 67(9): 1123–1143.

Murphy, K. and Tyler, T. (2008) 'Procedural justice and compliance behaviour: The mediating role of emotions.' *European Journal of Social Psychology*, 38(4): 652–668.

Neyroud, P. (2009) 'Civilianization.' In: J. Fleming and A. Wakefield (eds.) *The Sage Dictionary of Policing*. London: Sage, pp. 25–28.

Pogrebin, M.R. and Poole, E.D. (1991) 'Police and tragic events: The management of emotions.' *Journal of Criminal Justice*, 19(4): 395–403.

Punch, M. (1979) 'The secret social service.' In: S. Holdaway (ed.) *The British Police*. London: Edward Arnold, pp. 102–117.

Reiner, R. (1985) *The Politics of the Police*. New York: Harvester Wheatsheaf.

Reiner, R. (2013) 'Who governs? Democracy, plutocracy, science and prophecy in policing.' *Criminology & Criminal Justice*, 13(2): 161–180.

Schaible, L.M. and Gecas, V. (2010) 'The impact of emotional labor and value dissonance on burnout among police officers.' *Police Quarterly*, 13(3): 316–341.

Schaible, L.M. and Six, M. (2015) 'Emotional strategies of police and their varying consequences for burnout.' *Police Quarterly*, 19(1): 3–31.

Shuler, S. and Sypher, B.D. (2008) 'Seeking emotional labor: When managing the heart enhances the work experience.' *Management Communication Quarterly*, 14(1): 50–89.

Stinchcomb, J.B. (2007) 'Searching for stress in all the wrong places: Combating chronic organizational stressors.' *Policing, Police Practice and Research*, 5(3): 259–277.

Styhre, A. (2011) *Knowledge Sharing in Professions*. Surrey: Gower.

Toch, H. (2002) *Stress in Policing*. Washington: American Psychological Association.

Tracy, S.J. and Tracy, K. (1998) 'Emotion labor at 911: A case study and theoretical critique.' *Journal of Applied Communication Research*, 26: 390–411.

Van Gelderen, B., Heuven, E., van Veldhoven, M., Zeelenberg, M. and Croon, M. (2007) 'Psychological strain and emotional labor among police-officers: A diary study.' *Journal of Vocational Behavior*, 71: 446–459.

Van Maanen, J. (1978) 'The asshole.' In: P.K. Manning and J. Van Maanen (eds.) *Policing: A View from the Street*. Santa Monica, CA: Goodyear, pp. 221–237.

Van Stokkom, B. (2011) 'Dealing with defiant citizens: Building emotional intelligence into police work.' In: S. Karstedt, I. Loader and H.E. Strang (eds.) *Emotions, Crime and Justice*. Oxford: Hart Publishing.

Westmarland, L. (2016) 'Governance of policing and cultural codes: Interpreting and responding to policy directives.' *Global Crime*, 17(3–4): 352–369.

Williams, V., Ciarrochi, J. and Deane, F.P. (2010) 'On being mindful, emotionally aware, and more resilient: Longitudinal pilot study of police recruits.' *Australian Psychologist*, 45(4): 274–282.

Chapter 3

Emotional labour in the legal profession

Chalen Westaby and Andrea Subryan

Introduction

In this chapter, we present an overview of the emotional labour of legal professionals in their everyday work. For the purposes of this chapter, we will concentrate on those legal professionals which have been the focus of emotional labour research. In England and Wales, research has been undertaken on the emotional labour of barrister and solicitors, while in the US, research into the emotional labour of attorneys and paralegals has taken place. Furthermore, in Sweden defence lawyers have been the focus of research. Finally, in Australia, the emotional labour of magistrates has been documented.

More often than not the participation in the legal process is highly emotive. Consequently legal professionals regularly have to deal with extreme human emotion such as anger, frustration or sadness, whether it is through the representation of a client during a divorce, in relation to a violent crime or an attempt to remain within a country as an asylum seeker. However, traditionally emotional expression by legal professionals has been viewed as antithetical to law. This is in part due to the fact that historically, the legal profession has been established and maintained by men as a 'masculine cultural project' which is based on 'expertise, rationality, control, predictability and commitment' (Bolton & Muzio, 2007: 53).

Central to this conceptualisation of professional legal practice is the notion of impartiality. In order for law to be effective it needs to be impartial which, it has been argued, can only be achieved through the employment of rationality and reason (Daicoff, 1997). Emotions, on the other hand, are linked with affect and therefore related to bodily functions. This is seen to make them unpredictable and illogical (Maroney, 2006; Grossi, 2015) and antithetical to appropriate to legal practice (Binder et al., 2019).

Nevertheless, an increasing number of scholars consider the distinction between reason and emotion as not only unmanageable, but also harmful to legal practice (Silver, 1999; Lange, 2002; Montgomery, 2008; Bandes, 2011–2012; Flower, 2014):

> Legal scholars have, however, slowly begun to recognize the relevance of human psychology to a fuller understanding of legal systems

and actors and, thereby, to envision a more integral role for emotion in the law.

(Yakren, 2008: 142)

Rather, emotions are beginning to be seen by some as a vital element in the practice of law. Research relating to law and emotions has developed rapidly, moving from being associated solely with feminist and other critical schools of thought to 'an interdisciplinary effort aimed at exploring many dimensions of human affective response' (Abrams & Keren, 2010: 2004).

Additionally, it has recently been recognised that legal professionals conduct a significant amount of emotional labour in their everyday work (Yakren, 2008). Researchers have found that legal professionals are required to use a range of strategies to carry out emotional labour. These strategies are contingent upon factors such as the area of legal practice, legal culture both within and outside of the law firm, gender and stakeholder expectations more generally. Such strategies require the employment of surface acting, deep acting, the suppression of emotion and detachment in varying forms.

This chapter aims provide an overview of empirical research (which to date comes from the UK, US, Australia and Sweden) that focuses on the emotional labour of legal practitioners. It will focus on emotional labour in relation to challenging legal landscapes, women legal practitioners, adversarialism, the notion of superordinate and subordinate, empathy and 'iron self-control' and professionalism. An analysis of the consequences of performing emotional labour within legal practice will also be presented. The final part of the chapter takes the form of a case study of emotional labour in the legal profession which focuses on emotional labour conflict experienced by English family law practitioners. Subryan (2020) introduces the concept of emotional labour conflict which further highlights the complex nature of emotional labour performed by legal professionals working in family law as they traverse intra- and inter-display rule conflict.

Challenging legal landscapes and emotional labour

Traditionally, and particularly within England and Wales, lawyers as original status professionals (Harris, 2002) have occupied a position within society which afforded them high regard and respect for the legal services they provide (Abel, 1988).

However, barristers are self-employed, and this has always meant that they are required to perform emotional labour in order to gain work. This is particularly the case in relation to barrister's clerks who, due to their unique position, are responsible for controlling the flow of work to barristers. Therefore, in Harris's (2002) study barristers described the need to gain favours by performing emotional labour through surface acting. Furthermore, Harris discovered that this was often sexual in nature with barristers engaging in flirting with barrister's clerks.

It is also the case that barristers are actually hired by solicitors' firms. They are therefore reliant on legal services procured by solicitors and as such have to perform emotional labour. Thus, barristers are required to entertain solicitors engaging in surface acting to feign an interest in their 'squalid little lives – [interest] in their children their petty squabbles, their workload, their new house' (Harris, 200: 567 quoting Barrister with eight years' experience). Despite regarding this as a negative aspect of their job, barristers also understood that it was financially rewarding, so much so that it would often spill over into their home life and involve the emotion work of partners and wives.

There have been a number of shifts in the legal landscape meaning solicitors have had to adapt to a 'changing business context' (Muzio & Ackroyd, 2005: 616). There has been a rapid increase in commercial law firms as a result of the rapid expansion of the corporate sector. This has led to anxiety that what was once a collegial profession is now more concerned with the business of law, and that an entrepreneurial identity may replace professionalism (Sommerlad, 2007, 2011). Alongside this, change has come in the form of the convergent rise in consumer power, particularly of corporate clients (Dal Pont, 2009) as well as the opening up of 'reserved areas'. Before the passing of the **Legal Services Act 2007**, only firms which were subject to regulation by the Solicitors Regulation Authority (SRA) and had workers with particular legal qualifications and training could provide certain legal services described as 'reserved legal activity', which are legal activities reserved only for solicitors who are regulated by the SRA. However, the Act reduced the number of reserved legal activities, allowing unregulated companies to provide more legal services resulting in even further competition in the legal services marketplace. This has arguably affected the way in which solicitors are expected to work, and consequently the amount and type of emotional labour they are required to perform.

Client gathering and client loyalty have always been important to law firms, but the changes highlighted above have increased the importance of this aspect of solicitor's everyday work. They are therefore under increasing pressure to bring in clients and build up trust and rapport with current clients. Solicitors are also expected to provide legal advice quickly and efficiently, and often outside of traditional working hours (Thornton, 2016).

Not only does this add to the 'long hours culture' (Sommerlad, 2002; Webley & Duff, 2007; Epstein et al., 2014) already prevalent in the occupational culture of solicitors but also the need to engage in longer and more intense periods of emotional labour.

Furthermore, in her study of female solicitors Sommerlad (2016) highlights how the strong influence of both the client and the solicitor's firm, particularly as a result of commercialisation, has produced further demand for emotional labour by female legal practitioners in their interactions with clients. While legal knowledge is regarded as a given, the need to build rapport with clients is considered to be key. This means that the female solicitors in Sommerlad's study not only had to engage in 'chit chat' with clients, but also socialise with them and lawyers from other law firms outside the normal working day (2016: 73).

Women legal practitioners and emotional labour

Bolton and Muzio (2007: 47) comment that the 'effective closure regime', which in the past barred women from becoming lawyers, has over time been gradually eroded. Indeed, a study conducted by the SRA in 2017 found that 48% of women were working as lawyers in law firms in England and Wales (SRA, 2017). This can be contrasted with the figures for 1990 which stood at 23%, and less than 10% of lawyers in 1982 were women (Aulakh et al., 2017). A similar, if perhaps more moderated, trend can be seen in the US with 34.8% of women working as lawyers in 2018 (American Bar Association, 2019) in comparison to 1960 when only 25% of women were lawyers (Cheeseman Day, 2018).

The commercialisation of the profession in the UK has resulted in women being expected to engage in emotional labour, which is not associated with their role as lawyers, but as women (Sommerlad, 2016). Participants described how they were able to use emotional labour to build rapport with clients and thus increase the profitability for the law firm. Sommerlad also refers to the exploitation of women lawyer's 'erotic capital' and sexualisation and the ensuing emotional labour (2016: 63). It is clear from Sommerlad's analysis that this type of emotional labour is not only hard work but also potentially dangerous work. Women lawyers have to negotiate interactions with both solicitors and clients as powerful role receivers carefully whilst ensuring that both professional integrity and working relationships are maintained simultaneously.

The substantial increase in the number of women lawyers conceals the fact that the number of women working in other roles in UK law firms far outweighs men at around 75% (SRA, 2017). Similarly, in the US 87% of women were recorded as being paralegals who support attorneys in the provision of legal services (Anders, 2019).

In her study of the emotional labour of US paralegals, Pierce (1995) found that female paralegals were both interruptible, and in contrast, invisible depending upon the disposition of the attorney they supported. When attorneys did engage with female paralegals they would often treat them as if they were adversaries and consequently interrogate, intimidate and grill them. However, in accordance with gender stereotypes, female paralegals were expected to respond to this type of treatment by suppressing any unwanted emotion, and particularly anger. Where a female paralegal responded inappropriately, thereby not conforming to prescribed display rules, this could lead to poor appraisals, being passed over for promotion, or in – extreme circumstances – being dismissed (Pierce, 1999; Lively, 2000).

Female paralegals were expected to engage in the caretaking of attorneys (Pierce, 1999; Lively, 2000), which requires them to be pleasant despite being treated with contempt and disdain (Pierce, 1999). They were also required to 'hand hold' which consisted of reassuring attorneys in order to decrease stress and anxiety (1999: 131). This relationship is consequently one example of how the US law firm can be regarded as 'a site for the reproduction of gender' (Pierce, 1995: 3). Female paralegals are therefore expected to conform to 'gender-appropriate' displays (Pierce 1999: 132), and which, therefore, position men as dominant and women as subordinate.

Adversarialism and emotional labour

Adversarialism is 'a system of governance driven by three major forces: (1) formal legal contestation, (2) litigant activism including fact-finding and (3) decentred-decision making' (Scheffer, 2010: xvi). It is this system which generally dominates both the English and US legal systems, and it is within this environment that legal practitioners have to work. Adversarialism has been found to impact upon expected emotional labour.

In her study of US attorneys, Pierce (1995: 50) highlights the fact that the adversarial model encourages a 'macho ethic' whereby lawyers act as 'zealous advocates'. This has led to two types of emotional labour being used to persuade juries, judges and witnesses in the courtroom, in depositions and in communications with opposing counsel and clients.

The first is strategic friendliness, where charm or flattery is used to manipulate others and, is therefore directly linked to the adversarial model and importantly the need to win, which Pierce (1995: 73) links to masculinity and competition. An example can be seen in the cross-examination of a sympathetic witness, where a law student is coached to gently draw out information from a widower about his new girlfriend, thereby reducing credibility in his testimony without compromising the jury's perception of her as legal counsel (Pierce, 1995).

Westaby (2014) also describes strategic friendliness being used by some immigration solicitors in their interactions with United Kingdom Border Agency case owners. Participants pointed to the need to 'butter up' case owners in order to ensure a positive response to their requests on behalf of their asylum clients. While it may seem like deferential behaviour, there is a manipulative, and therefore masculinised, element akin to that utilised by US attorneys in Pierce's study.

Intimidation, which is also considered by Pierce (1995: 60) as a masculinising practice, requires the use of anger and aggression with lawyers portraying themselves as the 'Rambo litigator' in order to dominate the courtroom. For example, US law students were observed being trained by teachers to use deep acting to feel the requisite aggression towards witnesses to achieve a successful cross-examination. One student, Tom, was encouraged to think about how a particular witness made him angry when they lied to him. This translated into the cross-examination with Tom becoming angrier and angrier in response to the witness becoming more and more intimidated and confused. His cross-examination was considered to be the 'best in the class' (1995: 62).

In contrast to US attorneys, who use intimidation to dominate the courtroom, immigration solicitors describe acting in an intimidating manner in order to confront what they saw as unreasonable behaviour from case owners (Westaby, 2014). This is described by Westaby (2014: 6 quoting Strazdins, 2000: 233) as a form of 'emotional contagion' which is framed in such a way as to promote the professional status and, therefore, mental agility of the immigration solicitor.

While Pierce (1995) makes reference to the 'Rambo litigator' and the performance of different forms of emotional labour as masculinising practices in her study of US attorneys, Flower (2020) in her chapter later in this book describes more nuanced emotion management techniques by criminal defence lawyers in Sweden. While Tom was praised by his law teacher for becoming more and more angry with a witness (Pierce, 1995), defence lawyers in Sweden, and particularly those who practice outside Stockholm, regard displays of aggression and hardness as inappropriate. They favour 'straight and honest communication' (Lo, quoted in Flower, 2020: 176) and consideration of the witnesses they cross-examine. Flowers suggests that rather than displaying anger Swedish criminal defence lawyers take a more measured approach, which she describes as, '"Rambo-bambi"…Anger can therefore be shown by raised eyebrows, a shake of the head or a quiet exclamation such as "what!?"' (Flower, 2020: 177).

Superordinacy, subordinacy and emotional labour

It is clear that there has been a change in the legal landscape over the years, which has, particularly in commercial law service practice, meant a shift from a public service role to working within a service industry (Boon, 2005). However, lawyers remain original status professionals, and the specialised knowledge they possess provide them with an identity in which they align themselves with what might be described as the 'superordinate' simply as a result of their membership of this group (Pierce, 1995; Flood, 2016). Research shows how the performance of emotional labour is influenced by this perception. Pierce (1995), for example, references how strategic friendliness, as opposed to being deferential emotional labour performed by paralegals (Pierce, 1999; Lively, 2000), and perhaps barristers in their interactions with solicitors (Harris, 2002), can be linked to the superordinate perception of the role of the attorney and the need to manipulate and dominate others to win the case. Similarly, Westaby (2014) highlights how immigration solicitors situate themselves as superordinate in their interactions with case owners.

Where a case owner was junior and lacked the requisite knowledge, one immigration solicitor commented that this would result in them having 'less respect for them and so you perhaps become a bit more condescending towards them because you feel you know the law better than them' (Westaby, 2014: 5 quoting Solicitor with seven years' experience). As Westaby suggests, it is this specialised knowledge and their status as legal professional which informs the emotional labour they perform.

That said, there are situations where immigration solicitors have found themselves in subordinate positions, and this in turn has influenced the type of emotional labour they are required to perform. For example, in situations where case owners are not influenced by strategic friendliness or intimidation immigration solicitors spoke of how it was necessary to engage in deferential emotional labour. Therefore, negative or indifferent emotional displays must be met with politeness and courtesy (Westaby, 2014).

Where deferential emotional labour is required, both immigration solicitors and barristers felt they were expected to suppress genuine emotions (Harris, 2002; Westaby, 2014). As a consequence, for immigration solicitors, anger and frustration were considered inappropriate and surface acting used to portray emotionally neutral displays (Westaby, 2014).

Empathy and 'iron self-control' and emotional labour

Thus far, with the exception of discussion of the emotional labour of female solicitors in Sommerlad's (2016) study, the focus of this chapter has primarily been on what has been described by Harris as 'private emotional labour' (2002: 567). This type of emotional labour is non-public and concerns professional interactions with other legal practitioners: solicitors, barristers, barrister's clerks, paralegals, court clerks, ushers and judges. In contrast, Harris (2002: 568) describes the interaction with clients (or court users in the case of judges) as an example of 'public emotional labour'.

This type of emotional labour is arguably one of the most important aspects of a legal professional's everyday work. Research has revealed the distinct ways in which different legal practitioners perform emotional labour in their interactions with clients and service users. This can depend upon not only their job role but also the occupational culture which provides expected emotional display rules. Studies have focused on the use of empathy and in contrast, 'iron self-control' (Harris, 2002), in relation to the performance of emotional labour.

The role of empathy within legal practice has in recent years progressively become the focus of legal practice research. In the US in particular, there have been increasing calls for it to be regarded as a core lawyering skill, and one which underpins all other skills possessed by legal practitioners (e.g. Henderson, 1987; Rosenberg, 2002; Gerdy, 2008; Gallacher, 2012; Westaby &

Jones, 2018). In the UK, while there is less discussion of the concept in academic literature, it has been identified in the Legal Education and Training Review (2013) as a core legal competency. Additionally, in the Bar Standard's Board's (BSB) 'Professional Statement' for barristers it is also recognised that practitioners must 'know how and where to demonstrate empathy and act accordingly' (BSB, 2017: rule 3.4, 18). Empathy, however, still remains much debated as to whether it has a place in legal practice (Henderson, 1987; Maroney, 2006; Abrams & Keren, 2010; Grossi, 2015). As was highlighted in the introduction to this chapter, this is because traditionally law has been viewed as being based on impartiality, rationality and reason leaving no place for emotion in legal practice (Daicoff, 1997; Maroney, 2006; Grossi, 2015; Binder et al., 2019).

Nevertheless, empirical research suggests that empathy plays an important role in their interactions with asylum clients. Westaby (2010) comments on the fact that all the immigration solicitors in her study describe the necessity to display empathy and sympathy to clients in order to build a relationship of mutual trust and confidence. This is achieved through the use of deep acting and genuine emotional responses.

It could perhaps be predicted that empathy would be displayed by immigration solicitors given the highly emotive issues presented by asylum clients. Similarly, Kadowaki (2015) in her study of US 'consumer oriented attorneys' (practicing in, e.g., family law, criminal law and personal injury law) found that participants used deep acting in order to place themselves in the position of the client. Interestingly, this is not referred to as empathy, but instead participants described identifying and understanding the client and attempting to align their emotional displays to that expected by clients. It does, therefore, resonate with the emotional displays presented by immigration solicitors. Deep acting was also used by attorneys to align their personal feelings with the client rather than suppressing emotion in order to reduce frustration and gain 'inner peace' (Kadowaki, 2015: 334). Interestingly, then, the aim of displaying an emotion akin to empathy in this context is to conceal personal unprofessional feelings. Essentially deep acting is used by attorneys to remain professional when interacting with challenging and difficult clients.

The display of empathy is also considered important by Australian magistrates (Roach Anleu & Mack, 2005). This emotional display was primarily the result of having to directly interact with court users, and therefore required magistrates to manage unmediated emotion. This is described by participants as being achieved by displaying empathy such as that exhibited by a mediator or counsellor rather than an authoritative demeanour. Where this type of emotional labour was not productive then magistrates would record the proceedings or adjourn in order to allow court users to 'cool off' (2005: 608).

In contrast to those legal professionals above who commented on the need to use empathy in their everyday work with clients and court users, barristers highlighted the perceived need to use 'iron self-control' (Harris, 2002: 571

quoting Jackall, 1988: 47). Iron self-control is used to maintain emotional detachment and suppress any personal, and therefore, genuine emotional responses, which are denigrated as being unprofessional. Harris (2002) points out that this in fact contradicts Hochschild's (1983) assertion that genuine emotions are a natural part of the labour process. Barristers instead described the surface acting used to align their emotional displays with the emotional expectations of clients. Interestingly, it is in relation to clients that participants described the limited amount of deep acting they engaged in. Moreover, this occurred in extreme situations where the barristers found it difficult to even surface act to show loyalty to their client (Harris, 2002).

Barristers suggested that this way of performing emotional labour was necessary in order to ensure emotional detachment and consequently rationality when arguing their client's case (Harris, 2002). This is also related to the fact that barristers see themselves as having a particular standing as an original status profession and so it would be inappropriate to 'go running around after clients, holding their hands and fetching them cups of tea; that's what solicitors are for!' (Harris, 2002: 571 quoting Barrister of 12 years' experience). The barrister in this quote also alludes to the unique working environment inhabited by members of their profession. As mentioned in an earlier section, barristers only have limited direct interaction with clients given that their clients are actually solicitor's firms, and much of that interaction takes place in a public arena such as the court.

Professionalism and emotional labour

In the previous section, limited reference was made to professionalism and emotional labour. Both Kadowaki (2015) and Harris (2002) show how emotional labour is performed in particular ways in order to ensure that personal feelings are not revealed to clients, as this is considered to be unprofessional. Therefore, professionalism often requires the suppression of particular emotions.

For example, US paralegals commented on the link between the need to suppress anger in favour of deferential behaviour and the display of professionalism when being treated poorly by attorneys (Lively, 2000). Similarly, both immigration solicitors and US consumer-oriented attorneys considered the suppression of emotions as important in order to maintain professionalism in front of clients. Immigration solicitors spoke about suppressing emotions such as care and concern to provide a balanced emotional display (Westaby, 2010). In contrast, US consumer-orientated attorneys described suppressing anger, frustration and impatience in order to avoid being perceived as unprofessional (Kadowaki, 2015). Immigration solicitors did, nevertheless, talk about suppressing frustration and anger in order to maintain an appropriate demeanour, but this was in relation to case owners (Westaby, 2014). Australian magistrates also described the need to suppress unwanted emotions so that court users, their families and even members of the public in general were satisfied with their performance as an arbiter of justice. If unwanted emotions were not suppressed, then magistrates ran the risk of their behaviour being criticised as unprofessional (Roach Anleu & Mack, 2005).

It is clear that the suppression of unwanted emotion is not enough for legal practitioners to persuade clients and court users that their conduct is professional. Certain emotions must also be displayed. For example, US consumer-oriented attorneys described how they engage in surface acting as a way of dealing with difficult clients. This emotional labour is used for two main reasons: to suppress or disguise personal feelings regarded as unprofessional and to convey the display of professionalism. However, other emotions such as happiness and excitement were also tempered by these attorneys, as well as the urge to laugh at clients, and surface acting was used in order to conform to client expectations, and thus, for example, act sympathetic where appropriate (Kadowaki, 2015).

Flower (2020) also makes reference to professionalism in her study of Swedish defence lawyers. However, rather than suppressing emotions such as disgust, irritation and sadness her participants explain how they engage with these emotions and transform them into professional emotions and tools used to assist their client. Flower (2020: 179) describes one example as 'stoneface' – where the defence lawyer shows no discernible physical movement both facial and bodily – which is used as a professional tool to transform inappropriate emotions into professional instruments, such as drawing attention away from damaging information disclosed by a client.

The highs and lows of performing emotional labour in legal practice

It has been demonstrated in previous sections that legal professionals are expected to engage in diverse and often distinct forms of emotional labour depending upon the stakeholders they interact with, as well as the legal environment within which they perform. As a result of being required to perform emotional labour legal professionals described being affected both positively and negatively.

Both immigration solicitors and barristers described the performance of emotional labour to ensure tasks were performed more effectively (Harris, 2002; Westaby, 2010). Protection was also highlighted by both barristers and magistrates as being a positive consequence of performing certain types of emotional labour (Harris, 2002; Roach Anleu & Mack, 2005). For barristers, 'purposely simulating' (Harris, 2002: 575) certain emotions provided protection against displaying genuine emotion and thus acting unprofessionally. The importance of being able to enter into an emotional state described as 'the zone' or 'barrister mode' (Harris, 2002: 575) was highlighted as being important for success. On the other hand, some magistrates pointed to depersonalisation (where the unique qualities of court users are ignored or distanced from) as a protective measure, allowing the management of court user's emotions to become easier.

While legal practitioners highlighted some limited positive consequences of performing emotional labour, the negative consequences were significant and clearly deeply felt. Perhaps the most cited negative consequences related to mental health concerns. Emotional exhaustion was stated as being a consequence of performing emotional labour for magistrates (Roach Anleu & Mack, 2005); barristers described deep acting as resulting in physical and mental tiredness (Harris, 2002); and immigration solicitors went further in their descriptions of the mental effects of performing emotional labour linking such emotional displays to potential stress and depression. It is noted by Westaby (2010) that immigration solicitors were more forthcoming in describing the potential mental health issues arising from performing emotional labour than the barristers in Harris's (2002) study. However, there are serious concerns that legal professionals are socialised to see mental illness as a sign of weakness and are therefore unlikely to share their experiences. For example one barrister highlights the fact that admitting it was stressful was not the 'done thing' (Barrister of eight years' experience quoted in Harris, 2002: 573). Furthermore, Katzmann (2008: 13) in a speech as president of the New South Wales Bar Association, marking the beginning of Mental Health Week, drew attention to the fact that lawyers struggle with stress and tend to see those 'struggles as a symbol of our own failings. We regard it as a sign of weakness to admit to ourselves, let alone anybody else, that we need help' (see also Katzmann, 2015).

Magistrates and barristers make reference to spill over of their work, including its emotional component, into family life. Both barristers and magistrates highlight the negative effects on their home life (Harris, 2002; Roach Anleu & Mack, 2005). For example, a magistrate describes how they find it difficult to walk away from the distressing and traumatic situations that court users find themselves in, and try and be more patient with their own children as a result (Roach Anleu & Mack, 2005).

Some magistrates reported depersonalisation, with one describing the growing of 'a skin as thick as a rhino' (Roach Anleu & Mack, 2005: 612) as a result of having to engage in emotion management with court users who may in fact be experiencing inequality or social disadvantage. However, while it was acknowledged that this did result in negative effects on job satisfaction, it was also regarded as necessary in order to protect themselves.

Emotional labour dynamics among family law practitioners: a case study

In the first part of this chapter, we have seen that the practice of emotional labour in the legal profession is complex. Despite lawyers learning and internalising that they should have intolerance for their emotions at work

(Silver, 1999), most areas of law involve emotions. Legal professionals conduct a significant amount of emotional labour to meet the requirements of display rules and professional discourses (Yakren, 2008). As such, practitioners cannot avoid practising emotional labour at work. Put simply, emotional labour is an essential and vital facet of work for legal professionals (Pierce, 1995; Harris, 2002; Lively, 2002; Roach Anleu & Mack, 2005; Westaby, 2010) and thus, according to Jordan et al. (2006), it is essential that both employees and employers understand how to use emotions to influence other stakeholders' emotional reactions.

However, legal professionals have multiple roles as part of their job such as legal representatives for clients, colleagues and as practitioners within the profession (Ashforth & Humphrey, 1995). Each of these roles requires compliance with particular display rules, which are the implicit or explicit rules that postulate which emotions are appropriate and how they should be expressed to others (Grandey, 2000; Diefendorff & Richard, 2003). The display rules expected by stakeholders in relation to legal practitioners can be broadly split into two types: organisational display rules and professional display rules. Organisational display rules refer to the criteria for organisationally appropriate emotional expression in work-related contexts (Hochschild 1983; Rafaeli & Sutton, 1989; Sutton & Rafaeli, 1988), while professional display rules refer to explicit and implicit rules shaped by professional bodies that inform and guide practitioners (Bolton, 2005). In the case study, a third type of display rule was considered, that being informal client display rules. Such rules refer to a set of client expectations (societal norms) that relate to appropriate behaviours and emotional displays towards clients. Societal norms provide general, key rules regarding how and what emotions should be expressed during service encounters (Rafaeli & Sutton, 1989).

As a result of different emotional expectations, there may be instances when display rules can conflict, and this conflict occurs as a result of a tension in the underlying purposes of each display rule. Essentially, there is both intra- and inter-display rule conflict. Intra-display rule conflict refers to conflicts within the same display rule, and inter-display rule conflict refers to conflict among several display rules. An example of the latter within the field of family law practice sees the purpose of organisational display rules being to significantly influence customer satisfaction (Rafaeli & Sutton, 1989), whereas the purpose of a client display rule is to show support through demonstrating anger towards the other party. As display rules dictate emotional labour performances, it is when complying with display rules that display rule conflict can arise.

Inter-display rule conflict is, by its very nature, considered to be boundary spanning in that the emotional labour operates across organisational borders and agencies (Needham et al., 2017). As boundary spanners, legal professionals are required to possess an adaptive capacity to conform to display rules expected by different stakeholders as well as be aware of various social cues of different groups (Caldwell & O'Reilly, 1982). Such adaptation to multiple display rules, particularly among professionals who practice a high degree of emotional labour, could mean that boundary spanning roles are demanding. Importantly, the phenomenon of boundary spanning and intra- and inter–display rule conflict is under-researched.

Intra-display rule conflict

An example of intra-display rule conflict offered by one family law practitioner taking part in the study, Matt, pertained to tensions which existed when complying with competing organisational display rules. Matt noted that his immediate line manager expected him to 'emotionally support the client' which meant it was acceptable for him to discuss the emotional aspects of the case at work. However, Matt's department manager, who works at head office, did not see the need to discuss emotions at work. Matt explained the reasoning behind this to be because 'the family department is a small area of the business and the vast majority of the business is based on a commercial footing'. However, Matt found it challenging to comply with these competing organisational display rules when both his immediate manager and department manager were in the same meetings.

Another participant, Mary, who worked in the same firm as Matt said:

> We (the family department) are in our own little cocoon. I mean we do interact with everyone but when it comes to work other people don't want to know (about family law) so we're happy talking to each other really.

This demonstrates some of the intricacies of intra–display rule conflict as organisational display rules are not universal for the whole organisation but are contingent on the nuances of departmental practices, understandings and expectations.

Inter-display rule conflict

A few participants in the study indicated that a 'thick skin' is needed to deal with demands associated with choosing to prioritise and comply with one display rule over another. One participant, Madeline, highlights this dilemma, in a description of a conflict she experienced when faced with complying with both professional display rules and organisational display rules. Madeline notes that, on occasion, she advised clients to represent themselves at court to avoid the high costs associated with instructing a solicitor. While Madeline feels this is in line with professional display rules to act in the client's best interest, she notes that her manager discouraged such advice.

She states, 'I think that I'm acting more in my client's best interests than in making money for the firm and that's probably why I'm not climbing the greasy pole'.

Another participant, Jason, agrees with Madeline,

> the main difficulty is the client's expectations at the beginning of the case and that your role is to agree with them. Versus the firm's perspective that it would be a bad way to run a business to sit and agree with your clients and further that we would be doing a bad job if we did that.

Such inter-display rule conflict can occur often for practitioners, particularly as they deal with clients daily. Furthermore, where practitioners are identified by managers to have prioritised client display rules over organisational display rules, it may have an impact on the practitioner's career progression. In Madeline's case, she alludes to career stagnation, as she does not appear to be progressing in her career (Abele et al., 2012). It may be that progression opportunities are more likely to be offered to those practitioners who align themselves more with the commercial ethos of the firm. Interestingly, for both Madeline and Jason, it seems to be acceptable to prioritise the use of emotional labour to secure financial outcomes over practising emotional labour to manage the emotions of others.

Another participant, Oliva, discusses a further inter-display rule conflict between informal client display rules and organisational display rules. Olivia acknowledges the emotive nature of family law and said a challenging situation is, 'knowing that your client is going through a really difficult time emotionally. Actually, there will also be a big bill and you might have to pile on the pressure for them and that's a hard one'. This demonstrates a tendency of management to expect practitioners to prioritise organisational display rules over client display rules.

Consequences of display rule conflict

Key findings from the case study were that consequences of display rule conflict ranged from discomfort to professional identity conflict (in relation to the latter see, e.g., Robertson, 2010; Chenhall et al., 2016). Most participants said that they felt under pressure or stress when they experienced display rule conflict as they had to prioritise one rule over another. One participant, Emily, suffered from mental health issues when she could no longer reconcile the inter-display rule conflict she experienced between organisational display rules and her personal expectations arising from her professional identity. Emily disclosed that she worked for a firm with a reputation for being aggressive and ambitious. Unfortunately, for Emily, these expectations did not align with her personal expectations of being a paralegal. Ultimately, this inter-display rule conflict made Emily feel constantly under pressure and resulted in her leaving the legal profession altogether. This important finding paves the way for more research to be carried out in this area to explore the extent of potential consequences of intra- and, particularly, inter-display rule conflict.

Coping with display rule conflict

Regardless of the type of display rule conflict experienced by the participants, they all discussed the importance of coping communally in the work environment. Participants noted that coping and informal support at work were primarily obtained from their peers (Korczynski, 2003). However, some work cultures did not facilitate informal discussions for family law practitioners taking part in the study, which made them feel unsupported. This is because most participants felt that once they were able to offload with a trusted peer, they could continue with their working day.

A particularly interesting finding is that despite participants acknowledging the benefits of coping communally, some family law practitioners indicated that in order to preserve a good impression of themselves, they would falsify or alter their experiences on the job. Emily stated that she was constantly under pressure to present herself in a way that did not align with her personal identity. She confessed to downplaying her experiences at court to colleagues so that they would continue to consider her as a competent practitioner.

> Yes, I would limit it (experiences). I'll be honest with you. I would limit it. Yes. I would limit it I mean there were some things that you couldn't.... But knowing if the result wasn't in our favour going back and having to explain to 3 senior people on my own was never a pleasant thing.

This reveals the potential ongoing boundary spanning emotional labour within communities of practice which is currently under-researched. It also exposes nuances that take place among family law practitioners within a community of practice which could impact the quality of learning from such a community.

The case study uncovered interesting nuances of complying with display rules for family law practitioners. Participants discussed incidents of both intra- and inter-display rule conflict and noted the potential consequences of such conflicts. Moreover, participants said that being able to cope communally greatly assisted with minimising the impact of such consequences. Interestingly though, experiences of boundary spanning for family law practitioners within communities of practice could potentially impact on any learning arising from such communities. Further research is needed regarding display rule conflict and coping with consequences to gain deeper insights into the phenomenon described here.

Conclusions and future research

There are only a limited number of studies which focus on emotional labour in the legal profession. Additionally, to date there has been only limited analysis of legal professionals performing emotional labour within the criminal justice system. However, previous research does provide a number of interesting themes which could, whilst also being mindful of the jurisdictional differences involved in different legal fields, be the focus of analysis in future research conducted into practitioners working in the field of criminal justice.

Studies have highlighted gendered aspects of emotional labour. They shed light on the ways in which female legal practitioners are expected to perform gendered emotional labour, whether it be in the form of the exploitation of their 'erotic capital' (Sommerlad, 2016: 63), or to 'mother' (Pierce, 1995) higher status workers. Masculine stereotypes are also engendered within emotional labour expectations, and Pierce draws attention to how future attorneys are trained to act as 'zealous advocates' through intimidation and strategic friendliness (1995: 50). This leads Pierce (1995) to argue that law firms perpetuate traditional gender stereotypes. The SRA (2017), for example, reports that 40% of female lawyers mainly engage in criminal work, and it would be interesting to see whether Sommerlad's and Pierce's findings are replicated in relation to female legal practitioners working with the criminal justice system.

Research has explored the different types of emotional labour performed by legal practitioners and highlights the various approaches to performing emotional labour. For example, barristers make explicit reference to the fact that the display of genuine emotion is deemed to be unprofessional, preferring to engage in surface and some limited deep acting (Harris, 2002). Consumer-orientated attorneys in the US also do not report using genuine emotion, and instead use surface and deep acting in order to maintain professionalism (Kadowaki, 2015). In contrast, UK immigration solicitors emphasise the need to use genuine emotion and deep acting in order to build rapport with clients (Westaby, 2010). Therefore, a range of emotional labour techniques are considered appropriate by different legal practitioners at different times. These techniques differ according to perceived emotional labour expectation disseminated through formal and informal feeling rules and are designed to manage the emotions of the worker and those with whom they interact. Therefore, a comprehensive study of the emotional labour of legal professionals working within the criminal justice system may reveal some overlaps with other legal practitioners. However, such research would provide an important contribution to the field given the unique emotional displays which will inevitably influence those working within criminal justice.

What is also clear is that the way in which emotional labour is performed by legal professionals can ameliorate, and equally, contribute to the potentially negative consequences of performing emotional labour. In terms of the former, Kadowaki (2015) highlights the fact that US consumer-orientated attorneys use deep acting not only to ensure professionalism, but also to avoid the suppression of negative emotions. However, unless the legal professional is able to use deep acting in this way, or detach completely (Kadowaki, 2015), the suppression of genuine emotion is an intrinsic part of their everyday work. Paralegals commented on the need to suppress anger in favour of deferential behaviour, when being treated poorly by attorneys (Pierce, 1999; Lively, 2000). On the other hand, magistrates, despite occupying a senior position within the hierarchy of legal practitioners, also described the requirement for them to suppress unwanted emotions so that service users are satisfied with their performance as an arbiter of justice (Roach Anleu & Mack, 2005).

The suppression of emotion in most cases requires surface acting. There are some benefits of using this type of emotional labour highlighted by legal practitioners, such as task efficiency (Harris, 2002; Westaby, 2010) and protection (Harris, 2002; Roach Anleu & Mack, 2005). However, when surface acting is used to balance emotional engagement and detachment, this can potentially lead to stress and depression (Westaby, 2010). Further research which focuses on legal professionals within the criminal justice system that sheds light on the consequences, both positive and negative, would be welcomed. Moreover, recommendations as to how to support legal practitioners performing emotional labour would be a welcome addition to the growing literature in the field.

Finally, within the criminal justice system, legal professionals are expected to interact with a range of stakeholders such as clients, colleagues, Judges and other legal professionals. Each stakeholder will have their own display rules. It is an unwritten rule that legal professionals must engage with emotional labour in their roles as they comply with display rules. However, research carried out by one of the authors suggests that where display rules are open to interpretation, intra- and inter-display rule conflict can occur. Further research is needed to explore the nuances and complexities of emotional labour conflict and how it can influence employees, and importantly how communities of practice can both limit or indeed exacerbate the potentially negative consequences of such conflicts.

References

Abel, R. (1988) *The Legal Profession in England and Wales*, London: Blackwell.

Abele, A. E., Volmer, J., & Spurk, D. (2012). Career stagnation: Underlying dilemmas and solutions in contemporary work environments. In N. P. Reilly, M. J. Sirgy, & C. A. Gorman (Eds.), *Work and Quality of Life: Ethical Practices in Organizations*, London: Springer, 107–132.

Abrams, K. & Keren, H. (2010) Who's afraid of law and the emotions? *Minnesota Law Review*, 94(6) 1997–2074.

American Bar Association (2019) A Current Glance at Women in Law 2019, www. americanbar.org/content/dam/aba/administrative/women/current_glance_2019. pdf, accessed 14 June 2019.

Anders, G. (2019) Women are 87% of paralegals, but only 23% of law-firm partners. Let's find out why, Linkedin, www.linkedin.com/pulse/women-87-paralegals-only-23-law-firm-partners-lets-find-george-anders/ last, accessed 9 October 2019.

Ashforth, B.E. & Humphrey, R.H. (1995) Emotions in the workplace: A reappraisal, *Human Relations*, 48(2) 97–125.

Aulakh, S., Charlwood, A., Muzio, D., Tomlinson, J. & Valizade, D. (2017) Mapping advantages and disadvantages: Diversity in the legal profession in England and Wales, SRA, www.sra.org.uk/sra/how-we-work/reports/diversity-legal-profession.page, accessed 20 June 2019.

Bandes, S.A. (2011–2012) Moral imagination in judging, *Washburn Law Journal*, 51(1) 1–24.

Bar Standards Board (2017) *Bar Professional Training Course Handbook 2017/18*, London: Bar Standards Board.

Binder, D.A., Bergman, P., Tremblay, P.R. & Weinstein, I.S. (2019) *Lawyers as Counselors*, 4th Edition, St Paul, MN: West Academic.

Boon, A. (2005) From public service to service industry: The impact of socialisation and work on the motivation and values of lawyers, *International Journal of the Legal Profession*, 12(2) 229–260.

Bolton, S.C. (2005) *Emotion Management in the Workplace*, Palgrave: London.

Bolton, S.C & Muzio, D. (2007) Can't live with 'em; can't live without 'em: Gender segmentation in the legal profession, *Sociology*, 41(1) 47–64.

Caldwell, D.F. & O'Reilly, C.A. (1982) Boundary spanning and individual performance: The impact of self-monitoring. *Journal of Applied Psychology*, 67(1) 124–127. doi:10.1037/0021-9010.67.1.124.

Cheeseman Day, J. (2018) More than 1 in 3 Lawyers are Women, United States Census Bureau, www.census.gov/library/stories/2018/05/women-lawyers.html, accessed 14 June 2019.

Chenhall, R.H., Hall, M. & Smith, D. (2016) Managing identity conflicts in organizations: A case study of one welfare nonprofit organization. *Nonprofit and Voluntary Sector Quarterly*, 45(4) 669–687.

Daicoff, S. (1997) Lawyer know thyself: A review of empirical research on attorney attributes bearing on professionalism, *The American University Law Review*, 46 1337–1427.

Dal Pont, G. (2009) My client the bully, *Law Institute Journal*, 83(1/2) 76.

Diefendorff, J.M. & Richard, E.M. (2003) Antecedents and consequences of emotional display rule perception, *Journal of Applied Psychology*, 88(2) 284–294.

Epstein, C.F., Seron, C., Oglensky, B. & Saute, R. (2014) *The Part-Time Paradox: Time Norms, Professional Life, Family and Gender*, New York: Routledge.

Flood, J. (2016) Corporate lawyer–client relationships: bankers, lawyers, clients and enduring connections, *Legal Ethics*, 19(1) 76–96.

Flower, L. (2014) The (un)emotional law student, *International Journal of Work, Organisation and Emotion*, 6(3) 295–309.

Flower, L. (2020) Emotional labour, cooling the client out and lawyer face. In J. Phillips, J. Waters, C. Westaby and A. Fowler (Eds.) *Emotional Labour in Criminology and Criminal Justice*, 173–184. Abingdon: Routledge.

Gallacher, I. (2012) Thinking like non-lawyers "why empathy is a core lawyering skill and why legal education should change to reflect its importance", Syracuse

University, http://surface.syr.edu/cgi/viewcontent.cgi?article=1005&context=lawpub, accessed 4 January 2017.

Gerdy, K.B. (2008) Clients, empathy and compassion: introducing first-year students to the "heart" of lawyering, *Nebraska Law Review*, 87(1) 1–61.

Grandey, A.A. (2000) Emotional regulation in the workplace: A new way to conceptualize emotional labor, *Journal of Occupational Health Psychology*, 5 (1) 95–110.

Grossi, R. (2015) Understanding law and emotion, *Emotion Review*, 7(1) 55–60.

Harris, L.C. (2002) The emotional labour of barristers: an exploration of emotional labour by status professionals, *Journal of Management Studies*, 39(4) 553–584.

Henderson, L.N. (1987) Legality and empathy, *Michigan Law Review*, 85(7) 1574–1653.

Hochschild, A.R. (1983) *The Managed Heart: Commercialization of Human Feeling*, Berkeley: University of California Press.

Jordan, P.J., Lawrence, S.A. & Troth, A.C. (2006) The impact of negative mood on team performance, *Journal of Management & Organization*, 12(2) 131–145.

Kadowaki, J. (2015) Maintaining professionalism: Emotional labor among lawyers as client advisors, *International Journal of the Legal Profession*, 22(3) 323–345.

Katzmann, A (2008) Lawyering as Emotional Labour, Speech delivered to the New South Wales Bar Association.

Katzmann, A. (2015) Another inconvenient truth. Mental ill-health in the legal profession: What is wrong and how can it be fixed, *Public Defenders Conference*, http://classic.austlii.edu.au/au/journals/FedJSchol/2015/7.html, accessed 20th June 2019.

Lange, B. (2002) The emotional dimensions in legal regulation, *Journal of Law and Society*, 29(1) 197–225.

Legal Education and Training Review (2013). Setting standards: the future of legal services education and training regulation in England and Wales. London: Legal Education and Training Review.

Lively, K.J. (2000) Reciprocal emotion management: Working together to maintain stratification in private law firms, *Work and Occupations*, 27(1) 32–63.

Lively, K.J. (2002) Client Contact and Emotional Labour: Upsetting the Balance and Evening Up the Field, *Work and Occupations*, 22(2) 198–225.

Maroney, T.A. (2006) Law and emotion: A proposed taxonomy of an emerging field, *Law and Human Behavior*, 30(2) 119–142.

Montgomery, J.E. (2008) Incorporating emotional intelligence concepts into legal education: Strengthening the professionalism of law students, *University of Toledo Review*, 39(2) 323–352.

Muzio, D. & Ackroyd, S. (2005) On the consequences of defensive professionalism: Recent changes in the legal labour process, *Journal of Law and Society*, 32(4) 615–642.

Needham, C., Mastracci, S. & Mangan, C. (2017) The emotional labour of boundary spanning, *Journal of Integrated Care*, 25(4) 288–300. doi:10.1108/JICA-04-2017-0008.

Pierce, J.L. (1995) *Gender Trials. Emotional Lives in Contemporary Law Firms*, Berkeley: University of California Press.

Pierce, J.L. (1999) Emotional labor among paralegals, *The Annals of the American Academy of Political and Social Science*, 561(1) 127–142.

Rafaeli, A. & Sutton, R.I. (1989) The expression of emotion in organizational life, in Cummings, L.L. & Staw, B.H (Eds.) *Research in Organizational Behaviour*, Vol. 11, Greenwich, CT: JAI Press, 1–43.

Roach Anleu, S. & Mack, K. (2005) Magistrate's everyday work and emotional labour, *Journal of Law and Society*, 32(4) 590–614.

Robertson, C.B. (2010) Organizational management of conflicting professional identities, *Case Western Reserve Journal of International Law*, 43 603–623.

Rosenberg, J.D. (2002) Teaching empathy in law school, *University of San Francisco Law Review*, 36 621–657.

Scheffer, T. (2010) *An Ethnography of English Court Procedure*, Leiden: Brill.

Silver, M. (1999) Emotional intelligence and legal education, *Psychology, Public Policy and Law*, 5(4) 1173–1203.

Solicitors Regulation Authority (2017) How diverse are law firms? www.sra.org.uk/solicitors/diversity-toolkit/diverse-law-firms.page, accessed 17 April 2019.

Sommerlad, H. (2002) Women solicitors in a fractured profession: Intersections of gender and professionalism in England and Wales, *International Journal of the legal Profession*, 9(3) 213–234.

Sommerlad, H. (2007) Researching and theorizing the processes of professional identity formation, *Journal of Law and Society*, 34(2) 190–217.

Sommerlad, H. (2011) The commercialisation of law and the enterprising legal practitioner: Continuity and change, *International Journal of the Legal Profession*, 18(1–2) 73–108.

Sommerlad, H. (2016) 'A pit to put women in': Professionalism, work intensification and work-life balance in the legal profession in England and Wales, *International Journal of the Legal Profession*, 23(1) 61–82.

Sutton, R.I. & Rafaeli, A. (1988) Untangling the relationship between displayed emotions and organizational sales; the case of convenience stores, *The Academy of Management Journal*, 3193 461–487.

Thornton, M. (2016) Squeezing the life out of the lawyer: Legal practice in the market embrace, *Griffith Law Review*, 25(4) 471–491.

Webley, L. & Duff, L. (2007) Women solicitors as a barometer for problems within the legal profession - Time to put values before profits? *Journal of Law and Society*, 34(3) 374–402.

Westaby, C. (2014) What's culture got to do with it? The emotional labour of immigration solicitors in their exchanges with United Kingdom, Border Agency case owners, *European Journal of Current legal Issues*, 20(1) 1–26.

Westaby, C. (2010) 'Feeling like a sponge': The emotional labour produced by solicitors in their interactions with clients seeking asylum, *International Journal of the Legal Profession*, 17(2) 153–174.

Westaby, C. & Jones, E. (2018) Empathy: An essential element of legal practice or 'never the twain shall meet'? *International Journal of the Legal Profession*, 25(1) 107–124.

Yakren, S. (2008) Lawyer as emotional laborer, *University of Michigan Journal of Law Reform*, 42(1) 141–184.

Chapter 4

Emotions in context

The marginalisation and persistence of emotional labour in probation

Andrew Fowler, Jake Phillips and Chalen Westaby

Introduction

In this chapter, we explore and synthesise the limited extant research on the performance of emotional labour by probation practitioners. We begin by providing a chronological account of the appearance and disappearance of descriptions of emotions in probation practice. In doing so, we show how emotions can be seen to be inherent to probation work since the earliest accounts of probation work in the 19th century. We map the emotional labour expectations that would be associated with such work as well as consider how emotions are displayed by practitioners from this time until the last quarter of the 20th century.

We then track how the latter part of the 20th century and early 21st century saw the use – or at least acknowledgement – of emotion work in probation fall out of favour in probation policy in particular. In turn, we argue that this has led to a marginalisation of the use of emotion in probation practice with which comes certain ramifications for practitioners, who perform emotional labour as a core element of their work nonetheless. We then explore the small body of knowledge in the field to highlight the important role played by emotional labour in probation practice. We suggest that the performance of emotional labour in probation has the potential to impact upon the wellbeing of probation practitioners – although there is currently little evidence to support this hypothesis – and argue that support and training should be seen as vital in combatting these potential adverse effects.

How do we understand emotional labour?

Notwithstanding the introduction to the concept of emotional labour contained in the introduction to this volume, it is necessary to establish the way in which we have operationalised the concept of emotional labour in the course of our own research and in this chapter. Hochschild argues (1979) that social psychology overlooked emotions as governed by social rules and introduced terms like 'emotion work', 'feeling rules' and 'emotion management' to offer an interactionist account of how workers induce or inhibit emotion to make them appropriate to a particular workplace 'situation'. Hochschild argues that social psychology can be split into the organismic and interactive accounts of emotion. The former explains emotion as a visceral response to a stimulus, as capacities to be triggered whereas the interactionist account proposes that social situations influence emotion, guide and contribute to the management of emotion. In this chapter, Hochschild's (1979: 561) definition of 'emotion work' will be adopted:

...the act of trying to change in degree or quality an emotion or feeling.

This is used synonymously with 'emotion management' or to work or manage a feeling or emotion. The three types of emotion work Hochschild offers are cognitive, bodily and expressive. The 'cognitive' is where someone tries to change the feelings they associate with an image or idea, the 'bodily' is where someone tries to alter their physical symptoms of an emotion and 'expressive' is the attempt to change expressive gestures in relation to inner feelings. They are theoretically distinct but could occur together. In this analysis, the focus is on the bodily and expressive types of emotion work.

A history of emotion work in probation practice

Schnell (2005, cited in Plamper, 2017: 5) suggests that historical research into emotions involves two contrary positions: first, that human feelings have remained the same and means of expressing them change, and second, that each emotion has its own history determined by historical changes. It is beyond the scope of this chapter to enter this debate. However, this socially constructed view of emotion implicit in Schnell's latter understanding of emotions is a helpful way of understanding the use of emotion in probation work. Therefore, whilst the use of emotion is present in the early descriptions of the probation role the description of those emotions must be understood within that particular historical context.

The work of Police Court Missionaries of the 19th century is often cited as the 'origin of probation work'. Police Court Missionaries were the first people appointed by the Church of England Temperance Society (CETS) to work in the court and offer support to people sentenced by Magistrates (McWilliams, 1983). This represented the theological, Christian motivations and values that informed future probation work (McWilliams, 1983), and is best described by a Police Court Missionary at the time.

Grasp the hand of the one you would rescue, and with him ascend the mountain, instead of standing like an inanimate and unsympathetic signpost on the plain which you consider so unsafe for him. Love is the vehicle of all the medicines of Christ. (Ayscough, 1922, cited in Newton, 1958: 7)

The Christian faith played a significant role in the work of Police Court Missionaries, and the fundamental principle of probation work to support clients to make positive changes was prevalent. Moreover, the use of emotion was considered critical to this task with the work of the Police Court Missionaries being characterised as 'changing behaviour by changing feeling – through conversion' highlighting the necessity of missionaries having to use emotion to affect change (Newton, 1956, in King, 1958: 7). In these early accounts, missionaries used pledges, praying, friendship, advice and admonishment, or as Newton (1956, in King, 1958: 7) succinctly suggests 'persuasion, exhortation and support'. We see such examples of the importance of emotion in probation work in the commentary of Thomas Holmes (1900: 81–83) – a Police Court Missionary himself – when describing his work with a family where there is domestic abuse:

> I did not know whether to smite him or laugh [as a consequence of witnessing domestic abuse]. He was a big fellow, so I held my peace…I could have cried but I did not… He felt pleased that he did not owe me anything and I felt pleased that he should think so…so again and again, when I have been called to such homes, have I had to play the hypocrite and humour his delusion; to have done otherwise would have been madness.

An analysis of this example of 'rescue work' (see Auerbach, 2015; Gard, 2007; McWilliams, 1983; Vanstone, 2004) through the lens of emotional labour alerts us to the necessity of performing emotional labour in such circumstances. Due to the social situation, Holmes describes having to suppress the urge to cry or challenge the man's behaviour and instead engages in surface acting; displaying deference to the husband's position as 'man of the house'. This performance is required in order to build a relationship with the family, and in particular with the husband, who had recently been released from prison. Interestingly, Holmes also comments on the consequences of performing emotional labour when he refers to the need 'to play the hypocrite'. This could be regarded as an example of 'faking in bad faith' (Rafaeli and Sutton, 1989: 32), which is where surface acting is used to display 'fake' emotions.

King (1958: 7) argues that the success of statutory probation in Massachusetts and the work of the Police Court Missionaries demonstrated the 'practical possibilities' of supervising people who had committed crimes. This coincided with the passing of the English Probation of Offenders Act 1907, which established a statutory probation service. Leeson (1914: 86) cites The Departmental Committee on the English Probation of Offenders Act 1907 description of the type of worker to act as a probation officer:

> The value of probation must necessarily depend on the efficiency of the probation officer. It is a system in which rules are comparatively

unimportant and personality is everything. The probation officer must be picked man or woman, endowed not only with intelligence and zeal, but in a high degree with sympathy, tact and firmness.

The Departmental Committee therefore requires probation officers who are able to perform emotional labour effectively. The requirement to use feeling as a necessary part of the job was thus seen as an essential characteristic of the probation worker. The dualistic nature of the role, which often characterises probation work today (see Trotter, 2015), is also captured when sympathy is required but in conjunction with 'tact and firmness'. This enshrines the importance of the use of emotion in the early professionalisation of probation work.

In this 'professionalisation of feeling', Leeson further considers the dualistic nature of probation practice when he interprets the condition of the Probation of Offenders Act 1907 that requires probation officers to 'advise, assist and befriend' as meaning the development of a 'constructive friendship' (1914: 114). He maintains that a 'constructive friendship' is therefore one which demands the officer to not be a 'sentimentalist...nor a dictator or bully...' and that 'as well as [displaying] sympathy he must act up to his knowledge' (p. 114). Thus, the probation officer has always needed to perform emotional labour with clear boundaries in mind and balance sympathy with his knowledge.

Emotion has always been present in the work of a probation practitioner. However, we should also bear in mind Schnell's (2005) second position: that emotions have their own history and are determined by historical changes. The need to strike a balance between creating clear boundaries and connecting with the probationer resonates with contemporary probation practice. That said, 'sympathy' or 'pity' would be unlikely to feature in the description of helpful characteristics for a probation worker in the contemporary context. Gerdes (201: 233) argues that sympathy has been devolved in its level of meaning in the 20th century to 'pity' or 'sorrow,' representing 'feeling for the other' and empathy is now used for 'feeling with the other'. The use of 'sympathy' makes visible the early philosophical and theological underpinning of how people expressed this essential characteristic of the probation worker which was akin to the later social science and psychologically informed use of the word 'empathy' (see Gerdes, 2011). The use of 'sympathy' as an essential characteristic and contemporary use of 'empathy' represent an abiding commitment in probation practice to feeling as a necessary part of the job.

In the 1920s, the professionalisation of probation was given further attention through greater consideration of the training, payment and appointment of probation officers. Following a Departmental Committee report on these matters, the Criminal Justice Acts of 1925 and 1926 implemented changes to standardise working conditions, qualifications and qualities that were desirable in applicants including 'sympathy, tact, commonsense and firmness' (King, 1958: 15). Further to this the introduction of *The Probation Rules* of

1926 introduced a more standardised approach to probation work. Indeed, Le Mesurier (1935) offers a comprehensive account of probation work, albeit with less focus on the emotional aspects in practice. Interestingly, Le Mesurier (1935: 124) argued that the probationer should 'leave the Court with the feeling that he can rely on help and guidance from an understanding friend'. Here we see evidence of the existence of emotional labour in the description of the probation officer's responsibilities in that the officer's purpose was to invoke a positive emotional response in the probationer on receiving a sentence.

The 1930s saw even greater development of the probation officer role with the introduction of the American inspired social casework approach underpinned by one-to-one work where the probation worker built a relationship with the probationer. In her analysis of the social casework method, King (1958) draws a direct link between the tradition of social work and probation work, with both being informed by compassion for people's distress and an awareness of the consequences of this distress. Her work brings emotions to the fore in our understanding of probation practice, in a way which had not hitherto been seen. King (1958: 46) describes the importance of understanding people on probation 'intellectually, but with our feelings' as central to the case work approach and cites psychology and psychiatry, including the work of Freud, as a major influence at this time. In short, King argued that feelings felt subconsciously by clients as a result of their upbringing need to be worked with, as is the changing of feelings in clients to alter attitudes and behaviour. King describes the use of feeling in the social casework approach in more detail in a quote which is worth including at length:

> Apart from the general satisfaction derived from the opportunity casework gives for the worker to express their love and concern for fellow men, he should seek no special emotional gratification in individual relationships with clients. Emotional involvement of this kind restricts freedom of both participants by blinding the worker to certain aspects of his role, in particular his need for objectivity, and thus limits the amount of help he can give. For the worker, mere control of feelings by suppression is not what is required. He has to recognise and use these feelings in the client's interest. If he is preoccupied by the need to restrain his anger or appear unshocked or to control his excessive sympathy, his capacity to listen creatively to whatever the client is saying will be impaired.
>
> (1958: 52)

King (1958) captures the nuances of emotional labour in probation practice and articulates this performance perfectly in her description of casework: providing the opportunity to express concern without the need for anything in return, to maintain what the author later calls a 'professional relationship'. This is where the worker is objective and does not allow their emotions to cloud or impair their judgement. King also recognises the risks to merely suppressing emotion and suggests that the emotions felt by the worker should be used to 'help the client', and argues that the worker will reveal 'as little or as much…as is appropriate to this end' (p. 54). This reference to self-disclosure and the use of emotion is another feature of the current supervisory relationship in probation practice (Phillips et al., 2018). King's representation of the 'social casework' approach can be related to McWilliams' characterisation of the pressure in probation to embrace the 'science of social work' (McWilliams, 1983: 129).

Whilst King focused on the importance of emotion, Biestek (1961) introduces the use of emotion as an evidence-based skill. For Biestek (1961), the relationship relies on emotional skills which involve the use of empathy over sympathy, the building of rapport and 'transfer' which he defines as the emotional relationship between the client and the person on probation (p. 8). Thus, the casework relationship is regarded as a 'dynamic interaction of attitudes and emotions between the caseworker and the client' (Biestek, 1961: 12). Biestek describes the 'permissive atmosphere' (p. 41) in which the caseworker creates the environment for the client, as somewhere the client can express their feelings without fear of being judged, in a warm way showing the intention to help and feeling with the client. The recognition of the significance of the use of emotion as a skill to facilitate the casework relationship is clear. In practice, these ideas can be seen in St John's (1961) observations of probation practice in which he describes the use of emotion in probation work. For example, St John recognises the use of sympathy as a positive emotion to build trust and the negative consequences of too much sympathy which could result in gratitude that turns to resentment when the probation officer is required to engage in a more supervisory role (1961: 69) and his account of probation work puts emotion front and centre:

> The probation officer's function is not to impose reform from without, but to arouse a desire to change, to supply incentives, to rebuild and bolster stamina; to plant the seeds of self-recovery and then allow friendship, acceptance and sympathy to germinate and fertilise them.
>
> (1961: 76)

The development of the casework relationship and social work methods is argued to have eclipsed theological rationales and conceptualisations of probation work by the 1960s (Whitehead, 2017). Whitehead (2017: 39) characterises the period from the 1930s to the 1970s as a scientific, positivist approach to probation which becomes more about 'curing by casework to rehabilitate offenders'. This perspective borrows from the writing of McWilliams (1983, 1985, 1987) and the development of the 'non-treatment paradigm' (Bottoms and McWilliams, 1979). From this brief examination of the use of emotion in probation practice from the 19th century until the 1970s, we see clear acknowledgement – in policy, legislation, conceptualisations of 'good' probation work as well as training – of the need to perform emotional labour in course of doing probation work.

The marginalisation of emotion

However, there was a shift in the focus of probation policy in the 1980s and 1990s. This came about as a result of unease about the effectiveness of probation as well as its apparent 'softness' (Garland, 2001; Robinson and Ugwudike, 2012) and continuing government focus on market principles of efficiency, cost effectiveness and economy (the role of competition) (see Deering, 2011; Ranson and Stewart, 1994). The resulting National Standards (Home Office, 1992) prioritised enforcement over compliance, and punishment over rehabilitation with practitioners being urged to focus on targets, performance data and accountability to the system rather than the service user. This 'era' saw the pinnacle of the 'technicality' of routinised practice over the 'indeterminacy' of practice informed by specialist knowledge (Robinson, 2003).

This shift from 'case worker' to 'case manager' (see Burnett, 1996) in the late 1980s and 1990s, along with the prevalence of surveilling relationships and the 'authoritative professional' (National Probation Directorate, 2003: 7) constrained probation practitioners' opportunities to develop relationships with clients in the late 1990s and early 2000s. Indeed, as argued by Burnett and McNeill (2005: 224), policy documents in the 2000s gave 'little hint of the support, friendliness and warmth that once characterised the supervision of offenders'. Additionally, the deliberate separation of probation from social work through, for example, the replacement of the Diploma in Social Work with specific trainee probation training, as well as the replacing of person-centred work with cognitive behavioural approaches also had an effect on the relationship between probation practitioners and clients.

Another example of the marginalisation of emotions in the field of probation can be seen in the context of the so-called 'What Works' movement. The 'What Works' approach, which is based on the key principles of Risk, Need and Responsivity was introduced in the 1990s (see Andrews and Kiessling, 1980; Dowden and Andrews, 1999) and led to the development of Core Correctional Practice (Dowden and Andrews, 2004) and the Strategic Training Initiative in Community Supervision (Bonta et al., 2008). Both of these models of practice are underpinned by structured training, mentoring and evaluation of key skills and characteristics that are considered important for probation officers to possess. Research undertaken as part of the 'What Works' approach – despite its focus on interpersonal contact – missed the mark in terms of bringing emotions centre stage, most notably when it came to the lack of research into the concept of responsivity

(Porporino, 2010), as well as the favouring of consistency of practice over relationship building (Mair, 2004). Furthermore, while the characteristics and skills required for effective probation work remained the focus, the emotions required to supervise clients were not explicitly considered.

We might speculate that some of the changes in the expectations made of probation workers and their need to perform emotional labour are linked to the changing purposes of probation. Robinson's (2008) work on the shift towards late-modern forms of rehabilitation whereby rehabilitation is justified through utilitarianism, managerialism and expressive forms of rehabilitation is of particular use here. Utilitarian rehabilitation exists to 'promote the 'greatest happiness (or, more precisely, safety) for the greatest number'', not (primarily) the individual welfare of the offender (cf. Bentham, 1823). Importantly, this implies that it is not the offender who should be the beneficiary of probation but the general public. In such a political context, one can see how explicit directions to convey, for example, empathy and kindness to people on probation become untenable. With regard to managerial rehabilitation, effective rehabilitative work has become synonymous with effective risk management (Garland, 2001) and is legitimated with reference to its ability to classify and treat people on probation. Such a mode of practice prioritises a so-called objective approach to measurement and management which should not be influenced by the irrationalities (rightly or wrongly) implied through the use of emotion. For example, Karstedt et al. (2011) argue that the criminal justice system seeks to exclude emotion on the basis that emotion is likely to distort the process of justice. That historically the criminal justice process has been suspicious of emotions. Similarly, Knight (2014) argues the criminal justice system is constituted to respond to criminal behaviour in an objective rational and just manner. Thus, we see a reliance on actuarial risk assessment technologies which require little in the way of professional relationship building and work which is wholly focused on so-called criminogenic risk factors rather than the broader social contexts in which people on probation generally reside. Finally, whilst expressive rehabilitation initially sounds like it requires the use of emotion, Robinson (2008) argues that this form of rehabilitation is equivalent to a push towards the remoralisation and responsibilisation of people on probation. Thus, rehabilitative work in probation becomes legitimated by the punitive potential of rehabilitation rather than on the welfarist ethos which underpinned probation work in previous eras. Thus, these broader contexts and 'purposes' of probation shape the way in which practitioners can perform emotional labour. In essence, these policy and policy contexts will have shaped the organisational display rules (Ashforth and Humphrey, 1993) which dictate what emotions are considered appropriate in the field of probation. In probation, this led to a distinct move away from the explicit acknowledgement of emotion in policy and training.

The persistence of emotion work

Much of the previous section focused on changes in policy and how emotions were marginalised in the field of probation, partly as a result of the changing ways in which rehabilitation came to be legitimated in the 1990s and 2000s. However, policy is rarely neatly reflected in changes in practice. Thus, in spite of the hardening of the image of probation practice at an institutional level, practitioners in the field have – probably always – relied on emotional skills to build and maintain relationships with clients. Research undertaken in the late 1990s and early 2000s highlights the importance of emotions in effective practice. In Rex's (1999) study of probation officers and probationers, probationers would commit to, and engage in a positive way, with the probation process if their probation officer showed empathy, an ability to listen, conveyed interest and understanding, and provided space for the probationer to talk. Trotter's (1996, 2012) work has also highlighted the importance of empathy, with some indication that it is linked to lower levels of recidivism. More recently, Knight's (2014: 188) work on emotional literacy exposed the often 'invisible world of emotion' which significantly impacts on interactions between probation workers and people on probation. Knight's work highlights the positive and negative exercise of emotion, where the former can build positive relationships and the former is visible in the repressive control of offenders.

Our own research on the performance of emotional labour in probation practice has built upon the work of Knight (2014) by shedding light on the 'emotionful' in contemporary probation work. Thus, data that we have generated through interviews with probation workers in the last few years has exposed the different ways in which probation workers manage their emotion and why they do so. We have also explored the ways in which emotion work is critical to effective probation practice due to the way in which it is used to create constructive, professional relationships between officers and their clients.

It is clear that, in spite of a relative neglect of the role of emotion in policy, practitioners regularly use and manage emotions when interacting with a client (Westaby et al., 2020). The emotional labour required in the everyday work of probation officers is one way of exposing the values of probation work. Thus, we have explored the organisational, occupational and societal 'feeling rules' or 'display rules' that shape the display of emotion in probation. This illuminates how probation workers display emotions in different ways, through integrative, neutral and differentiating emotional displays (Wharton and Erickson, 1993) in their interactions with clients.

Practitioners talked to us about how they would engage in surface acting when working, for example, with a client who was non-compliant in that they would mask true emotions such as disappointment. Interestingly, this might be done for a range of reasons such as an awareness of the risk that expressing negative emotion would be deleterious to the professional relationship. On the other hand, emotions would be suppressed because the practitioner felt that to be neutral was the most effective way of gleaning more information about risk. We can see that the performance of emotional labour is tied closely to the aims of the service. Importantly, we also see that the way in which practitioners talk about surface acting is linked to key aspects of being a probation 'professional', a point also highlighted in Tidmarsh's (2020: 5) recent study of professionalisation in a privatised probation providers:

> to *display* appropriate feelings, attitudes, and emotions, can be considered a crucial aspect of practitioner understandings of professionalism.

Interestingly, Tidmarsh (2020) highlights the intuitive way in which practitioners in his study knew what was, and was not, appropriate. In turn, we can link this to the occupational display rules (Ashforth and Humphrey, 1993) that are evident in the field of probation (Westaby et al., 2020). Partly as a result of occupational display rules that are at play in probation we see much reference made to positive emotions such as empathy when practitioners discuss their emotion work which can be linked to the underpinning values of probation practitioners whereby rehabilitation, individualised support and help are considered key to 'quality' probation work (Deering and Feilzer, 2015; Robinson et al., 2014).

In probation policy, models of effective practice and the contemporary emotional discourse in probation emotions like anger or disappointment are not discussed as frequently as empathy, praise or humour. However, we have seen evidence of the use of these less discussed emotional displays. Whilst initially considered unprofessional – as probation officers value the importance of pro-social modelling and see the risk that negative emotions can play in terms of affecting relationships – some of our participants talked about how they would sometimes feel anger towards clients who had, variously, been non-compliant or disrespectful. Whilst examples of deep acting negative emotions were rare, they were performed in order to represent the officer as a human – as a citizen agent rather than state agent, again making links to how probation practitioners see their role. Deep acting does not only occur in relation to negative emotion with participants engaging in deep acting when it came to clients who were doing well. Several participants talked about how they would genuinely be happy when someone made progress, or display genuine emotion to convey their belief in the ability of people to change.

Indeed, we have also explored (Fowler et al., 2017) the emotional labour undertaken by probation practitioners explicitly when fulfilling the building relationships aspect of Skills for Effective Engagement and Development and Supervision (SEEDS) – a programme implemented in England and Wales to encourage the engagement of offenders in their Order as well as support practitioners with the emotional demands of the job. In order to conform to this element of SEEDS practitioners get to know and understand the individual, which requires a complex understanding and performance of empathy. Participants must also develop clear boundaries by being honest, remaining emotionally detached and suppressing emotions such as disappointment and frustration. Importantly, participants describe how these expectations must be achieved at the same time leading to even more complex emotional displays, which can result in stress and burnout.

Interestingly, the lens of emotional labour sheds light on the identity of probation workers as an historical bricolage of social work, counselling, psychotherapy, and adaptation to the penal-welfare complex which has underpinned much probation work since the 1960s (Phillips et al., 2018). In probation practice, self-disclosure is used to develop a constructive working relationship with clients in orderto facilitate behaviour change and manage risk. The management of emotion is significant in achieving the goals of the organisation, for example, public protection. The emotional displays inherent in the act of self-disclosure reveal the 'feeling rules' (Hochschild, 1983) or values of the organisation, where the probation worker seeks to express empathy or model a pro-social response to behaviour.

The impact of emotional labour on practitioners

It is clear that probation involves emotional labour. Moreover, probation requires particularly onerous forms of emotional labour due to the nature of the job. In Steinberg's (1999: 151) model of different levels of human relations, skills and demands around the performance of emotional labour, probation work fits the highest level in terms of complexity:

> Level E: [The job requires the incumbent to exercise] interpersonal skills in combination, creating a climate for and establishing a commitment to the welfare of clients or the public... coaching and guiding clients through difficult emotional, attitudinal and developmental change around issues that are sensitive, controversial, and about which there is... individual resistance. [It requires] providing comfort... where people are in considerable pain, dying or gravely ill, angry, distraught,..., in drug-induced states, or otherwise unpredictable, physically violent or emotional.... crowd control when crowd gets out of hand.

Probation workers also work at the highest level in terms of emotional effort:

> Level E: [Incumbents] deal regularly with highly physically dangerous and unpredictably hostile or violent people or groups. [They] may also work directly to meet the needs of people (including family members) who are facing death, through caring for or discussing this or other, comparable, extremely sensitive topics with them.

(Steinberg, 1999: 153–154)

The implications of this complex, emotionally demanding work on workers' wellbeing is well documented, with high levels of emotional labour being associated with burnout and other adverse health outcomes (Jeung et al., 2018). There has, as yet, been no systematic study of the link between emotional labour in probation and burnout participants. However, participants in our own study talked about the relentlessness of probation work, especially when it came to working primarily with clients who had been assessed as posing a high risk of harm (Phillips et al., 2016).

One element of burnout is the process of desensitisation (Maslach, 1982), and this was also apparent in our participants' responses. This was particularly evident when it came to how workplace spillover affects probation practitioner's family lives. That said, we also saw evidence of hyper-sensitisation when it came to certain offences such as sex offending, especially when the practitioner had children (Westaby et al., 2016).

Conclusion

This chapter began by exploring the historical changes in the societal, organisational and cultural 'feeling rules' influencing the performance of emotional labour in probation practice beginning with the zealous Christian origins to the humanistic value-based view of the importance of emotions to the psychotherapeutic skills-based appreciation emergent in the 1950s. Moreover, the evidence-based literature of the 1980s and 1990s reveal how the importance of emotions is neglected. On another level, it represents the abiding and deep-rooted presence of emotions in descriptions of probation work in calls to convert offenders to change their feelings, the professionalisation of probation officers, the boundaries of emotion work, emotion skills and emotional literacy required to achieve the organisational goals of probation.

The chapter went on to explore what we know about the ways in which contemporary probation practitioners perform emotional labour. There is evidence of high levels of both surface and deep acting which are, in turn, closely tied to the aims of the organisation. There is also evidence of the potential for high levels of burnout and other adverse effects of this type of work, especially when considered in light of Steinberg's (1999) model of human relation skills.

However, the overarching argument that should be taken from this chapter is the lack of knowledge around emotional labour in probation. Beyond our own work and that of Knight (2014) and Tidmarsh (2020), very little research has been conducted in this area. This is perhaps surprising when we consider the enduring nature of emotion work in probation as well as in comparison to the amount of research conducted in other areas of criminology such as the police (see Chapter 2, this volume) and prisons (see Chapter 5, this volume). Moreover, what research has been undertaken has, hitherto, focused solely on generic front-line officers. There are, in all likelihood, differences in terms of the emotional labour required for probation workers working in different contexts such as prisons, the courts and hostels especially because emotional labour is linked to the aims of the job (which differs according to context) as well as broader macro structures such as differing levels of privatisation and governance structures. It is also the case that management plays an important role in supporting staff when it comes to their emotional wellbeing, yet there is no understanding of the emotional labour required by senior probation officers in fulfilling their roles, nor any research on how best to support staff who have to deal, on a daily basis, with emotional demanding situations.

There is a link between the performance of emotional labour, the effectiveness of a service and staff wellbeing. Quite how this works in the field of probation is currently unknown. The National Probation Service in England and Wales is currently embarking on rolling out a new version of the SEEDS programme which will – in theory at least – support staff with the emotional demands of the job. This is a positive policy development which, in conjunction, with more research on this important topic should lead to healthier workers and more effective practice as well as, more broadly, a better understanding of the purpose of probation and the way in which these purposes manifest in practice.

References

Andrews, D. and Kiessling, J. (1980). Program structure and effective correctional practices: A summary of the CaVIC research. In: R. Ross and P. Gendreau (eds.) *Effective Correctional Treatment*. *Toronto*. Canada, Butterworth, 441–463.

Ashforth, B.E. and Humphrey, R.H. (1993). Emotional labor in service roles: the influence of identity. *Academy of Management Review*, 18(1), 88–115.

Auerbach, S. (2015). "Beyond the pale of mercy": Victorian penal culture, police court missionaries, and the origins of probation in England. *Law and History Review*, 33, 621–965.

Bentham, J. (1823). *An Introduction to the Principles of Morals and Legislation*. Oxford: Clarendon Press.

Biestek, F.P. (1961). *The Casework Relationship*. London: George Allen & Unwin.

Bonta, J., Rugge, T., Scott, T.-L., Bourgon, G. and Yessine, A.K. (2008). Exploring the black box of community supervision. *Journal of Offender Rehabilitation*, 47(3), 248–270.

Bottoms, A.E. and McWilliams, W. (1979). A non-treatment paradigm for probation practice. *The British Journal of Social Work*, 9(2), 159–202.

Burnett, R. (1996). Fitting supervision to offenders: Assessment and allocation in the probation service. Home Office Research Study, 153. London: Home Office.

Burnett, R. and McNeill, F. (2005). The place of the officer-offender relationship in assisting offenders to desist from crime. *Probation Journal*, 52(3), 221–242. doi:10.1177/0264550505055112.

Deering, J. (2011). *Probation Practice and the New Penology: Practitioner Reflections*. Farnham: Ashgate.

Deering, J. and Feilzer, M. (2015). *Privatising Probation: Is Transforming Rehabilitation the End of the Probation Ideal?* Bristol: Policy Press.

Dowden, C., & Andrews, D. (1999). What works for female offenders: A meta-analytic review. *Crime & Delinquency*, 45(4), 438–452.

Dowden, C. and Andrews, D. (2004). The importance of staff practice in delivering effective correctional treatment: A meta-analytic review of core correctional practice. *International Journal Of Offender Therapy And Comparative Criminology*, 48(2), 203–214. doi:10.1177/0306624X03257765.

Fowler, A., Phillips, J. and Westaby, C. (2017). Understanding emotion as effective practice. The performance of emotional labour in building relationships. In: P. Ugwudike, P. Raynor and J. Annison (eds.) *Evidence-Based Skills in Community Justice: International Research on Supporting Rehabilitation and Desistance*. Bristol: Policy Press, 243–262.

Gard, R. (2007). The first probation officers in England and Wales 1906–14. *The British Journal of Criminology*, 47(6), 938–954. doi:10.1093/bjc/azm028.

Garland, D. (2001). The culture of control: Crime and social order in late modernity. Oxford: Clarendon.

Gerdes, K.E. (2011) Empathy, sympathy and pity: 21st definitions and implications for practice and research. *Journal of Social Service Research*, 37(3), 230–241. www.tandfonline.com/doi/full/10.1080/01488376.2011.564027?src=recsys&.

Hochschild, A.R. (1979). Emotion work, feeling rules, and social structure. *American Journal of Sociology*, 85(3), 551–575. doi:10.1086/227049.

Hochschild, A.R. (1983). *The Managed Heart: Commercialization of Human Feeling*. Berkeley: University of California Press.

Home Office (1992). *National Standards for the Supervision of Offenders in the Community*. London: Home Office.

Holmes, T. (1900). *Pictures and Problems from London Police Courts*. London, Edinburgh, Dublin and New York: Thomas Nelson and Sons.

Jeung, D.-Y., Kim, C., & Chang, S.-J. (2018). Emotional Labor and Burnout: A Review of the Literature. *Yonsei Medical Journal*, 59(2), 187–193.

Karstedt, S., Loader, I. and Strang, H. (2011). *Emotions, Crime and Justice*. Oxford: Hart Publishing.

King, J.F.S. (1958). *The Probation Service*. London: Butterworth and Co. Ltd.

Knight, C. (2014). *Emotional Literacy in Criminal Justice Professional Practice with Offenders*. Basingstoke: Palgrave Macmillan.

Leeson, C. (1914). *The Probation System*. London: P.S. King and Son.

Le Mesurier, L. (1935). *A Handbook of Probation and Social Work of the Courts*. London: National Association of Probation Officers.

Mair, G. (2004). *What Matters in Probation*. Cullompton: Willan.

Maslach, C (1982) Burnout: The Cost of Caring. Eagledwood Cliffs: Prentice Hall.

McWilliams, W. (1983). The mission to the english police courts 1876–1936. *Howard Journal of Penology*, 22, 129–147.

McWilliams, W. (1985). The mission transformed. *Howard Journal*, 24(4), 257–272.

McWilliams, W. (1987). Probation, pragmatism and policy. *Howard Journal*, 26(2), 97–121.

National Probation Directorate (2003). *Careers in the National Probation Service*. London: National Probation Directorate.

Newton, G. (1958) 'Recent Developments in Probation', *Case Conference*, 4(8), 219–226.

Phillips, J., Fowler, A. and Westaby, C. (2018). Self-disclosure in criminal justice: What form does it take and what does it achieve? *International Journal of Offender Therapy and Comparative Criminology*, 62(12), 3890–3909.

Phillips, J., Westaby, C. and Fowler, A. (2016). "It"s relentless': The impact of working primarily with high-risk offenders. *Probation Journal*, 63(2), 182–192.

Plamper, J. (2017). *The History of Emotions*. Oxford: Oxford University Press.

Porporino, F.J. (2010). Bringing sense and sensitivity to corrections: From programmes to 'fix' offenders to services to support desistance. In: J. Brayford, F. Cowe and J. Deering (eds.) *What Else Works? Creative Work With Offenders*. Cullompton: Willan, 61–85.

Rafaeli, A. and Sutton, R.I. (1989). The expression of emotion in organizational life. In: L.L. Cummings and B.M. Staw (eds.) *Research in Organizational Behavior*, vol. 11. Greenwich, CT: JAI Press, 1–42.

Ranson, S. and Stewart, J. (1994). *Management for the Public Domain: Enabling the Learning Society*. Basingstoke: The Macmillan Press Ltd.

Rex, S. (1999). Desistance from offending: Experiences of probation. *Howard Journal of Criminal Justice*, 38(4), 366–383.

Robinson, G. (2003). Technicality and indeterminacy in probation practice: A case study. *The British Journal of Social Work*, 33(5), 593–610.

Robinson, G. (2008). Late-modern rehabilitation: The evolution of a penal strategy. *Punishment & Society*, 10(4), 429–445.

Robinson, G. and Ugwudike, P. (2012). Investing in 'toughness': Probation, enforcement and legitimacy. *Howard Journal of Criminal Justice*, 51(3), 300–316.

Robinson, G., Priede, C., Farrall, S., Shapland, J. and McNeill, F. (2014). Understanding 'quality' in probation practice: Frontline perspectives in England & Wales. *Criminology & Criminal Justice*, 14(2), 123–142.

St John, J. (1961). *Probation-the Second Chance*. London, Vista Books.

Steinberg, R.J. (1999). Emotional labor in job evaluation: Redesigning compensation practices. *The Annals of the American Academy of Political and Social Science*, 561(1), 143–157.

Tidmarsh, M. (2020). 'The right kind of person for the job'? Emotional labour and organizational professionalism in probation. *International Journal of law, Crime and Justice*, 61.

Trotter, C. (2015). Working with involuntary clients: A guide to practice. Abingdon: Routledge.

Trotter, C. (2012). Effective community-based supervision of young offenders. *Trends & Issues in Crime and Criminal Justice*, 448, 1–7.

Trotter, C. (1996). The impact of different supervision practices in community corrections. *Australian and New Zealand Journal of Criminology*, 29(1), 29–46.

Vanstone, M. (2004). Mission control: The origins of a humanitarian service. *Probation Journal*, 51, 34–47.

Westaby, C., Phillips, J., & Fowler, A. (2016). Spillover and work–family conflict in probation practice: Managing the boundary between work and home life. *European Journal of Probation*, 8(3), 113–127.

Westaby, C., Fowler, A. and Phillips J. (2020). Managing emotion in probation practice: Display rules, values and the performance of emotional labour. *International Journal of Law, Crime and Justice*, in press.

Wharton, A.S. and Erickson, R.J. (1993). Managing emotions in the job and at home: understanding the consequences of multiple job roles. *Academy of Management Review*, 183, 457–486.

Whitehead, P. (2017). *Transforming Probation: Social Theories and the Criminal Justice System*. Bristol: Policy Press.

Chapter 5

The emotional labour of prison work

Per Åke Nylander and Anders Bruhn

Introduction

This chapter is concerned with how prison staff, especially prison officers, manage prisoners' emotions as well as their own emotions within the prison arena. The chapter uses current literature from other researchers as well as our own studies on this topic. The sociology of emotions is a field that has grown substantially and gained increasing importance in recent decades. This includes how to understand and manage emotions in all kinds of social relations, how emotions affect actions and behaviour, and how emotions are managed in working life (Barbalet, 2001; Hochschild, 1983).

Prison life has often been described in emotional terms in movies and popular literature, and ranges from boredom to fear, from revenge to hope. However, research studies that explicitly focus on emotions and emotional life in prisons have emerged only relatively recently. This is perhaps surprising considering this environment is known to create numerous – mostly negative – emotional challenges that are constantly present for prisoners in their daily prison life. Emotions such as anger because of a negative decision, frustration over isolation from family life, or depression following from long-term powerlessness are all common in prison settings (Crawley, 2004a; Crewe, 2009).

There are some early scholarly writings and research that have indirectly described the negative emotions experienced by prisoners. To mention the most famous example, Gresham Sykes (1958) argued that prisoners suffer from at least five deprivations common in prisons: liberty, goods and services, heterosexual relations, autonomy, and personal safety, all of which cause frustration and other emotions. Goffman (1961), often referring to Sykes, saw prison life as leading to a process of 'mortification' of the prisoner's identity. Michel Foucault (1977) showed the painful effects of the disciplinary ideas that were the reasons for the expansion of prisons in society in the 19th century. Nonetheless, prison research has often overlooked, underestimated, or has not sufficiently highlighted the importance of emotions in prisons and especially in the relationships between staff and prisoners (Crewe et al., 2014).

How prison staff interact with prisoners in the processes of adjustment to prison life is also sparsely described and analysed in previous prison literature (Crawley, 2004a). In sum, there is knowledge about how prisons emotionally affect the prisoners, while research on how prisons emotionally affect staff is more limited.

It is important to note that prisons are not all the same. Rather, the prison 'estate' comprises a manifold of different types of prison. First, prison conditions differ between countries and prison systems, owing to differences in prison policies and criminal justice systems. Even within a prison system, size, security category, management, and staffing are just a few examples of differing preconditions forming each individual prison. Furthermore, some have argued that there are large differences in the emotional or caring work in women's and men's prisons (Tait, 2008). Others have emphasized the differences between prisons according to their regimes as crucial (Liebling et al., 2011). Prison cultures are found to differ between prisons, but also between wings and workgroups within each prison (Bruhn et al., 2011). One implication of these variations in prisons and their cultures is how prison officers create and manage emotional issues. Later in the chapter, we describe some trends that, to varying degrees, affect many prison systems, namely 'punitive turns' – that shaped prison-security thinking – but also new forms of managerialism and evidence-based practice that have influenced most public organisations. It is important to bear in mind that even if we are aware of the differing conditions of prison systems, most of the previous research presented here comes from the Western hemisphere, especially from Anglophone or Scandinavian countries, due to its dominant position in prison research and publishing at present.

Prison officers are the largest group of prison employees, and they are also the 'front-line staff', working most days face-to-face with prisoners. Hence, they are also the emotional key-group, the most important group encountering and managing emotions in prisons. Prison officers must get the 'right' relationships with prisoners (Liebling et al., 2011: 111) by using parts of their own personality. An inevitable part of that is to manage their own emotions as well as the emotions of prisoners in the most appropriate way. This emotion work, when performed as part of their everyday prison work, is what Hochschild (1983) terms 'emotional labour', and this kind of labour will be scrutinized in detail later in this chapter.

The aim of this chapter is to describe and discuss the emotional labour of prison staff under the prevailing conditions of prison life in the changing prison systems of today. In the following section, we will briefly review some theoretical concepts connected to emotional labour and to the prison literature. We will then discuss the recent development of most Western prisons and prison policies and its impact on preconditions for emotional labour in prisons. We further review important research on emotional life in prisons, particularly emotional labour and its consequences for prison officers. Finally, we briefly discuss the possible future and challenges of emotional labour in prisons.

Some concepts used in emotional labour research

Departing from the theory presented earlier in this book, we will briefly remind the reader about some of the central concepts. When Hochschild developed her concept of emotional labour (from the wider emotion work/management in private life), she described it as having exchange value and being sold for a wage, but also that emotional labour was restricted by feeling/display rules set by the employer and workplace culture. In prisons, the feeling/display rules are often both formal and informal. Furthermore, feeling/display rules are conformed to through the use of surface and deep acting in emotional labour. Hochschild (1983) argues that deep acting – really trying to involve in emotions – demands emotive effort and hence risks staff exhaustion, whereas surface emotional labour – more akin to distant feigning – often leads to emotive dissonance and the risk of cynicism. The possible consequences in terms of emotional strain, exhaustion, and cynicism have been widely discussed in recent years with many occupations which demand high levels of emotional labour being comparable to prison work. Before delving into emotional labour in prisons, we will look at the prison as an emotional arena and some current trends in prison policy mirrored by the literature.

Emotion management and staff in prisons

The classical prison literature provides several descriptions of emotional and social life in prisons, i.e. the conditions under which the emotional labour takes place. In his seminal study of an American high-security prison, Sykes (1958) says little explicitly about this emotional life but more about the emotional effects upon prisoners of prison structures and conditions. He has argued that the system of power within a prison can never be totalized for several reasons. One is that the 'custodians' (mainly the prison officers) are fallible human beings, not machines, and another is that their core mission is not to exercise power but to keep order within the prison and to prevent escape. The underuse of power leaves space for prisoners to develop strategies to manage their time in prison. The social interactions between staff and prisoners are a crucial tool for the negotiation of a basic order which, in turn, means that prison officers have to handle different kinds of emotional expressions from prisoners. However, most of the emotional exchange is argued by Sykes to rest on prisoner-to-prisoner interactions, and they will always suffer from prevalent deprivations such as lack of liberty, heterosexual relations, goods and services, autonomy, and safety. Sykes argues that prisoners also handle this frustration without support from staff. That staff may help them manage their emotions is not reflected upon. The sparse description of emotional expressions and interactions in Sykes's book could be a sign that the 'emotional turn' (Barbalet, 2001) in sociology had not yet reached the prison literature at that time.

Emotional labour is contingent on formally prescribed (often by the employer) but informally performed (by staff) rules of behaviour. As we have argued above, the social relationships between prison officers and prisoners is the foundation for emotional management in prisons. The conditions for these relationships are set by the organisational framework, not least the division between different kinds of prison wings depending on the sorting of prisoners on the basis of crimes committed, risk assessments, and so forth. In each prison wing, the relationships are related to the wing subculture, formed by prison officers and prisoners through interaction. But staff culture is also connected to individual ambitions and moral disposition of each officer. In the prison literature, staff culture is often discussed in terms of patterns of thought, mutual understanding of emotional issues, and certain accepted behaviours (Bruhn et al., 2011; Liebling et al., 2011), while prison officers have often been studied as individuals in terms of their individual professional orientation.

There is a body of research, predominantly conducted in the US prison system, focussing on prison officers' professional orientation towards prisoners. Professional orientations are often measured and described as punitive, custodial, or rehabilitative. According to Griffin, professional orientation 'reflects the values, goals, and attitudes of an individual as he or she functions within a specific organization' (2002: 251) which, in turn, might have some impact on the emotional approach taken by the individual prison officers.

Orientation measures are often compared with individual demographic variables. Gender has shown differences in many but not all studies. Some have shown that female staff prefer the human service/rehabilitative approach to the role more than male colleagues (e.g., see Griffin, 2002; Hemmens & Stohr, 2000), whilst other studies found fewer or no gender differences in rehabilitative thinking (e.g., see Cullen et al., 1989). Age, entry age in prison work, and years in service have similarly shown contradicting impacts on orientation. The contradictions in the findings could be explained by the many small and local studies within this tradition (Philliber, 1987). The question is still whether orientation can explain how prison officers work and behave emotionally. This leads us to a more collectively developed understanding of how prison officers think and act.

Emotion management and cultures in late-modern prisons

Since 2000, a growing number of articles have argued that prisons are emotional arenas. This has to be because a large number of human beings are forced together in a relatively limited area. Hence, emotional expressions of many different kinds can be expected (Crawley, 2004b). This is the foundation for expressions of negative and sometimes positive emotions within the prison environment, something staff have to tackle on a daily basis. Goffman (1959) argues that people in everyday life act like they are on a stage when in front of people, and they act in quite a different way when they are without an audience or backstage. The homelike character of a prison wing contributes to developing a setting, or a stage, where certain emotions are 'performed' by prisoners and officers (Crawley, 2004b). Emotional expressions in prisons are not only about masculinity and toughness as some may expect. It has much greater variety which is contingent upon different prison situations. Thus, there are emotion zones which enable the display of feelings other than the traditionally described ones of fear, aggression, and mistrust (Crewe et al., 2014). Many of these emotion zones cannot be regarded as either front-stage, acting in front of spectators, or backstage – private spaces with only friends and peers (Goffman, 1959) but rather as something in between. Visiting rooms after family visits and many classroom situations (e.g., cooking or pottery lessons, and theoretical classes) are examples of such emotion zones where other emotions are allowed (Crewe et al., 2014). The prison officers who are present in these 'in-between' zones will therefore encounter greater variation in emotions and emotional displays.

The question of culture is pivotal for understanding what kind of emotional labour staff perform in the wing. Regarding professional orientation as part of one or several prison cultures there is acknowledgement of the collective nature of prison work, and the collective impact upon how emotional labour is performed. When discussing prison officer discretion and peace-making, several authors touch on emotional issues in prison work without explicitly connecting them to emotional labour (see e.g., Liebling et al., 2011; Tait, 2008). There is a somewhat divergent understanding of how to think about 'culture' among prison officers. On a higher organisational level, we must understand that different kinds of prisons shape different staff cultures (Crewe et al., 2014; Liebling et al., 2011). Concerning staff culture, some authors regard it as fairly homogenous (Crawley, 2004a), while others have argued that there are several subcultures among prison officers, which ought to be regarded separately. Specialization and the division of work inside these prisons often develop diverging subcultures in separate prison wings, units, and work groups within the same prison (Kolind et al., 2013; Nylander et al., 2011).

Thus, we would argue that 'professional orientation', and ways to develop emotional work is to a large extent determined by the staff culture in each prison wing or unit, which is formed by the prison policy, organisational preconditions, and division of work. The most evident subcultures are those among staff with treatment tasks and staff in security work (Bruhn et al., 2011). These types of cultural bases are important to bear in mind when we explore the emotional labour that takes place in prisons.

In late-modern prisons, at least those of the Western countries, several new characteristics affect the prison environment and also the emotional labour to be performed there. There are technical solutions for constant monitoring of prison areas and prisoners, but there are also more sophisticated systems for registering behaviour and risks. Some have argued that the CCTV-monitoring of every part of the prison area, which, together with the hidden complicated systems for sanctions (such as the Incentives and Earned Privileges system in English and Welsh prisons), has created a new environment in prisons affecting the behaviour of prisoners. The power is now more invisible, and in adapting to this new prison world, prisoners use new strategies to cope (Crewe, 2009). Similarly, the emotional impact and consequences of having a TV monitor in the cell, and the privilege of in-cell television for prisoners, have been studied in a male adult prison. It is suggested that in-cell TV for prisoners has changed the way prisoners are controlled by occupying prisoners' attention and limiting the time in contact with others in the prison (Knight & Layder, 2016). The constant monitoring and assessment has, combined with some important trends presented below, resulted in more distant surface emotional labour in prisons, while the deep emotional labour is reserved for program staff and treatment units.

Punitive turns and other trends affecting emotional labour

Prison organisation and structure, as well as new techniques of surveillance, must be seen in relation to at least three important ongoing developmental trends of policy and governance in the public sector in the Western hemisphere – trends that altogether work towards more distanced relations and surface variants of emotional labour in prisons.

First, we have witnessed what some have termed a 'punitive turn' (Garland, 2001: 142) in prison policy which has dispersed into prison systems at different points of time and at different paces. The United States in the 1980s (e.g., see Garland, 2001), the United Kingdom in the 1990s (e.g., see Liebling et al., 2011), and Sweden around 2005 (Bruhn et al., 2011) are examples of such turns affecting prisons and emotional labour.

This is only partly connected to the second trend, the implementation of new ways of governing in public organisations (Liebling et al., 2011). The doctrine of New Public Management (NPM) could be seen as an umbrella term covering different institutional standards or as a cluster of ideas about how to develop the organisation of public authorities. Essentially, NPM rests on the idea of implementing market logic in the governance of public services (Power, 1997). It is heavily influenced by, or rather imported from, the private business sector. At the core of NPM are ideas about professional leadership, performance targets (explicit criteria for productivity and efficiency), control of results, disaggregation into self-governed units, competition between units, and privatization (Hood, 1991).

In Sweden, for example, the trend of NPM has, since the 1990s, continued to reshape the prison system. There has been both a process of centralization as well as decentralization to 'production units'. Under the slogan 'One Authority', the regional reform moved most decisions from the local to the regional level and further to the Swedish Prison and Probation Services (SPPS) Head Office. Several official audits scrutinizing the prison services around the turn of the millennium (1999 and 2002) have criticized the SPPS for the overuse of resources and issues in the implementation of routines as well as insufficient control of results and costs. Several 'Annual Prison Orders' from the Department of Justice have demanded different detailed performance measures or 'indicators' to be used concerning urine samples, cell searches, and program participation. Centralized decisions about a heavily increased number of security measures are accompanied by a standardization of common rules and security routines in all prisons from 2005 onward (Bruhn et al., 2017).

The third trend is the emphasis on evidence-based practice in many areas of the human service organisations. In prisons, this means that all interventions should be proven – through rigorous academic research – to be effective in reducing crime and/or reoffending before being implemented. This began with the drug and crime programs, many of which were first developed in Canada and US prisons. Some of them showed small but significant effects on relapse into crime rates. They were implemented in European prisons mainly starting in 1990. Whether the effects are small or non-existent, they are symbolic of a determination among prison authorities in their efforts to reduce crime. Another example of this trend is the development of the increased importance of risk which has seen widespread implementation of risk-assessment instruments and procedures (e.g., see Bruhn et al., 2017; Carlen, 2008).

These parallel and partly intertwined trends affect emotional labour in prisons in several ways. It is an understatement to argue that if time and resources are spent on security measures and technical solutions, the opportunities for, and the nature of, emotional management will be affected. But it also signals to staff that the everyday encountering of prisoners and the building of good relationships with them on a daily basis is less important. This, then, means that the relational work and emotional labour in each prison wing will rely on the informal subculture of the wing as well as the personal views of each officer (see, e.g., Nylander et al., 2011).

Emotional labour among prison officers

Arlie Hochschild never specifically discussed prison work as emotional labour, but what she expressed concerning other occupations in several cases shows interesting similarities to prison work. In her seminal work *The Managed*

Heart (1983: 16), she considers a number of occupations from flight attendants to bill collectors and sees these two as the 'toe and the heel' of emotional labour. This span in the modes of emotional labour presented above clearly comprises prison officer work. Other researchers have applied her theoretical framework to other public occupations like the police (see Chapter 2 of this volume) and to caring occupations such as nurses. Yet, it took almost two decades until it was specifically and rigorously used to understand prison officer work. In general, prison officer work has many similarities with caring work as well as policing tasks, although it also has its own character.

A crucial question to raise is whether prison officers see themselves as performing emotional labour. In our nation-wide survey in 2009 with 1,218 Swedish prison officers (answered by 806 officers, 20% of the workforce), we asked if they agreed with various statements, some of which were related to emotional labour. We found that Swedish prison officers of all kinds agreed with the statements to a high degree. For example, only 19.4% of the prison officers disagreed with the statement, 'To be professional in this job is to hold back what you really feel'. As argued elsewhere, sub-groups of prison officers varied in their agreement to these items according to the different kinds of wings and units in which they worked, and the tasks they were expected to perform (e.g., see Nylander et al., 2011). Those working in treatment wings and with personal officer tasks, agreed to a much higher extent than those with security tasks.

Briefly returning to Sykes, we can gain some further insights into the nature of prison officer work. Importantly, he describes the many shifting roles any prison officer ('guard') in the US must adopt in order to fulfil their job, ranging from counsellor to boss (Sykes, 1958: 54). In the UK context, Crawley (2004a,b) has extensively described the emotional labour among prison officers. The domestic character of a prison wing and the day-to-day continuity of the personal relationship between prisoners and officers makes prison work different from police work in general. Within a homogenous prison officer culture, Crawley argues that the most important thing is getting the work right, by displaying the right emotions according to the formal and informal feeling and display rules of the workplace. This is something that new recruits learn in their basic training. In rare situations in the prison work when this performance fails, when a prison officer is losing the professional mask, the contrast to the regular emotional labour is obvious (Crawley, 2004b). So, the de-personalization argued to be required in fulfilling the professional role and its emotional labour, is not always working.

From a US perspective, Tracy (2004) argues that prison officer work is a profession for which being tough, macho, and hardened is considered a badge of honour. Crawley (2004a) has stated that the foundation for prison officer culture and emotion management is masculinity, and even though not every prison officer will conform to this, one should not overlook this important element of officer culture in the workplace. Hence, it is argued to have a significant impact on the display rules which are at play. Others have argued that an extreme macho-style among male staff is less useful in most prisons and wings today, and there are often negotiations between alternative male images instead (Liebling et al., 2011). In a Scandinavian context, this expressive macho-style of being a prison officer is uncommon and, importantly, rarely accepted among the majority of prison officers or in the official codes of conduct for prison staff (Bruhn, 2013).

Today, both female and male prison officers work in women's as well as men's prisons, although the proportions can differ. This, we would argue, also affects the emotional climate as well as the emotional labour performed, for example, by creating a gender-division of labour concerning which tasks male and female officers are expected to perform. Crawley (2004a) has described the different attitudes male and female staff might have on this issue. While some male officers see women as a risk or unable to match the performance of officers in men's prisons, others emphasize their calming impact in the wings. However, female prison officers often experience sexist attitudes and harassment from male colleagues. Other studies have argued that there is a gendered division of labour in prison wings today, as female staff are expected to think more about rehabilitation and do more deep emotional labour (e.g., counselling and caring tasks), whereas male staff are supposed to be more active in security matters (e.g., when there are conflicts with staff or violence among prisoners). This means that a balanced gender distribution among prison officers could further increase the rehabilitative work in the prisons (Bruhn, 2013; Tait, 2008), which affects the performance of emotional labour.

From an emotional labour perspective, Knight and Layder (2016) have argued that in-cell television might affect the work of prison officers in several ways. A prison officer in the study argued that TV receivers in prisoners' cells might reduce the time and opportunities for staff to interact with prisoners. As in-cell television is a valuable privilege for most prisoners, it might also contribute to reducing the emotional expressions among prisoners and work to keep the peace in the prison. Nylander et al. (2011) have argued that prison officers first and foremost try to keep a calm and friendly attitude towards prisoners. By departing from this common 'low-key style', a kind of friendly surface acting among prison officers in general, means they perform their emotional labour in accordance with the subculture in their own wing or workgroup. The emotional labour is found to be performed more through deep acting in the treatment units and many regular wings in low- and medium-security prisons with a 'rehabilitative' culture, whereas surface acting is the dominant way of performing emotional labour in special security units/groups and in regular wings of high-security prisons (Nylander et al., 2011).

To manage the emotional labour in prison wings and units, prison officers are argued to use some common strategies. Crawley (2004a) states that prison officers use banter with colleagues as a general pattern of interaction. Others have described that when (US) prison officers try to fulfil the contradictory organisational norms in their work practice (be suspicious, do not take things personally, follow rules but be flexible), they construct 'emotionally harnessed identities, marked by paranoia, withdrawal, detachment and an us-them approach towards inmates' (Tracy, 2004: 529). Hochschild (1983) observed that the flight attendants were able to retreat to the 'backstage' (Goffman, 1959) where they could express their real feelings about a passenger or at least drop the smiling mask for a while. Similarly, Crawley (2004b: 420) noticed that some areas without prisoners present, like the staff room, served as 'emotional zones' where prison officers could 'blow off steam' and drop their professional emotional attitude. Staff who had counselling sessions in programs for sex offenders especially needed these zones. Other ways to manage frustrations in prison work are black humour, bantering with colleagues backstage, and socializing with their fellow prison officers in leisure time (Crawley, 2004b). Within drug-treatment wings and other units with little security, where prisoners and staff interact more frequently, the emotional zones are few, and the time in contact with prisoners is extended. In these, and similar environments, prison officers have been observed to create a sort of 'temporary backstage' or micro-pauses in the work group, for example by tacitly closing the office door and relaxing for a moment with colleagues, until a prisoner shows up outside the office windows and wants something from them, at which time they adopt the professional attitude again (Nylander et al., 2011: 481). Also, the strategies to manage emotional labour seem to be connected to the different subcultural patterns in prisons, wings, and units, even if there might also be individual components in these strategies. Emotional zones and strategies to cope might help prison officers to manage the impact of emotional labour, but only to a certain extent.

The outside view of prison work

Prison work is often argued to be either an unknown or a disrespected line of work for several reasons. In the media, the selection of information concerning this occupation contributes to a weak and stereotypical view of prison officer (Jewkes, 2007). Limited information and stereotypes affect the prison officers working there. Prison officers often sense that they are invisible and misunderstood, owing to the media reporting and the lack of reliable knowledge (Crawley, 2004a; Liebling et al., 2011).

Media and other sources have been argued to form a public view of occupations as more or less favourable or preferable in society. The concept of 'dirty work' developed by Hughes (1951) to describe less accepted occupations in society is useful here. Prison officer work is argued to belong to the category of dirty work (Ashforth & Kreiner, 1999), which is originally described as being tasks and occupations that are likely to be perceived as disgusting or degrading among people in society. Hughes argued that the people working in these occupations become regarded as dirty workers; 'a symbol of degradation, something that wounds one's dignity' (Hughes, 1951: 319). It is work that is physically, socially, or morally 'tainted', and prison officers are argued to belong to the second category owing to the low occupational prestige this group derives from their regular contact with stigmatized people in prisons (Ashforth & Kreiner, 1999; Hughes, 1951). This has two important consequences. First, it affects people's relationships with the 'dirty workers' in different ways. Second, 'dirty workers' try to manage the stigma connected to their work, for example by creating strong occupational or workgroup cultures. They use defence mechanisms like ideological reframing and social restructuring processes to change the meaning of dirt and moderate the pressure from outside perceptions. This 'taint management' is important to making and sustaining identity (Ashforth & Kreiner, 1999: 429). Tracy (2004: 517) similarly argues that the stigma associated with prisoners rubs off onto staff in the eyes of outsiders. This also serves as societal display rules for staff. One could argue that the transition of the labour market today has changed the jobs as well as our apprehensions of them. Still, this has probably only changed what occupations we consider, or socially construct, as more or less tainted, and the fact that dirty work can comprise several dimensions of dirt remains. However, it is shown that the status, the training, and the public view of prison officers also vary a lot between countries, owing to organisation, tradition, and prison policy (Bruhn et al., 2017).

Others have elaborated the view further and argued that 'emotional dirt' is a fourth part of the negative taint associated with certain occupations (McMurray & Ward, 2014: 1140). Through observations and interviewing telephone-call workers (Samaritans), they found that their responses to different severe emotional problems over the phone made the workers see themselves as tainted emotionally, at least in the eyes of the general public. This implies that emotional dirty work could form part of the emotional labour performed by certain occupations. Such a suggestion can be found in Crawley (2004a) in her description of the prison officers working as tutors on the Sex Offender Treatment Program (SOTP). Many of these officers were suffering from hearing about serious offences to children and needed counselling from tutor colleagues to cope with it. Many felt that their tutoring caused problems in connection to their own family lives, and they also felt disrespect from colleagues not working as SOTP-tutors. This taint did not come from being a prison officer; rather, it came from their tutoring and association with a disregarded group of prisoners, something comparable to 'emotional dirt'. Also, other prison staff might have similar problems. In a study of prison nurses, their emotional labour with prisoner patients, knowing about the severe crimes the prisoners had committed, risked nurses distancing themselves and doing their work with less humanity (Walsh & Freshwater, 2009). These preconditions involving the general public's view of prison officers, as well as the officers' awareness of this, form a kind of societal display rules. This might be important for everyday emotional labour, which is both necessary and unavoidable in prisons.

Consequences of emotional labour among prison staff

There is a lot of research on stress among prison staff, especially in the US context. Prison officer stress can take different forms and be connected to individual or organisational factors, where the latter seems to have the most impact (Finn, 1998; Triplett et al., 1996). While the relation between work and private life as a source of stress has been studied, the emotional strain and stress resulting from the demand to perform emotional labour in prisons has not been researched. Hochschild (1983) argues that deep emotional labour demands emotive effort and hence a risk of strain and exhaustion, whereas surface emotional labour might lead to emotive dissonance and a risk of cynicism. A meta-analysis including many other typical emotional labour jobs found that performing surface acting had more adverse consequences for well-being and job attitudes than performing deep acting (Hülsheger & Schewe, 2011). Other studies have shown that prison officers describe high psychological distress (e.g., see Harvey, 2014). Even if some prison officer strategies serve to reduce the personal costs and negative effects of performing emotional labour, it is still a source of emotional strain and stress to prison officers (Crawley, 2004a; Nylander et al., 2011).

Our study also found that emotional strain as well as the nature of emotional labour differs significantly according to tasks and between wings and units in the same prison (Nylander et al., 2011). As argued earlier, emotional labour is more likely to be performed through deep acting in the treatment and regular wings compared to security units. The personal officer tasks seem to be more seriously and deeply conducted in treatment and regular wings. In our study, emotional strain in terms of exhaustion is found to be higher among prison officers with personal officer tasks than among security and night staff (Nylander et al., 2011). This could be compared with what Hochschild (1983) called emotive effort often resulting in exhaustion, being more present due to the large amount of time spent with prisoners. As female prison officers are often overrepresented among personal officers and often are expected to perform caring tasks in a limited time, this might contribute to the differences in emotional strain between officers with different tasks (see Bruhn, 2013). The prison officers working in security units and high-security prisons are often men with less time in personal contact with prisoners, and they use a more distanced surface-approach to prisoners. We can assume – based on Hochschild's theory – that this creates more alienation and cynicism among these prison officers, and further research might go some way to corroborate this assessment.

It seems that the consequences for prison staff of their emotional labour, in terms of exhaustion from emotive effort and/or alienation/cynicism caused by emotive dissonance, is not occasional but occurs in accordance with the different occupational subcultures that exist in the field of prison work. Managing the dilemma between treatment ambitions and security requirements, in different parts of the prisons, seems to be the most important mechanisms behind the cultural patterns comprising emotional labour in prisons (also see Nylander et al., 2011).

Conclusions

In this chapter, we have reviewed a substantial body of literature on emotional labour in prison work. In doing so, we have connected this research with the recent development of prison policy, organisational changes, and cultural differences between and within prisons. Punitive turns in criminal justice policy, especially in prison policy, limit the opportunities for relational work and good relationships between prisoners and prison officers on a daily basis. This is because it results in more administrative work, security routines, and technical monitoring which consumes resources and time. The concentration on control and risk will affect officer-prisoner relationships, creating distance between staff and prisoners. In addition, new managerialism emphasizes centralization, efficiency, and measurable targets, which demand manual-based programs and evidence-based interventions at the expense of daily personal officer work and the necessary building of human social relationships with prisoners. This development is not uniform everywhere but differs across prisons, wings, and units. Even if the whole prison system is affected by changes in policy and organisation, there are differences owing to prison officer tasks and units, which create informal cultural patterns among prison officers in the balancing of security routines and rehabilitative treatment ambitions.

How does this affect the emotional labour in prisons? While some prisons, wings, and units manage to uphold a rehabilitative subcultural pattern, which makes a deep acting emotional labour possible, others fall into pure custodial work where distanced surface emotional labour is predominant. If small groups of officers tried to perform emotional labour through deep acting in the harsher prison environment of today, they would risk exhaustion, as the support within the organisation for this kind of work is decreasing. The organisational support for more custodial control and monitoring will probably increase the surface mode of emotional labour in general, but the organisational support for this mode of working paradoxically does not protect these prison officers from alienation and cynicism.

The general public's view of prison work as having low status and appreciation in society could tighten the collegiality among prison officers, but the emotional labour of some prison officers working in programs with vulnerable or other disrespected prisoners might also be regarded as 'tainted' not only by the general public but also by other groups of prison officers.

Where is emotional labour in prison work heading? Punitive turns, new managerialism, and evidence-based practice seem to be the continuing reality for prison work in many countries. Swedish prisons are traditionally part of a Scandinavian welfare tradition with low incarceration rates and decent prison standards. However, we are currently experiencing an increasing prison population and a concentration to larger closed prisons, a development that some other countries have already experienced. Referencing the literature on prison work and emotional labour, it is all about getting the relationships with prisoners right for prison officers (Crawley, 2004a; Liebling et al., 2011). This could mean very different things in different prisons. In the future, even if there might be small islands of good human relationships in prisons, with opportunities for prison officers to perform emotional labour through deep acting in some units or programs, most prison work will be at risk of becoming increasingly distant, requiring increasing amounts of emotional labour through surface acting. The research on emotional labour in prison work is limited. The long-term consequences of different kinds of emotional labour on staff, and the effects of this work on their prisoners, should be further researched. These results might help to change today's dominating view on prison work, and lead to more commitment, motivation, and therefore deeper emotional work.

References

Ashforth, B. E., & Kreiner, G. E. (1999). "How can you do it?" Dirty work and the challenge of constructing a positive identity. *Academy of Management Review*, 24(3), 413–434.

Barbalet, J. M. (2001). *Emotion, Social Theory and Social Structure: A Macrosociological Approach*. Cambridge: Cambridge University Press.

Bruhn, A. (2013). Gender relations and division of labour among prison officers in Swedish male prisons. *Journal of Scandinavian Studies in Criminology and Crime Prevention*, 14(2), 115–132.

Bruhn, A., Lindberg, O., & Nylander, P. Å. (2011). A harsher prison climate and cultural heritage working against it – Sub-cultural divisions among Swedish prison officers. In J. Dullum & T. Ugelvik (Eds.), *Penal Exceptionalism? Nordic Prison Policy and Practice*. Abingdon: Routledge, 215–232

Bruhn, A., Nylander, P. Å., & Johnsen, B. (2017). From prison guards to...what? Occupational development of prison officers in Sweden and Norway. *Journal of Scandinavian Studies in Criminology and Crime Prevention*, 18(1), 68–82.

Carlen, P. (2008). Imaginary penalties and risk-crazed governance. In P. Carlen (Ed.), *Imaginary Penalities*. Cullompton: Willan Publishing, 1–25.

Crawley, E. M. (2004a). *Doing Prison Work: The Public and Private Lives of Prison Officers*. Portland, OR: Willan Publishing.

Crawley, E. M. (2004b). Emotions and performance: Prison officers and the presentation of self in prison. *Punishment and Society*, 6, 411–427.

Crewe, B. (2009). *Power, Adaption and Social Life in an English Prison.* Oxford: Oxford University Clarendon Studies in Criminology.

Crewe, B., Warr, J., Bennett, P., & Smith, A. (2014). The emotional geography of prison life. *Theoretical Criminology,* 18(1), 56–74.

Cullen, F. T., Lutze, F. E., Link, B. G., Link, & Wolfe, N. T. (1989). The correctional orientation of prison guards: Do officers support rehabilitation? *Federal Probation,* 53, 33–42.

Finn, P. (1998). Correctional officer stress: A cause for concern and additional help. *Federal Probation,* 62(2), 65–74.

Foucault, M. (1977). *Discipline and Punish: The Birth of the Prison.* New York: Vintage.

Garland, D. (2001) *The Culture of Control. Crime and Social Order in Contemporary Society.* Oxford/New York: Oxford University Press.

Goffman, E. (1959). *The Presentation of Self in Everyday Life.* Garden City, NY: Doubleday Anchor Books.

Goffman, E. (1961). *Asylums.* Garden City, NY: Doubleday Anchor Books.

Griffin, M. L. (2002). The influence of professional orientation on detention officers' attitudes toward the use of force. *Criminal Justice and Behaviour,* 29(3), 250–277.

Harvey, J. (2014). Perceived physical health, psychological distress, and social support among prison officers. *The Prison Journal,* 94(2), 242–259.

Hemmens, C., & Stohr, M. K. (2000). The two faces of the correctional role: An exploration of the value of the correctional role instrument. *International Journal of Offender Therapy and Comparative Criminology,* 44(3), 326–349.

Hochschild, A. R. (1983). *The Managed Heart: Commercialization of Human Feeling.* Berkeley: University of California Press.

Hood, C. (1991). A public management for all seasons? *Public Administration,* 69, 3–19.

Hughes, E. C. (1951). Work and the self. In J. H. Rohrer & M. Sherif (Eds.), *Social Psychology at the Crossroads* (pp. 313–323). New York: Harper & Brothers.

Hülsheger, U. R., & Schewe, A. F. (2011). On the costs and benefits of emotional labor: A meta-analysis of three decades of research. *Journal of Occupational Health Psychology,* 16(3), 361–389.

Jewkes, Y. (2007). Prisons and the media: The shaping of public opinion and penal policy in a mediated society. In Y. Jewkes (Ed.), *Handbook on Prisons* (pp. 447–466). Cullumpton: Willan Publishing.

Knight, V. & Layder, D. (2016). Concept-formation, complexity and social domains: Investigating emotions in a prison setting. *Sociological Research Online,* 21(4), 107–120.

Kolind, T., Frank, V. A., Lindberg, O., & Turunen, J. (2013). Prison-based drug treatment in Nordic political discourse: An elastic discursive construct. *European Journal of Criminology,* 10(6), 659–674.

Liebling, A., Price, D., & Shefer, G. (2011). *The Prison Officer* (2nd ed.). Cullompton: Willan Publishing.

McMurray, R. & Ward, J. (2014). *The Dark Side of Emotional Labour.* Abingdon: Routledge.

Nylander, P. Å., Bruhn, A., & Lindberg, O. (2011). Emotional labour and emotional strain among Swedish prison officers. *European Journal of Criminology,* 8(6), 469–483.

Philliber, S. (1987). Thy brother's keeper: A review of the literature on correctional officers. *Justice Quarterly,* 4(1), 9–37.

Power, M. (1997). *The Audit Society: Rituals of Verification.* Oxford: Oxford University Press.

Sykes, G. M. (1958). *The Society of Captives: A Study of a Maximum Security Prison.* Princeton, NJ: Princeton University Press.

Tait, S. (2008). Prison officers and gender. In J. Bennett, B. Crewe, & A. Wahidin (Eds.), *Understanding Prison Staff* (pp. 65–89). Cullompton: Willan Publishing.

Tracy, S. J. (2004). The construction of correctional officers: Layers of emotionality behind bars. *Qualitative Inquiry*, 10(4), 509–533.

Triplett, R., Mullings, J. L., & Scarborough, K. E. (1996). Work-related stress and coping among correctional officers: Implications from organizational literature. *Journal of Criminal Justice*, 24(4), 291–308.

Walsh, E., & Freshwater, D. (2009). The mental well-being of prison nurses in England and Wales. *Journal of Research in Nursing*, 14(6), 553–564.

Chapter 6

Emotional labour in the penal voluntary sector

Kaitlyn Quinn and Philippa Tomczak

Introduction

Studies of emotion and emotional labour have recently gained significant attention in sociology, social work, organisational studies and criminology. The emotional labour of criminal justice practitioners is a burgeoning and important area of inquiry. Whilst we have some understanding of emotion in the legal professions (e.g. Bergman Blix and Wettergren, 2018), prisons (e.g. Crawley, 2004a,b; Nylander et al., 2011) and probation (e.g. Knight and Modi, 2014; Fowler et al., 2018), absent from this scholarship is the emotion work and emotional labour of criminal justice *volunteers*, *paid practitioners* and *voluntary organisations* (Tomczak and Buck, 2019a,b): practitioners that work within and often across criminal justice institutions (Quirouette, 2018). The penal voluntary sector (PVS) comprises non-profit, non-statutory agencies whose volunteer and paid practitioners work principally with criminalised individuals, their families and victims through prison, community and advocacy programmes, from the micro to macro levels (Tomczak, 2016). There are further statutory volunteers, organised directly by prison and probation agencies, and quasi-statutory volunteers, organised at arm's length from prison and probation agencies (Tomczak and Buck, 2019b).

The PVS is not a niche sector. It impacts the experience of punishment, along with penal and social policy, in *at least* the UK, Nordic countries, France, the USA, Canada, Australia, New Zealand, Brazil and Uganda (Tomczak, 2016; Darke, 2018; Marshall, 2018). It increasingly undertakes complex work for some of the least powerful in societies around the world. In fact, the growth of the PVS is one of the defining shifts in the global management of criminalised populations (Tomczak and Buck, 2019a). The voluntary sector working in criminal justice has a workforce larger than that of the prison and probation services *combined* in England and Wales (Tomczak and Buck, 2019a), and in the USA manages "more people, more poor people, and more poor people of colour than the prison system itself" (Miller, 2014, p. 307)—the jurisdiction that is the world leader in incarceration.

Although the voluntary sector has a long history of working with criminalised individuals (as well as their families and victims) (e.g. Maurutto, 2003), its role in criminal justice service delivery is expanding due to enduring government funding crises and the (near) global retrenchment of welfare state protections (Mills et al., 2011). In England and Wales, the austere, neoliberal economic climate since 2008 has further reduced the PVS's already chronically limited resources. The Conservative government's welfare reforms, lack of safe housing and widespread difficulties accessing community mental health provisions are increasingly straining voluntary 'organisations already experiencing significant pressures' (Drinkwater, 2018, p. 5). Similarly, in Canada the retrenchment of the welfare state has had 'profound implications for the non-profit and voluntary sector', particularly as 'levels of funding for many organisations [have] declined—in some cases dramatically—while the need and demand for services [has] increased' (Hall et al., 2005, p. 23). PVS practitioners across these contexts are attempting to respond to increasingly complex and urgent social needs, including: 'housing, debt and financial management, problematic substance misuse and poor mental health' (Drinkwater, 2018, p. 25).

Whilst voluntary organisations and volunteers comprise a large and rising proportion of the criminal justice and social services workforces and 'deliver important services on a not-for-profit basis', their experiences and voices have thus far received minimal analysis (Teicher and Liang, 2019, p. 217). This is especially true of PVS practitioners' emotions, emotion work and emotional labour. This oversight means we have very little knowledge about *why* people work in this sector, *what* doing their work is like, and *how* they cope with challenges. It is especially troubling given that volunteers and staff are often identified as voluntary organisations' "greatest resource" (e.g. Hall et al., 2003, p. viii). With the responsibility for public service delivery "increasingly entrusted to the voluntary sector" (Hall et al., 2003, p. 62), the need to understand the widespread effects of this work (on practitioners, service users and for societies) is imperative. Better understanding the emotions and emotional labour of (paid and volunteer[1]) PVS practitioners has implications for their well-being, that of their service users and potentially society.

Conceptualising emotion, emotion work and emotional labour in the PVS is a challenging, multi-faceted task deserving of scholarly attention around the world. Our approach in this chapter considers emotional labour in and across (overlapping) experiential, organisational and sector levels of analysis (Dean and Wood, 2017) in two national settings: England and Canada. We consider the experiential and organisational levels in Canada, followed by the sector level in England. Our goal is to highlight the complexity and diversity of emotional labour in the PVS in order to stimulate future research. We hope that this examination of PVS practitioners as boundary-spanning agents (Marchington et al., 2005), straddling institutions and goals across criminal and social justice, will also create avenues for interdisciplinary and participatory research.

Emotional labour in the PVS

PVS practitioners around the world work with and for often marginalised individuals facing complex psychosocial problems and traumatic pasts involving poverty, violence and addiction (Jansen, 2018). The emotional heft of supporting criminalised individuals through such circumstances can be considerable on its own, but PVS practitioners must simultaneously navigate *how* to conduct themselves amid the display rules of their organisations and criminal justice institutions. As Hochschild (1983, p. 148) notes, in the gap "between the 'what' and the 'how'...lies the line between technical and emotional labour". More specifically, emotional labour refers to the regulatory process by which individuals align their behaviour and/or feelings with organisational and institutional goals (Grandey, 2000). This concept is typically associated with occupations involving: face-to-face (or voice-to-voice) contact with members of the public, soliciting emotional responses from others as a core task and employer control over emotions (Hochschild, 1983). For employees in these roles, their emotions are "processed, standardised and subjected to hierarchical control" (Hochschild, 1983, p. 153).

Individuals in caring professions, including PVS practitioners, experience various emotional states that they are expected to hide or suppress in their interactions with service users, including: manifold pressure and stress (e.g. Gibson et al., 1989), role strain (e.g. Clare, 1988; Lev and Ayalon, 2016), existential crises (e.g. Picardie, 1980), burnout (e.g. Savaya et al., 2018), vicarious traumatisation (e.g. Joseph and Murphy, 2014; Merhav et al., 2018), shame (e.g. Gibson, 2016) and compassion fatigue (e.g. Robinson, 2014; Baugerud et al., 2018). The management of these emotions in the workplace is accomplished by adherence to organisational feeling rules—or "display rules" (Ashforth and Humphrey, 1993). These rules and norms are communicated by induction training programs, employee manuals and organisational materials, as well as through management and supervisors. Employees respond by engaging in "surface acting" and/or "deep acting" as different forms of emotional labour (Hochschild, 1983): the former involving a particular external performance and the latter calling for an internal state that is consistent with observable behaviour. Both techniques require sustained effort, "either in creating the inner shape of a feeling or in shaping the outward appearance of one" (Hochschild, 1983, p. 36).

In the criminology and criminal justice literatures, the concept of emotional labour has been widely employed in studies of organisations, including policing (e.g. Schaible and Gecas, 2010; Lumsden and Black, 2018), prisons (e.g. Crawley, 2004a,b; Nylander et al., 2011) and probation (e.g. Knight and Modi, 2014; Fowler et al., 2018). The majority of emotional labour research focusses on *front-line statutory sector* service staff and health professionals (Maxwell and Riley, 2017), neglecting the wider implications for the voluntary sector and many other professions. The effects of emotional labour are widespread and diverse, ranging from: fun, excitement and rewarding experiences (e.g. Shuler and Sypher, 2000; Baugerud et al., 2018), to employee alienation (Hochschild, 1983) and burnout (e.g. Gibson et al., 1989; Robinson, 2014; Maxwell and Riley, 2017). The relative invisibility of PVS practitioners' emotions amidst studies of criminal justice institutions and actors (Tomczak, 2016) means that we know very little about experiences of working in the PVS. This is a surprising and significant gap in knowledge, particularly as "people are the heart of non-profit and voluntary organisations" (Hall et al., 2003, p. 47).

Whilst existing studies of emotion amongst police, prison and probation officers do not examine homogeneous groups, they have focused on frontline practitioners with relatively clearly defined roles facing a group of service users (e.g. the public, prisoners or criminalised individuals in the community). In contrast, PVS practitioners' roles and interactions are especially diverse. They undertake varying programmes underpinned by different theoretical assumptions, seeking radical change and regulation of individuals and societies (Tomczak and Buck, 2019a). Paid, volunteer and "professional-ex"[2] practitioners, although all ostensibly involved in the same goal of helping criminalised individuals, draw on distinct discursive frames to understand and legitimate their perspectives (Quinn, 2019). Together they perform (often overlapping) roles, ranging from leadership and campaigning to front-line intervention. In so doing, they interact with a variety of audiences, including: criminalised individuals, their families and victims; other volunteers and practitioners; institutional gatekeepers; government policymakers; trustees, funders and donors; and the general public. Practitioners also have differing access to social, cultural, economic and symbolic resources as well as drawing from distinct life experiences as they form dispositions, habits and expectations at work (Bourdieu, 1984; Bourdieu, 1986). These differences lead to different patterns of thinking, feeling and acting in this sector (Quinn, 2019). Although police and prison staff and their work are not homogeneous, PVS practitioners and their work are particularly varied.

As boundary-spanning agents straddling criminal and social justice (Wharton, 1993; Marchington et al., 2005), PVS practitioners move between multiple working environments with different expectations, rules and norms regarding emotional display. While compliance with emotional display rules of an autonomous workplace can be stressful and psychologically harmful in and of itself (Hochschild, 1983; Bono and Vey, 2005), PVS practitioners must contend with numerous—often dissimilar—contexts. As a result, their emotional conduct is not only guided by their own organisation, but also their (shifting) work contexts (e.g. their offices, prisons, probation offices and community settings), stakeholders (e.g. their organisational trustees, statutory and private sector prison and probation staff, criminalised individuals and funders) and audiences (e.g. local and national policymakers, gatekeepers and the general public). PVS practitioners must adapt to, fit in with and challenge the emotional displays demanded by their varying audiences.

Methods

The data presented in this chapter are drawn from two separate qualitative research projects undertaken in: (i) England (drawing on 13 semi-structured interviews with voluntary sector practitioners at 12 organisations in 2012) and (ii) Canada (drawing on over 400 hours of participant observation conducted in seven penal voluntary organisations between 2013 and 2018). The England research inspired the Canada research, but these projects were undertaken independently by the authors. Pseudonyms have been used throughout.

Each penal voluntary organisation in the England sample provided supplementary support services for prisoners, probationers or families, and were principally funded by charitable trusts and foundations. None were involved in competitive contracting, but one held a statutory contract and another received statutory grant funding. Organisations included a women's centre in the north of England, a charity providing support through "pen pals" for prisoners throughout the UK and a housing/resettlement support service for released prisoners in the south of England. The quotations presented are from four paid practitioners in management and front-line roles.

The Canada analysis presented in this chapter is based on observations of seven volunteer (unpaid) practitioners completing 30 hours of induction training over six sessions at one voluntary organisation in Autumn 2017. This organisation sought to help criminalised women through services including: mentorship, community reintegration support, employment, housing and crisis counselling. It was predominantly funded by the federal, provincial and local governments, receiving further income from non-profit organisations, private donations, foundations, corporations and religious institutions. All unpaid practitioners observed in Canada were training to provide mentorship and emotional support to criminalised women. Fieldnotes were recorded by hand during each training session and later typed.

The theme of "emotions" emerged independently during thematic analysis and coding in both projects. Relevant coded data were then combined and reanalysed using ethnographic content analysis (Altheide, 1987), distilling themes from the data and revising these themes as new understandings emerged. Our analysis is neither representative of the heterogeneous PVS nor voluntary sector social services more broadly, but provides a useful preliminary analysis. These complementary bodies of original data allow us to offer a useful and rare analysis of penal voluntary organisations in two jurisdictions. Considered together, they are more analytically rewarding: providing a stronger data set to underpin future analyses, combining multiple observers and participants and a wider set of case studies. Our combined data speak to the overlapping emotional labour of different practitioner groups in the PVS(s) of Canada and England. Though our data are drawn from two Westernised countries, voluntary sector provision of social services to meet human needs is an issue relevant to many further countries, given attention to contextual differences (Tomczak, 2016).

PVS emotional labour across experiential and organisational contexts in Canada

In this section, we consider the emotion work and emotional labour of PVS practitioners in Canada within micro-level interactions with service users and meso-level organisational environments. These contexts are discussed concurrently as practitioners' relationships with service users are mediated by organisational display rules. As Hochschild (1983, p. 185) explains, "it is not simply individuals who manage their feelings in order to do a job; whole organisations have entered the game". Therefore, in examining practitioners' emotional experiences, we must also consider the role of occupational display rules (Harris, 2002; Orzechowicz, 2008). As a result, our analysis weaves together practitioners' experiences and organisational expectations to provide a layered perspective of emotional labour in this sector, encompassing the multi-dimensionality of deep acting, surface acting and spontaneous emotions (Ashforth and Humphrey, 1993).

In training, PVS practitioners were taught how to interact with service users according to organisational display rules. In particular, they learned that "the emotional style of offering the service is part of the service itself" (Hochschild, 1983, p. 5). For the practitioners we observed, their organisational roles were constructed around the successful embodiment of particular emotions as part of "good service delivery" (fieldnotes). The style of practitioners' service delivery was dictated by organisational display rules, which provided a normative scaffolding for the cultivation of a helping relationship on the basis of "empathy", "connection", "rapport", "trust" and "intuition" (fieldnotes). The purpose of these rules was to create a relationship that felt "healing, safe, predictable, consistent and attuned" to service users (fieldnotes). The responsibility for developing such a relationship was exclusively placed on practitioners—predominantly through the dutiful management of their emotions.

When the organisational manager, Karen, spoke about the relationship between practitioners and service users, her focus was on "empathy and genuine interest", explaining that "it is important for [practitioners] to connect with [service users] on a feeling level" (fieldnotes). This involved "show[ing] concern, build[ing] a comfort level and develop[ing] trust" (fieldnotes). In order to accomplish this, practitioners were taught that the essential difference between empathy (encouraged) and sympathy (discouraged) lay in the prepositions: feeling *with* versus feeling *for* (fieldnotes). The key to performing empathy was recognising emotion in others and responding with appropriate emotion—"feeling *with* people" (fieldnotes). Practitioners were required to demonstrate that they could "relate to the feelings clients were describing" by carefully managing their own emotions (fieldnotes). Practitioners engaged in deep acting by putting themselves "in the [service users'] shoes and imagining what [they] would do in that situation" (fieldnotes). The experience of emotions (rather than simply the performance) was vital in this context.

Despite a meta narrative of practitioners' authentic emotional connections with service users, this organisation carefully controlled the conditions under which these relationships were formed. Through organisational display rules, the interactions between practitioners and service users were "forced into narrow channels" (Hochschild, 1983, p. 119). When speaking to service users, practitioners were instructed to: "smile and gesture appropriately, nod, face and lean toward service users, be alert, maintain eye contact and be attentive to their physical proximity to service users" (fieldnotes). They were told to match service users' "softness/loudness of speech and speed of talking to mirror the mood that they are in". For example, if service users were "depressed and quiet", practitioners were told not to be "too bubbly and energetic". Or, if a service user was "angry and swearing", practitioners were given permission to "match those swear words" in their responses (fieldnotes).

When told "shocking stories" by service users, practitioners were expected "not to react at all because their reactions [were] something that [service users] might hold onto for a long time" (fieldnotes). They were expected to behave as if they had no emotional response to the pain and trauma of service users—for the sake of "good service delivery". Practitioners were also expected to refrain from the following "unacceptable" behaviours when interacting with service users:

> "diminishing expressed feelings", "using clichés", "empty reassurance", "disapproving", "ordering or demanding", "rejecting", "warning or threatening", "criticising or blaming or disagreeing", "admonishing or moralising", "persuading or arguing or lecturing", "advising or providing answers", "inappropriate praising or agreeing", "sympathising or reassuring", "probing or inappropriate questioning", "interpreting or diagnosing", "diverting or avoiding" and "kidding or using sarcasm".
>
> (Fieldnotes)

Recognising the complexity of suppressing spontaneous emotional reactions in stressful, real-time interactions with service users, this organisation encouraged practitioners to memorise (and internalise) scripted responses. Practitioners were provided with handouts containing hair-splitting detail about the kind of language that should be used when speaking with service users.

One handout listed 77 validating statements that practitioners were encouraged to use. Selected examples included:

> "you're a survivor!", "how frightening that must have been for you!", "one of the things I appreciate is your resilience", "tell me more so I can better understand you", "you are not alone", "let me listen to your story", "I believe you", "that must have made you feel bad", "most people would have that reaction, it's normal", "I care about you and what happened to you" and "no wonder you have nightmares! Any person would".
>
> (Fieldnotes)

This sheet had been photocopied with certain phrases crossed out or edited, demonstrating the organisation's very specific ideas about what was, and was not, acceptable. For example, "it will get better" was crossed out and replaced by "this too will pass" (fieldnotes). These examples illustrate the extent to which practitioners would ideally be "restricted to implementing standard procedures" in their relationships and emotional exchanges with service users (Hochschild, 1983, p. 120).

Despite the specificity of these materials, practitioners sometimes received contradictory messages about what was expected of them. At times, organisational display rules conflicted with one another. Such moments of contention and instability acted to reveal the complex emotional terrain that PVS practitioners must navigate in their work. For example, a central tension emerged between the expectation that practitioners form genuine connections with service users and the rigid channels through which they were permitted to engage in these relationships. In one training session, Karen explained to practitioners that "in order to connect with [service users] you need to connect with something in yourself that knows that feeling" (fieldnotes). Yet in a later session, she told practitioners "not to bring up similar feelings and problems from [their] own experience[s]" (fieldnotes, see also: Phillips et al., 2018). Many practitioners, like Danielle, expressed significant anxiety about navigating this complexity:

> **Danielle**: (unpaid, fieldnotes) I am so terrified of saying the wrong thing. I get in my head about it. I try to tell myself to just be normal and react how you normally would if this was your friend or something, but then immediately I'm like "oh I would definitely try to make her feel better by saying I've been through something similar" and I'm not supposed to do that, so yeah I just feel stuck and it makes me really awkward when I'm talking to people and trying to help them. I feel a lot of stress about it.

Danielle's perspective illustrates the complex interplay between the experiential and organisational levels of analysis. Her emotions at the experiential level, in her relationships with service users, were impacted by organisational display rules. She experienced emotional dissonance as a result of trying to fulfil conflicting organisational demands. Typically, when emotional dissonance is discussed in the context of emotional labour, it reflects "the separation of felt emotion from feigned emotion expressed to meet organisational expectations" (Mastracci et al., 2006, p. 126). This definition does not easily account for the kinds of scenarios Danielle described (above) in which the dissonance did not lie between felt and feigned emotion, but rather as a result of contradictory organisational demands on practitioners' emotions. Danielle felt an authentic connection (as is expected of her), but struggled to align her spontaneous expression of empathy with organisational display rules. Therefore, it is not simply that practitioners must feel (through deep acting) or perform (through surface acting), but also that they navigate the (sometimes fraught) relationship between these demands.

Scholarship on the harmful effects of performing emotional labour in the workplace tends to focus on burnout, stress, poor self-esteem, depression, cynicism, role alienation, self-alienation and emotional deviance (Mastracci et al., 2006). Despite the emotionally taxing nature of surface acting, deep acting, and the blurry relationship between them, very little organisational attention was paid to the well-being of practitioners. By contrast, the mental health and well-being of service users was a frequent topic of discussion in practitioners' training. For example, in the five-hour training session that was specifically focussed on mental health and trauma, practitioners were shown 116 PowerPoint slides, with only 13 slides (~11%) specifically addressing the emotions that they may experience at work. In fact, during training practitioners were told that personal distractions (e.g. "personal issues") caused "mistakes, misunderstandings, [and] poor service" (fieldnotes). Accordingly, practitioners were instructed to "try to leave [their] emotions behind" and to "get rid of distractions" (fieldnotes). Practitioners were asked to "be present with [the] distress" of service users, yet there was little concern over their own potential distress (fieldnotes).

Nevertheless, the practitioners observed considered the emotional cost to themselves as "worth it" because "[they] made someone feel better", or "[they] made a change in someone's life" (fieldnotes). The enjoyment of emotional labour has recognised potential antecedents, including personality and interaction characteristics (Diefendorff et al., 2005; Hsieh et al., 2012):

> any set of conversations with individuals in the helping professions (teaching, nursing, social work) will reveal that self-selection biases operate. Individuals choose such professions precisely because they provide an opportunity for normative rewards, one of which might be the use of emotional labour.
>
> (Meier et al., 2006, p. 906)

In nursing, Theodosius (2008, p. 34) notes "the significance of satisfaction nurses receive as a result of their work, and the importance of the gratitude they receive from their patients". Indeed, multiple PVS volunteers discussed enjoyment of their role because of the emotional labour required by their work. They found great satisfaction in "making a meaningful human connection" with service users, explaining that "it's a privilege to be on the receiving end of someone's story" and "it is an honour for people to share with you" (fieldnotes). However, this coping strategy may be a source of tension if practitioners are unable to form the meaningful connections they stake their well-being on, if the difference they can make is perceived to be insufficient or if they experience difficulties such as secondary traumatisation and compassion fatigue.

In this section, we have considered the experiential (micro) and organisational (meso) levels of PVS emotional labour in the context of face-to-face relationships with service users. Volunteer practitioners in Canada described how their diverse relationships with service users elicited powerful (positive and negative) emotions, whilst also requiring intense emotion work. At these overlapping levels of analysis, practitioners predominantly spoke about deep acting and spontaneous emotions as they sought to form authentic, empathetic connections with service users, and surface acting as they navigated the minutiae of these relationships with strict guidance from organisational display rules. This duality produced tension between the performativity required of organisational display rules (e.g. using particular validation statements) and the overarching narratives communicated during training about the kinds of genuine feelings that should motivate this work (e.g. empathy, intuition, trust and connection).

PVS emotional labour at the sector level in England

Though discussion of emotional labour often ends at the organisational level, as boundary-spanning agents (Wharton, 1993), PVS practitioners must also navigate environments beyond their workplace. Extending our view of emotion work and emotional labour to the sector level, illustrates how macro-level features that impact the (penal) voluntary sector as a whole influence practitioners' emotions. Faced with an austere political climate and continuing welfare state retrenchment at the macro level (Dean and Wood, 2017), paid and volunteer PVS practitioners in both England and Canada (among other nations) are responding to service users' increasingly complex and urgent needs with fewer resources and less support (Drinkwater, 2018). These sector-level developments diffuse across multiple levels of analysis as organisations and individuals alike are put "under increasing pressure as they work to address and meet the needs of their clients" (Drinkwater, 2018, p. 24). As "government funding has become more short-term, more competitive and less predictable [...] organisations and the people who work and volunteer with them are under considerable strain" (Hall et al., 2005, p. v).

In addition to confronting the consequences of a shrinking and shifting welfare state on the front-lines, PVS practitioners must also negotiate a complex set of relationships with the state (and privatised) criminal justice apparatus. These relationships are particularly high-stakes because for many organisations, their work with service users depends on gaining and maintaining access to prisons and/or other correctional facilities. The relationship between the voluntary sector and the prison is complicated because the priorities of these institutions are often dissimilar (or antagonistic) to the goals of PVS organisations. As practitioners Katrina and Adrian explained:

> **Katrina** (paid, manager): Well, I mean, I'm assuming you know about what prisons are like *(laughs)*. They can be really hard to work with [...] like on the ground there can often be problems. And prisons, you know, may believe in rehabilitation some of them anyway these days, but you know obviously their primary focus is security [...]
>
> **Adrian** (paid, Chief Executive): The thing I think about prison is... they're always slightly gonna think that you are these stupid little voluntary sector people getting in our prison and you know, kind of being annoying. I think it's fundamentally quite a tense relationship.

The nature of these relationships required that actors in the PVS approached interactions with correctional institutions mindfully and strategically. To do so, practitioners had to suppress their feelings and maintain a particular emotional façade consistent with surface acting in order to have a productive relationship with correctional institutions and their staff. As Solomon and Katrina explained, with reference to prison staff:

> **Solomon** (paid, Chief Executive): We very much, you know, try to make the most of those personal relationships with prison staff, that we have. And a big part of our work is about cultivating those relationships, you know, keeping friendly with them and trying to be sympathetic to the pressures that they're under, trying to offer what we offer in a way that doesn't cause disruption or headache to them, that fits in as smoothly, er, with them as possible.
>
> **Katrina** (paid, manager): I mean, I deal with them constantly basically [...] Some of them are just completely sealed off and its really difficult to build a relationship. [...] I think once you understand how it works and you understand that things take a really long time and that there's no point fighting against that, you have to work *with it*, then you can achieve quite a lot. [...] if you have any kind of aggressive stance against *(intake of breath)* prison, with the prison atmosphere, then you won't get anywhere, they'll actually dig their heels in, that's my experience.

While the presence of emotional labour in these interviews is obvious, it is more difficult to disentangle surface acting from deep acting. On the one hand, practitioners were required to "play nice" with prisons, which given their conflicting goals and ideologies would seem to call for surface acting. However, on the other, they expressed a genuine willingness to work with prisons (and their staff), rather than in spite of them.

The practitioners we spoke with were critical of prisons and frustrated by both their power and restrictions, yet had developed emotion management strategies for forming positive relationships with prison staff amidst such constraints. For example, Jacqui described how she self-regulated during interactions with prison staff:

> **Jacqui** (paid, frontline staff): [...] particularly around prisons, you have to be very careful about choosing your battles with the prison. And how you respond to things or do anything, the worst thing really is to piss off that prison, to really piss off that prison governor, to the point where they can say "actually, I don't want you in my prison any more" [...] If a Probation Officer's trying to recall her and I'm saying "I don't think that's a good idea", unfortunately I don't have a lot of say *(laughs)* [...] I guess it's about recognising what I can control and what I can't control. For me to fall out with that person's probation officer, with that prison officer, with that prison health and advice worker, the only person who's gonna be affected is that woman, [...] So we're quite careful.

Practitioners, like Jacqui, engaged in deep acting as they cultivated particular dispositions toward seeing the bigger picture, and recognised that their limited involvement or access to service users on the prison's terms was preferable to being prohibited entirely. However, this disposition simultaneously required practitioners to employ surface acting as they watched their words and suppressed their frustration during interactions with prison staff. As Jacqui explained, practitioners consciously put the best interests and needs of their service users above their own—an emotionally taxing decision that must be continually re-made in each interaction.

This examination of practitioner relationships with prisons and prison staff illustrates how macro-level developments impacting the voluntary sector as a whole (e.g. welfare state retrenchment, financial crises, changing political ideologies) play out in the workplace (and emotional) conditions faced by PVS practitioners. As was the case at the interface of experiential and organisational levels of analysis in Canada, emotional labour at the sector level often blurred the easy distinction between surface acting and deep acting. On the ground practice in the PVS required that practitioners engage in both, juggling the complex demands of a fundamentally tense and unstable relationship with criminal justice institutions.

Conclusion

In this chapter, we have presented preliminary data that highlight the previously unacknowledged emotion work and emotional labour—and consequent unaddressed well-being needs—of penal voluntary sector practitioners. We have considered the emotional labour of PVS practitioners across the overlapping experiential (micro), organisational (meso) and sector (macro) levels in Canada and England. Our data support existing studies of emotional labour that highlight the importance of both surface acting and deep acting (e.g. Hochschild, 1983), yet also encourage scholars to consider the boundaries between different forms of emotional labour as often blurry and sometimes tense or contradictory. As boundary-spanning agents, the diversity of PVS practitioners, their organisations, roles, audiences and workplace contexts has provided a generative ground upon which to investigate the multiplicity and complexity of emotional labour in this sector.

In particular, our data indicate that jurisdictions around the world that use voluntary organisations and volunteers to provide criminal justice services to marginalised populations, and the individual statutory, private and voluntary organisations that organise this, need to take the emotion work and emotional labour of voluntary sector practitioners seriously. Paid and volunteer practitioners in voluntary organisations are increasingly stepping in to fill widening gaps in statutory provision, and responding to a higher degree of service user need. It is unacceptable to overlook the emotional needs of practitioners confronted with human needs in the absence of alternative provisions. Overburdened and unhealthy practitioners may further disadvantage or damage their service users. This presents an urgent need for further scholarship and sustained attention in policy and practice at individual, organisational and sector levels.

Notes

1 Although Hochschild (1983) only considers emotional labour within paid contexts, scholars such as Steinberg and Figart (1999) have widened understandings of emotional labour to unpaid (volunteer) contexts.
2 Professional exes (LeBel et al., 2015) are often former clients of voluntary organisations who go on to volunteer or work helping other criminalised individuals. There has been a push by many organisations in the penal voluntary sector to employ formerly incarcerated individuals (Buck, 2018).

References

Altheide, D.L. (1987) Reflections: Ethnographic content analysis. *Qualitative Sociology.* 10(1), 65–77.
Ashforth, B.E. and Humphrey, R.H. (1993) Emotional labor in service roles: The influence of identity. *The Academy of Management Review.* 18(1), 88–115.

Baugerud, G.A., Vangbæk, S. and Melinder, A. (2018) Secondary traumatic stress, burnout and compassion satisfaction among norwegian child protection workers: Protective and risk factors. *British Journal of Social Work*. 48(1), 215–235.

Bergman Blix, S. and Wettergren, Å. (2018) *Professional Emotions in Court: A Sociological Perspective*. New York: Routledge.

Bono, J.E. and Vey, M.A. (2005) Toward understanding emotional management at work: A quantitative review of emotional labor research. In: Härtel, C.E., Zerbe, W.J. and Ashkanasy N.M. (eds) *Emotions in Organizational Behavior*. Mahwah, NJ: Lawrence Erlbaum Associates Publishers, pp. 213–233.

Bourdieu, P. (1984) *Distinction: A Social Critique of the Judgement of Taste*. Cambridge, MA: Harvard University Press.

Bourdieu, P. (1986) The forms of capital. In: Richardson, J.G. (ed) *Handbook of Theory and Research for the Sociology of Education*. Westport, CN: Greenwood, pp. 241–258.

Buck, G. (2018) The core conditions of peer mentoring. *Criminology & Criminal Justice*. 18(2), 190–206.

Clare, M. (1988) Supervision, role strain and social services departments. *British Journal of Social Work*. 18(5), 489–507.

Crawley, E.M. (2004a) *Doing Prison Work. The Public and Private Lives of Prison Officers*. New York: Routledge.

Crawley, E.M. (2004b) Emotion and performance: Prison officers and the presentation of self in prisons. *Punishment & Society*. 6(4), 411–427.

Darke, S. (2018) *Conviviality and Survival: Co-Producing Brazilian Prison Order*. Palgrave London: Macmillan.

Dean, J. and Wood, R. (2017) "You can try to press different emotional buttons": The conflicts and strategies of eliciting emotions for fundraisers. *International Journal of Nonprofit and Voluntary Sector Marketing*. 22(4), 1–7.

Drinkwater, N. (2018) *The State of the Sector: Key Trends for Voluntary Sector Organisations Working in the Criminal Justice System*. London: Clinks.

Diefendorff, J.M., Croyle, M.H. and Gosserand, R.H. (2005) The dimensionality and antecedents of emotional labor strategies. *Journal of Vocational Behavior*. 66(2), 339–357.

Fowler, A., Phillips J. and Westaby C. (2018) Understanding emotions as effective practice in English probation: The performance of emotional labour in building relationships. In: Ugwudike P., Raynor, P. and Annison, J. (eds) *Evidence-Based Skills in Community Justice: International Perspectives on Effective Practice*. Bristol: Bristol University Press, pp. 243–262.

Gibson, F., McGrath A. and Reid N. (1989) Occupational stress in social work. *British Journal of Social Work*. 19(1), 1–18.

Gibson, M. (2016) Social worker shame: A scoping review. *British Journal of Social Work*. 46(2), 549–565.

Grandey, A.A. (2000) Emotion regulation in the workplace: A new way to conceptualize emotional labor. *Journal of Occupational Health Psychology*. 5(1), 95–110.

Hall, M.H., Andrukow, A., Barr, C., Brock, K., de Wit, M., Embuldeniya, D., Jolin, L., Lasby, D., Lévesque, B., Malinsky, E., Stowe, S. and Vaillancourt, Y. (2003) *The Capacity To Serve: A Qualitative Study of the Challenges Facing Canada'a Nonprofit and Voluntary Organizations*. Toronto: Canadian Centre for Philanthropy.

Hall, M.H., Barr, C.W., Easwaramoorthy, M., Worjciech Sokolowsi, S. and Salamon, L.M. (2005) *The Canadian Nonprofit and Voluntary Sector in Comparative Perspective.* Toronto: Imagine Canada.

Harris, L.C. (2002) The emotional labour of barristers: An exploration of emotional labour by status professionals. *Journal of Management Studies.* 39(4), 553–584.

Hochschild, A.R. (1983) *The Managed Heart: Commercialization of Human Feeling.* Berkeley: University of California Press.

Hsieh, C.W., Yang, K. and Fu, K.J. (2012) Motivational bases and emotional labor: Assessing the impact of public service motivation. *Public Administration Review.* 72(2), 241–251.

Jansen, A. (2018) 'It's so complex!': Understanding the challenges of child protection work as experienced by newly graduated professionals. *British Journal of Social Work.* 48(6), 1524–1540.

Joseph, S. and Murphy, D. (2014) Trauma: A unifying concept for social work. *British Journal of Social Work.* 44(5), 1094–1109.

Knight, C. and Modi, P. (2014) The use of emotional literacy in work with sexual offenders. *Probation Journal.* 61(2), 132–147.

LeBel, T.P., Richie, M. and Maruna, S. (2015) Helping others as a response to reconcile a criminal past: The role of the wounded healer in prisoner reentry programs. *Criminal Justice and Behavior.* 42(1), 108–120.

Lev, S. and Ayalon, L. (2016) Coping with the obligation dilemma: Prototypes of social workers in the nursing home. *British Journal of Social Work.* 46(5), 1318–1335.

Lumsden, K. and Black, A. (2018) Austerity policing, emotional labour and the boundaries of police work: An ethnography of a police force control room in England. *The British Journal of Criminology.* 58(3), 606–623.

Marchington, M., Vincent, S. and Cooke, F.L. (2005) The role of boundary-spanning agents in inter-organizational contracting. In: Marchington, M., Grimshaw, D., Rubery, J. and Wilmott, H. (eds) *Fragmenting Work: Blurring Organizational Boundaries and Disordering Hierarchies.* Oxford: Oxford University Press, pp. 135–156.

Marshall, H.J. (2018) "Once you support, you are supported": Entrepreneurship and reintegration among ex-prisoners in Gulu, northern Uganda. *Economic Anthropology.* 5(1), 71–82.

Mastracci, S.H., Newman, M.A. and Guy, M.E. (2006) Appraising emotion work: Determining whether emotional labor is valued in government jobs. *The American Review of Public Administration.* 36(2), 123–138.

Maurutto, P. (2003) *Governing Charities: Church and State in Toronto's Catholic Archdiocese, 1850–1950.* Montreal: McGill-Queen's Press-MQUP.

Maxwell, A. and Riley, P. (2017) Emotional demands, emotional labor and occupational outcomes in school principals: Modelling the relationships. *Educational Management Adminstration & Leadership.* 45(3), 484–502.

Meier, K.J., Mastracci, S.H. and Wilson, K. (2006) Gender and emotional labor in public organizations: An empirical examination of the link to performance. *Public Administration Review.* 66(6), 899–909.

Merhav, I., Lawental, M. and Peled-Avram, M. (2018) Vicarious traumatisation: Working with clients of probation services. *British Journal of Social Work.* 48(8), 2215–2234.

Miller, R.J. (2014) Devolving the carceral state: Race, prisoner reentry, and the micro-politics of urban poverty management. *Punishment & Society.* 16(3), 305–335.

Mills, A., Meek, R. and Gojkovic, D. (2011) Exploring the relationship between the voluntary sector and the state in criminal justice. *Voluntary Sector Review.* 2(2), 193–211.

Nylander, P.Å., Lindberg, O. and Bruhn, A. (2011) Emotional labour and emotional strain among Swedish prison officers. *European Journal of Criminology.* 8(6), 469–483.

Orzechowicz, D. (2008) Privileged emotion managers: The case of actors. *Social Psychology Quarterly.* 71(2), 143–156.

Phillips, J., Fowler, A. and Westaby, C. (2018) Self-disclosure in criminal justice: What form does it take and what does it achieve? *International Journal of Offender Therapy and Comparative Criminology.* 62(12), 3890–3909.

Picardie, M. (1980) Dreadful moments: Existential thoughts on doing social work. *British Journal of Social Work.* 10(4), 483–490.

Quinn, K. (2019) Inside the penal voluntary sector: Divided discourses of "helping" criminalized women. *Punishment & Society.* 22(2), 161–180.

Quirouette, M. (2018) Community practitioners in criminal courts: Risk logics and multiply-disadvantaged individuals. *Theoretical Criminology.* 22(4), 582–602.

Robinson, K. (2014) Voices from the front line: Social work with refugees and asylum seekers in Australia and the UK. *British Journal of Social Work.* 44(6), 1602–1620.

Savaya, R., Melamed, S. and Altschuler, D. (2018) Perceptions of service providers' burnout: Comparison of service users and service providers. *British Journal of Social Work.* 48(2), 339–352.

Schaible, L.M. and Gecas, V. (2010) The impact of emotional labor and value dissonance on burnout among police officers. *Police Quarterly.* 13(3), 316–341.

Shuler, S. and Sypher, B.D. (2000) Seeking emotional labor: When managing the heart enhances the work experience. *Management Communication Quarterly.* 14(1), 50–89.

Steinberg, R.J. and Figart, D.M. (1999) Emotional labor since: The managed heart. *The Annals of the American Academy of Political and Social Science.* 561(1), 8–26.

Teicher, J. and Liang, X. (2019) The politics of voice: Voice and volunteering in a third sector organisation. In: Holland, P., Teicher, J. and Donaghey, J. (eds) *Employee Voice at Work.* Singapore: Springer, pp. 217–229.

Theodosius, C. (2008) *Emotional Labour in Health Care: The Unmanaged Heart of Nursing.* New York: Routledge.

Tomczak, P. (2016) *The Penal Voluntary Sector.* London: Routledge.

Tomczak, P. and Buck, G. (2019a) The penal voluntary sector: A hybrid sociology. *British Journal of Criminology.* 59(4), 898–918.

Tomczak, P. and Buck, G. (2019b) The criminal justice voluntary sector: Concepts and an agenda for an emerging field. *The Howard Journal of Crime and Justice.* 58(3), 276–297.

Wharton, A.S. (1993) The affective conseqences of service work: Managing emotions on the job. *Work and Occupations.* 20(2), 205–232.

Chapter 7

Doing criminological research

An emotional labour perspective

*Jaime Waters, Chalen Westaby,
Andrew Fowler and Jake Phillips*

Introduction

Emotional labour is becoming increasingly recognised and utilised within the disciplines of criminology and criminal justice (as this book is a testament to). This chapter takes a 'peek behind the curtain' and looks at the emotional labour performed by the criminological researchers themselves. As is the case with all those engaged in empirical research, criminological researchers – particularly those who adopt a qualitative research design – are required to interact with other people as part of their research in order to gain and maintain access to the field of study as well engage in data collection. This inevitably results in the need to perform emotional labour in order to manage both their emotions and the emotions of their gatekeepers and participants. This is perhaps unsurprising given the nature of work, as is the fact that often such research requires criminological researchers to engage with vulnerable and sometimes dangerous populations and often in challenging environments. In spite of all of this, little research has been conducted in this area.

One of the reasons for this can be attributed to the way in which criminological research is structured as a 'social science' (Wakeman, 2014), and the historical masculinisation of the discipline (Wykes and Welsh, 2008). Furthermore, and arguably related to the masculinity of the discipline, is the traditionally positivistic nature of criminology. As such, 'objectivity', 'restrained language' and 'methodology' are often seen as key to its rigour, and to the detriment of 'any form of biographical or emotional intrusion by the researcher' (Wakeman, 2014: 705, quoting Jewkes, 2012: 65). This, therefore, not only means that the researcher should not be present in the data, but also must stay silent about the emotional investment that they put into the research. As Jewkes (2012: 64) suggests, 'the academic environment arguably trains researchers to be rational and objective, to "extract out" emotion and not disclose feelings of anxiety, confusion, vulnerability, or anything of themselves'. As such, only a limited discussion of emotional labour in criminological research has been forthcoming. What little there is has primarily been in the area of prisons research and has led to the understanding that expressing, absorbing, and responding adequately to the expression of emotions in others, and handling it in oneself, can be among the most pressing challenges of prison researchers [both in terms of] our professional identities as well as our emotional wellbeing.

(Liebling, 2014: 481, 483)

It is therefore imperative that we understand not only the emotional labour undertaken by criminological researchers, but also the potential impact on their professional identity and wellbeing.

This chapter is divided into two parts. The first part is an overview of the existing literature around the emotional labour performed by researchers. We begin by looking at the emotional labour required to gain access to a field of study, before moving on to consider emotional labour in data collection, specifically looking at ethnography, autoethnography and research interviews. We conclude this part by focusing on exiting the field, both temporarily and following the conclusion of research. The second part of the chapter provides a case study on emotional labour and criminological researchers, drawing on research conducted by the authors. We end the chapter by considering the implications for criminological researchers, particularly those early on in their career and doctoral students, and providing some recommendations for going forward.

Gaining access to the field

In order to gain access to a research field, and therefore individuals within or linked to an organisation, it is generally necessary to contact gatekeepers, and negotiate access with those gatekeepers (Okomus et al., 2007; Patton, 2002; Shenton and Hayter, 2004). This process, while being crucial to the study, is hard work and requires both strategy and luck (Van Maanen and Kolb, 1985). It rarely proceeds neatly nor predictably and almost always requires a variety of interpersonal skills in order to be effective (Burgess, 1984). Furthermore, where there is direct contact with gatekeepers, either face-to-face or on the phone, this also involves the performance of emotional labour.

There remains little research in this area for criminology. However, there is, albeit limited, discussion of the emotional labour required in accessing the field more generally (Bergman Blix and Wettergren, 2015). Bergman Blix and Wettergren (2015) identify and explore the emotional labour researchers have to perform in order to build trust and rapport with gatekeepers in order to gain access to, secure and maintain that access. Their research focuses on the Swedish judiciary. Therefore, they consider emotional labour required in relation particularly to elites, or 'researching up' as they describe it (2015: 689). The distinction between this and 'researching down' (ibid) is important given the different emotional labour required to undertake each type of research.

Emotional labour is analysed by Bergman Blix and Wettergren (2015) along three dimensions, and of particular relevance to maintaining access to the field is the first they discuss, strategic emotion work to access the field. Given the risks associated with being excluded from the field of study, researchers are required to quickly develop rapport with gatekeepers. This requires engaging in preliminary work to understand the field of study in order to ensure a confident and trustworthy appearance, even where self-confidence might not be forthcoming, particular in the early stages of the project. As Bergman Blix and Wettergren (2015) suggest, this necessitated surface acting, which also served to project understanding when actually the researchers were still working out what outward countenance was expected by gatekeepers. Once initial access had been gained, it was still necessary to engage in emotional labour in order to gain further access, and Bergman Blix describe how surface acting became deep acting as a result of the understanding that certain emotional displays proved successful.

Bergman Blix and Wettergren (2015) also talk about reflexivity in terms of gaining – and, for that matter, maintaining – access to the field and often involves a process of learning about their identity. This is because it requires researchers to place themselves in situations which they may not have chosen to be in outside the research. The consequences of this may be self-development, but inevitably requires the researcher to consider the distinction between their 'private' self and the 'professional researcher' they may become in the field (692).

In the field

Once a researcher has gained access, data collection begins. It could be argued that nearly all data collection methods will require some amount of emotional labour from the researcher, with a heavier burden generally falling on those using qualitative methods. The two which have had the most consideration and will be discussed here are research interviews and ethnography/autoethnography.

Interviewing and emotional labour

The most commonly used form of qualitative data collection in the field of criminology has traditionally been interviews, with a heavy reliance on semi-structured interviews. However, the performance of emotional labour by criminological researchers during interviews has thus far received little attention. Although there is little writing on this in criminology, we can look to related research areas where it is acknowledged that emotional labour is required in interviews and indeed that it can be challenging, not least because, as Hoffman suggests, 'decisions about what level of emotion and which emotions to share are very difficult' (2007: 339). This is particularly the case given the fact that while emotional labour is expected from researchers during interviews, the autonomous nature of their role (Lee-Treweek, 2000) means there is little guidance on how to manage emotions both in relation to the researcher and participants. Moreover, as emotions in research are linked to a lack of scientific rigour, the suppression of emotion is often favoured (Bellas, 1999; Kleinman, 1991).

Nevertheless, emphasis has been placed on the need for researchers to display empathy during interviews, and particularly to be used as a tool to build relationships (Dickson-Swift et al., 2009), which is key to a successful interview. This is because it encourages trust leading to participants 'opening up' and discussing often sensitive issues (Hubbard et al., 2001). However, as a result of the autonomous nature of the researcher, there might be a lack of consensus in terms of the extent to which empathy should be displayed. For some, while the importance of displaying empathy is not to be underestimated, there is also the need to portray the 'competent detached researcher' (Fitzpatrick and Olsen, 2015: 52). In contrast, there may be those researchers whose empathic displays could result in them becoming 'part of the experience themselves' and displaying emotions similar to their participants (Dickson-Swift et al., 2009: 65).

This also raises the question of which emotions should be expressed by researchers, and which should be suppressed. Dickson-Swift et al. (2009: 65) comment on how some researchers highlighted the importance of 'becoming emotionally open' so that they could connect with their participants on a personal level, while for others emotional displays such as crying would be considered inappropriate. Seear and McLean (2008) comment on how, for example, they felt it necessary to suppress emotional reactions because to display those emotions would result in losing or alienating their participants because it would be deemed to be unprofessional. They add that feelings were also suppressed as a result of being doctoral students, commenting that they felt accountable to their supervisors, as well as the institution and discipline more generally.

The suppression of emotion can lead to frustration in researchers and the need to release emotion after exiting the field (Dickson-Swift et al., 2009). Performing emotional labour can also result in feelings of guilt. This feeling of guilt is often linked to the notion of 'using' participants for qualitative data, and is not uncommon following interviews (Glesne and Peshkin, 1992: 112). Moreover, such feelings might be exacerbated by the expectation to display empathy. However, the display of empathy in particular can also foster further commitment from the researcher and the undertaking to give voice to participants taking part in the research (Emerald and Carpenter, 2015).

Ethnography (autoethnography) and emotional labour

Ethnography in the discipline of criminology is a relatively underused methodology. Only 10% of articles in US criminology and criminal justice journals make use of ethnographic methods. That said, there has been a recent growth in its use as a method of data collection, which has seen the publication of books such as *Doing Ethnography in Criminology: Discovery through fieldwork* (Rice and Maltz, 2018) and the recently published *Criminological Ethnography: An Introduction* (Treadwell, 2019). A quick glance at the contents of *Doing Ethnography in Criminology* tells us that whilst ethnography is still relatively rare – certainly in comparison to surveys and interviews – researchers have used ethnography to explore a broad range of topics such as courts, crime, drug dealing, prisons and the police. There are also examples of ethnography being used to research probation and women's experiences of being supervised (Harding, 2018) – football hooligans (Poulton, 2014) and boy racer culture (Lumsden, 2009). A review of the literature also reveals a range of types of ethnography including overt, covert and autoethnography. Whilst much of the previously mentioned research was overt, Calvey (2018) identifies a range of settings in which covert ethnography has been used including police and prison culture, football hooliganism, recreational drug use and sexual deviance. Authoethnography has increasingly been used in criminology to reverse the 'ethnographic gaze' and thus problematise the ways in which criminology reifies objectivity and restrained language which, by necessity, excludes the researcher from the process of data generation and analysis. Thus, autoethnography in criminology seeks to consider the biography of the researcher and uses that biography as a heuristic device for exploring the phenomenon under consideration (Wakeman, 2014; Waters, 2016a, b).

Therefore, ethnographic research in criminology has been used to explore different groups of people and criminal justice organisations although, interestingly, Copes et al. (2011) found that race and gender tended not to be specific units of analysis except where the focus is 'offender-based' ethnographic research. Despite ethnography being used less frequently than other methods, there is then a reasonable body of criminological literature which uses these methods to explore criminological phenomena.

Mirroring broader ethnographic work which recognises the emotional commitment required in ethnographic research there is an implicit assumption in much of this criminological work that ethnography requires the use of self. References to Goffman are abound and it is fair to say that there is a general recognition that emotions play a role in the generation, analysis and presentation of findings. In spite of this, there are only a handful of publications which explicitly explore the emotional labour of doing ethnographic research. This is an important observation because, as we see in later chapters in this volume, face-to-face research will always involve the management of emotions. Moreover, ethnography demands the researcher to adopt multiple personae – sometimes simultaneously – such as participant, observer, researcher, expert and novice. Thus, it will – almost inherently – involve the management of emotion in order to achieve the goals of the job being undertaken by the researcher.

There is inherent role conflict in any ethnographic research. Moreover, there is a combination of implicit and explicit feeling rules at play all of which guide the ways in which emotions should be used. Thus some display rules are formalised in codes of ethics and health and safety guides for researchers, whilst implicit rules that researchers learn through experience, contact with other colleagues and rules which are underpinned by their own theoretical and political standpoint will also dictate the appropriate and inappropriate display of emotion. There is also no getting away from the fact that in today's higher education context, research is considered a key part of the job and academics do research not only for the normative justification of making a contribution to knowledge but also to meet personal and institutional goals such as publishing in high-quality journals, gaining external funding, obtaining promotion/tenure and, in the UK context the Research Excellence Framework and demonstrating impact. There are, thus, a range of feeling rules – both explicit and implicit – which guide ethnographers' emotional labour during fieldwork and beyond.

Interestingly, much of the writing on the emotional labour of ethnography comes out of an ethnographic study that was exploring something else rather than being the product of a study in its own right. This is something which we hope to address in our own work on the emotional labour of criminological research which we discuss in more detail below. Even though this body of literature is small, some interesting themes emerge in terms of the emotions that require managing in ethnographic research as well as the implications of it for the researcher.

Jewkes (2012: 69) highlights the fact that,

> introspection, anxiety, vulnerability, and trauma are present—if generally downplayed—in much prison research, positive emotional experiences are equally under discussed. As previously noted, the fact that prison research can be an ordeal has been documented by a handful of, mostly female, ethnographers. But prisons can also be stimulating, exhilarating, and curiously life-affirming environments in which to do qualitative research, and emotional identification with prisoners and prison staff, like all research participants, is often a positive and powerful stimulus in the formulation of knowledge.

Whilst more autoethnographic in nature, Jewkes makes a strong case for seeing researchers' emotional responses to a research situation as something which are 'subjective judgments about objective experiential worlds' in much the same way that our interpretivist forms of thematic analysis are subjective understandings of someone else's reality. Indeed, Phillips and Earle's (2010) account of fieldwork in prisons sheds important light on how the emotional reaction of a researcher is key to understanding the generation of data; thus, the way in which ethnographers manage their emotions is likely to result in data that takes on a particular shape. As an example, they describe an emotional reaction to a skinhead participant which 'conflicted directly with professional principles of resisting judgment of research subjects' attitudes and behaviour' (Phillips and Earle, 2010: 368). In a rare explicit engagement with the emotions of doing criminological – and specifically prison – research, Drake and Harvey (2014: 490) describe prison ethnography as 'emotionally exacting' and argue that prison ethnography will involve 'significant levels of impression management'. This, they argue, has an affective toll on the researcher which emanates from having to negotiate and re-negotiate access on a daily basis which, in turn, accounts for some of the emotional demand of prison research because this rests on having to constantly gain and re-gain trust from gatekeepers. They also discuss 'role strain' which is critical to prison research whereby researchers must adopt a range of 'virtual identities' and engage in impression management in a constantly changing set of contexts (Drake and Harvey, 2014: 494). A final emotion associated with this type of research is that of 'meaninglessness and fragmentation' whereby they would experience a sense of their own weakened identity and, as we have found in our own research, a tension between feeling like mere 'receptacles and sponges for other people's pain and suffering' and a 'sense of mastery on the other (that we were really 'getting' the prison environment)' which led to what might be described as a form of existential crisis (Drake and Harvey, 2014: 496).

The attentive reader will have noticed that much of writing on the emotional toll of doing criminological ethnographic work has been based on prison research. This is, perhaps, unsurprising considering that institution's relatively long history as the subject of such analysis (going back to Goffman) as well as the idea that prisons are 'special places'. Literature which explores the emotional labour in non-custodial settings are much less common. Harding's (2018) reflection on the emotional labour of doing research with people on probation is a rare example of this. Again, her work is more autoethnographic in nature but nevertheless highlights some of the ways in which this type of research demands certain emotional displays. Harding (2018) highlights the 'messy' nature of her research and uses the concept of 'emotional moments' to elucidate the untold stories of her participants. For Harding, her emotions and the process of suppressing and displaying emotion were critical to the way in which she 'generated data'.

Harding's analysis is underpinned by both an autoethnographic but also gendered analysis. Interestingly, despite Copes et al. (2011) suggesting that gender plays a relatively minor role in criminological ethnography except those which deal with specific groups of offenders, much of the writing on the emotional labour of doing ethnographic work does take a gendered perspective. Poulton (2012, 2014) reflects on her role as a female academic who was engaging with the overwhelmingly male and masculine world of football hooliganism. In one example, she loses her well-earned rapport with a key informant and employs a series of impression management techniques to get him back on board. This involved the extensive use of emotion such as humility, ego-massaging and 'apologetic manner', and the situation was resolved resulting in a sense of pride for the researcher. Poulton describes the experience as 'emotionally exhausting' and involved her having to 'compromise some of my personal principles and manage my normal expressive behaviour to preserve what I now knew was a very precarious professional relationship' (2012: 5.8). Because ethnography depends on good relations, it might be expected that this type of emotional labour would be relatively common to this particular methodology.

For Poulton, this needed to be understood in terms of the gender dynamic between herself and her informant, but the inherently relational aspect of ethnography underpins much of the writing on emotional labour in ethnography. For example, Copes (2018) describes how, in the course of conducting research with drug dealers and users in the US, he had to become more open with emotions and engage in more 'emotionally open' to participants through a greater use of deep acting. This, he argues, allowed him to collect more meaningful data than he otherwise would have.

Exiting the field

Gobo and Molle (2017) explain that in ethnography, there are various rituals to start research and live in the field but very little about how to disengage. They argue that disengagement from the field is both a methodological and an emotional problem, as the ethnographer must devise an exit strategy. This is significant to avoid 'burning' the field (Gobo and Molle, 2017) for future researchers and also if the researcher returns to the field. Moreover, our own findings from interviews with criminological researchers suggest the regular 'exiting' and 'returning' during ethnographic fieldwork or when completing qualitative interviews in a challenging context requires further consideration. As we see in the chapters of this book and from our own research, researchers are aware of the intensity of the emotional experience; however, there is a temptation to dismiss examining feelings as: (i) distracting from the subject matter (ii) trumped by the traumatic experience of the participant and too self-indulgent. We would argue, however, that the intensity and duration of the research needs to be acknowledged as part of the performance of emotional labour (Morris and Feldman, 1996). Such an approach would be helpful in supporting researchers to devise coping strategies and consider approaches for exiting and returning to the field.

A final reflection is whether it is possible to disengage from the field following the emotional impact of work undertaken by researchers. A helpful distinction here is Gobo and Molle's (2017) proposal to consider institutional, interpersonal and intrapersonal reasons for exiting the field. The former might be the end of funding whilst the latter two can be related to emotional labour. Interpersonal reasons for ending research might be, for example, conflict between the role of researcher and parent. Intrapersonal reasons, on the other hand, might include mental exhaustion from being on stage and having to perform. Gobo and Molle (2017) then list some of the emotional consequences, for example: the development of close relationships with participants; indebtedness, when leaving feels like a betrayal (which can be intensified if participants experience social deprivation or hardship) and even relief following tiresome relationships. It is suggested that these emotional consequences need to be acknowledged in the development of an exit strategy.

In criminological research there is evidence of these considerations, for example, in Sloan's prison ethnography considering men and masculinities, in which she reflects on when to leave the field (2016: 30) citing King and Liebling's (2008) maxim to discontinue research 'once compassion fatigue sets in'. In Ellis's ethnographic study of violent men and masculinities (2016), he talks about the emotional consequences during and after the field work when he experiences poor sleep, paranoia and guilt about exploiting people who had welcomed him into their homes. Moreover, Ellis (2016: 16) describes feeling guilt about how he actually had the choice to 'exit' the 'drudgeries, various difficulties and potential threats' when those he met did not have the same option. It could be argued that these both strongly relate to intrapersonal and interpersonal reasons for exiting the field.

Both Sloan (2016) and Ellis (2016) refer to the emotional costs during and at the end of their ethnographic research. A further consideration is the regular exiting and returning to fieldwork to complete qualitative research interviews. Whilst conducting qualitative semi-structured interviews with sex offenders, Blagden and Pemberton (2010) explain how they always close their interview with a positive, focusing on the participant's hopes and future plans. Further to this they explain how they debrief participants, thanking them for their time, offering reassurance about data management and signposting them to support services. Cowburn (2005) and Blagden and Pemberton (2010) also mention that informed consent is an ongoing process when returning to interview a participant and should be continually checked. Cowburn (2005) suggests that the boundaries of confidentiality should be checked at the start of each day when conducting in-depth interviews with people who have committed sexual offences. When exiting and returning to interviews being aware of the potential harm caused by the interview, a positive end, praise, reassurance and continual checking of informed consent form aspects of the emotional labour performed as part of ethical considerations in qualitative research. In ethnographic research Gobo and Molle (2017) consider returning to the field and how a positive relationship may be discussed, how you will stay in touch or reconnect following the development of work products. They make suggestions of giving a card or photograph and expressing feelings about the good parts of the project to participants.

We should note that the emotional consequences of the work do not always allow for a full withdrawal from the field. Ellis, later in this book, alludes to this issue by suggesting that one can physically leave the field, whereas it may be more difficult to emotionally disentangle from the experience. Whilst Gobo and Molle consider disengagement and return to the field, Watts (2008) questions whether anyone truly leaves the field due the emotional consequences of the fieldwork. Indeed, Drake and Harvey (2014) argue that some emotions can be examined in situ to alleviate emotional pressure and that the emotional dimensions of the research need to be revisited after some distance from the work through structured reflection. In our research with criminological researchers, we see examples of the enduring emotional impact of the research. This involves disclosures about how our participants severed their ties with the field of research for interpersonal reasons, experiencing permanent change in their world view (both positive and negative) and citing intrapersonal reasons around looking after their mental health. Therefore, to describe leaving the field for good could be misleading when we consider the performance of emotional labour in qualitative criminological research.

Case study: emotional labour and criminological researchers

Thus far we have argued that there has been very little research explicitly exploring and documenting the emotional labour undertaken by criminological researchers. In an attempt to address this dearth of literature, we have investigated the experiences of criminological researchers in order to create a better understanding of the emotional labour they perform. The aim of the research was to bring to light both the emotions felt and the emotional labour employed by criminological researchers in the fieldwork they undertake.

Thirty semi-structured interviews were conducted with researchers who either self-identified as 'criminologists' or identified their research as 'criminological'. Participants self-selected into the study having heard about the project via Twitter, academic conferences, or word-of-mouth. Interviews lasted approximately one hour, were conducted either in person or via online telephony, and were audio recorded for accuracy. They were then transcribed verbatim for analysis. The research was conducted ethically and in accordance with ethical protocols. All participants provided informed consent and were assigned a pseudonym to protect their privacy and assure confidentiality. The research team also took special care to anonymise identifiable pieces of research carried out by participants.

Overall our sample consisted of 24 women (80%) and 6 men aged between 23 and 52 years (mean age of 35.3 years). All participants were based in the United Kingdom and were predominantly White (90%): 19 (63%) were 'White British', 3 (10%) were 'White Irish', 5 were (17%) 'White Other'.

Two (7%) participants identified their ethnicity as 'Mixed'. Our researchers were at various stages of their academic careers and had varied educational backgrounds: 3 held masters degrees as their highest qualification, 12 were working towards their PhDs, and 15 had completed their doctorates.

A thematic analysis (Braun and Clarke, 2006) of the transcribed interviews was carried out and a number of themes identified. The remainder of this chapter will develop some of these, focusing on the emotional labour performed, the consequences of that performance, and how our researchers coped with those consequences.

Emotion labour performed

The criminological researchers we interviewed were keen to discuss the emotions they experienced. They described facing and processing a variety of emotions throughout all stages of the research process, with the most common being during data collection, data analysis and writing-up. Positive emotions identified by the participants included feelings of gratitude, humility, responsibility and sympathy:

> I felt really grateful as well [...] interesting to feel grateful to your participants for their participation.
>
> (Sofia)

> I was aware it was quite shocking but if anything it just made me thankful for the life I have had [...] It just made me very thankful and very humble for what I had.
>
> (Zoe)

Negative emotions included sadness, grief, depression, vulnerability, anger, frustration and disgust:

> I found that very difficult and I found it hard, because on the one hand what they were telling me was evoking quite profound anger in me and on the other hand it was provoking quite a lot of sadness, it was provoking some very kind of turbulent and tumultuous kinds of feelings of resentment, of anger, of hurt, of sadness for the experiences.
>
> (Mark)

Researchers also dealt with high levels of guilt around their research and their research participants:

> I don't think that I will ever really be free of guilt because [...] is still struggling so much and you can't help but feel a little bit helpless about that and I think the more I research [...] the more I understand that, so

there is not really any way to soothe that and I don't really think that that's a bad thing as such, I don't think that I need to kind of shy away from that emotion.

(Natalie)

Other common emotions comprised imposter syndrome, a wariness of showing emotion or uncertainty about what level of emotion to show. This final point leads us to explore empathy and suppression as emotional labour in greater detail.

Empathy as emotional labour

In terms of the emotional labour expected of our researchers, one of the most referenced was that of empathy. In line with the previous literature on emotional labour and qualitative researchers (Dickson-Swift et al., 2009; Fitzpatrick and Olsen, 2015), the criminological researchers we interviewed, whilst highlighting the importance of empathy, did not necessarily agree on how empathy should be displayed to participants.

On my part empathy really. I tried very much to give them space to express themselves and not allow my emotions to affect their stories that they were sharing with me...So it's negotiating that process of being sympathetic but not trying to move on or trying to over..., [pause] or not trying to affect their story.

(Grainne)

Grainne clearly believes that the empathy displayed needed to be controlled. Dickson-Swift et al. (2009) link this controlling of empathy, and the subsequent suppression of inappropriate emotion, to the rigour of the research method being used, and the consequent questioning of the trustworthiness of the research. However, for Grainne, while it may be an underlying concern, it is not articulated in this way. Rather, for her, it is about allowing those being interviewed to be placed at the centre of the interview.

In contrast, Trina and Sandra describe a very different understanding of empathy, something more akin to sympathy:

Showing as much empathy as you can...So very much validating each story...I've hugged quite a few participants and shed tears in a couple of interviews where I felt it was appropriate.

(Trina)

I am not embarrassed to say that on more than one occasion I've had tears dripping down my face while I've been speaking to women... I think it really helped the women to see me emotional because they knew I...

understood, probably, and recognised the weight of what they were tell-ing me and how important it was to them. So I think if I had sat there as a blank slate I don't think my interviews would be anywhere near as rich as they are, at all.

(Sandra)

Both Trina and Sandra highlight the appropriateness of displaying empathy in this way. Furthermore, Sandra makes a direct link between her emotional displays of empathy and respect for the participant's stories. It is also seen as intrinsic to the development of the relationship and consequently the richness of the data gathered.

Suppression as emotional labour

The suppression of emotion was a strong theme that came out of the in-terviews. Participants highlighted a variety of reasons why they needed to suppress emotions. Nicki presents interesting commentary on the potential insecurity and vulnerability of criminological researchers:

I think probably not masking them but probably didn't show - I defi-nitely would try not to show any extreme emotion during the inter-view. Certainly not anything like nervousness or my personal worries. I would just try and mask those and come across really positive and friendly.

(Nicki)

However, it is clear that the negative emotions of nervousness and worry need to be 'masked' in favour of presenting positive emotions. This type of emotional labour therefore requires surface acting, the suppression of one emotion in favour of the display of another (Hochschild, 1983).

Susan and Emily describe a different situation where the suppression of emotion is required:

I've also had judgement, like so working, doing research groups with sex offenders, really, really difficult, like to set aside feelings of absolute disgust and horror.

(Susan)

...when someone's telling you something that's emotional and you get emotional that's probably not necessarily going to be great for them. If they're telling you something and your primary emotional response is like, 'Wow, that's bad', again, you don't want that look to come on you face and them to feel judged.

(Emily)

There is an understanding that it is important not to display any negative emotion relating to, for example, an offence that has been committed in the past. The suppression of this type of emotion is considered important in order to develop and maintain trust and confidence. This form of emotional labour resonates particularly with the suppression of emotions such as shock and disgust highlighted, for example, by probation practitioners in their everyday work with clients (Westaby et al., 2019).

Consequences of performing emotional labour

The emotional labour performed while conducting their research impacted our researchers in a variety of ways. Five of the key consequences will be discussed: resilience, responsibility, emotional overload, feeling unsupported and isolation.

Resilience is seen as moving from 'something that is happening to them' to starting to look for or creating the networks to move them to a different place in their ability to cope. This is in response to the negative emotions of guilt, anger, frustration, disgust, sadness and empathy. It challenges the 'emotional-ness' that is sometimes expected while doing research.

> I love the field that I work in but I expect anything and everything now, so I can kind of take it with a pinch of salt, have some resilience as to what I hear and balance that in a way that won't affect me and my emotions too much I guess [...] Everyone's story that you hear are very different but the more different experiences that people share with you the more the resilience has built up for me in some sense.
>
> (Rose)

Second, our criminological researchers felt a strong responsibility in wanting to do their research justice and give a voice to their participants. They also found this positive responsibility motivated them to be more productive in their writing and other outputs:

> I want to help people individually because I had horrible feelings of guilt...I can't help the women because I know that's unprofessional...but what I can do...is bring that information into the light...into the kind of public awareness.
>
> (Trudy)

> Well I feel like I've helped people sometimes and I feel like - like I said, on a professional level I think sometimes the stuff that I can get from people really helps and I've got some really good projects where reports that have been generated through peer research as evidence have affected commissioning. I've seen like real changes in services for people as a

consequence. So that makes me really proud and makes me want to carry on doing it.

(Susan)

Responsibility could also be negative in that researchers felt like they were not doing enough and not doing justice to their participants. This consequence linked to feelings of guilt and gratitude.

The third consequence was emotional overload, or as described by one participant as an 'emotional hangover' (Lindsey). This, along with emotional exhaustion, depression, spillover, desensitisation, or burnout, were experienced by many of our participants as well as those in Dickson-Swift et al.'s (2006) research who had experienced both physical and mental symptoms including insomnia, nightmares, exhaustion, depression, headaches and gastrointestinal problems as well as emotional stress and difficulties which affected relationships outside the field. Watts (2008) too points to the potential for emotion deluge and fatigue linked to feelings of guilt, sadness, grief, responsibility, anger, frustration, sympathy and disgust. This emotional overload often 'bled' into other aspects of their lives – sometimes linked to altered identity, nightmares and insomnia:

[I felt a] bit of guilt, that small aspects of exploitation...research to get these people to tell their hard story and then we go and get a career from it. That I struggle with sometimes.

(Trina)

Fourth, researchers often felt unsupported by institutions and supervisory teams. This included no appreciation of the emotions they were experiencing and the emotional labour they were performing, and a lack of training and practical support:

I guess it's about the importance of anonymity...and how long you're going to keep someone's data...and much less focus on actual, the messiness of human interaction...So on the whole, I would say I think that universities are quite bad at anything to do with emotional competency training.

(Emma)

Not having official institutional support in part compounded the sensation of imposter syndrome, including feeling out of one's depth and outside of one's areas of knowledge. This lack of support was connected with feelings of grief, depression, trauma, disgust, isolation and not wanting to appear 'weak' or 'vulnerable':

I wasn't aware of the boundaries or the limit I could reveal sensitive information without affecting my relationship with my supervisors and colleagues.

(Elena)

It always felt a bit self-indulgent to me to talk about our own emotions. Like the people who were the subject of the research were going through such horrendous periods of their life. They had just been in prison, they had come out, lots of them had been split up from their families and so they were going through the mental agony of staying in a hostel overnight when they had kids and a family back home. It felt really indulgent to be wanting to talk about my own emotions.

(Tom)

... just checked in every now and again [with a prison psychologist] because she was really busy [...] they were all so busy and I don't want to be a burden to anyone. That term we always hear, 'I don't want to be a burden'.

(Amy)

At the same time as well like I was also aware that I didn't want to make a really bad impression and you would think about saying, 'I'm having a really difficult time with this' about being a bad impression you're making on someone...when she's writing a reference for me.

(Aoife)

The final consequence of emotional labour in research is, perhaps, the culmination of feeling unsupported and emotionally overloaded: isolation. Misconceptions around confidentiality and self-imposed isolation meant that, as can be seen above, many researchers felt they were not able to offload emotionally: 'I can't talk about this, it's confidential' was a common theme. There are also issues around a lack of self-care: 'I don't deserve to be looked after', 'I don't want to bother people', and 'I can't be seen to be weak'.

Coping strategies

In order to deal with the consequences of the emotional labour performed, our participants engaged a number of coping strategies. These can be roughly organised into six non-mutually exclusive approaches: self-care, escapism, communities of coping, space creation, rituals and doing justice.

Many of the criminological researchers we interviewed described engaging in self-care with examples including taking a shower, changing clothes, reading, swimming, reflective writing, going to the gym, talking to a partner and having a counsellor or clinical supervision:

I try and have a bath or a shower and change my clothes, just sort of do some sort of mental closure...I think it just creates a sense of its over, like the connectivity with that person, you've moved on past it. So whether it's symbolic or whether it's real at some vibes level I don't know, do you know what I mean, but that's the technique that I do.

(Susan)

Wray et al. (2007) note that ordinary daily routines can have therapeutic value for qualitative researchers. It is therefore important to openly discuss simple self-care strategies which can aid in reducing the stress and anxiety resulting from performing emotional labour. However, Wray et al. (2007: 1399) also note that this did not always have the desired effect of remaining 'connected to our data without living in a fused state' particularly where researchers were less experienced. Therefore, as James and Platzer (1999: 76) maintain,

> self-care is crucial, but where there is considerable emotional labor involved in research interviews [and for us other forms of qualitative research] we suggest that there is a requirement for formal supervision, not only of the academic, but also of the therapeutic kind.

Common examples of escapism were alcohol, trash TV, violent video games, or any other activities that would give mental and physical space. One particular way of escaping the negative emotional consequences of performing emotional labour reported by the criminological researchers in our study was the consumption of alcohol. While engaging in such an activity, some commented on it being a rather unhealthy coping mechanism. As Natalie maintains, 'I would go out and drink too much, so I would describe that as a dysfunctional response'. However, interestingly, for a couple of participants when drinking was combined with social interaction with colleagues this was regarded as a form of self-care:

> So we would spend a lot of time in the pub afterwards, in the evenings, pretty much every evening would involve a degree of drinking and sometimes quite a lot of drinking and just talking through stuff...I wouldn't say they were deliberate choices or particularly around managing emotions, but incidentally they may well have helped manage emotions, if that makes sense.

(Richie)

Arguably, the difference between the two quotes is the social interaction in the second example, in contrast to drinking alone, which was the case for Natalie. The latter therefore could be regarded as a form of a community of coping.

Indeed, such communities of coping (Korczynski, 2003) were often described by our participants as a way of dealing with the emotional challenges of engaging in qualitative research:

There is a sense of solidarity I suppose isn't there with people who just know what interviews are like and who know what it's like to turn up at somebody's house and its 10am and they've already finished a bottle of wine and offering you some…Yeah so it that was useful to have the [postgraduate] resources in the form of people to offload onto.

(Raegan)

These informal groups are important given the fact that there is a tendency for workers to cope 'communally and socially' (Korczynski, 2003: 58) with the potentially negative consequences of having to perform emotional labour. As Wincup (2001: 29) suggests, peer discussion 'can provide reassurance and helps to overcome feelings of isolation by recognising your own emotional experiences are not unique'.

The remaining three coping strategies are as follows:

1   Space creation. These are the explicit ways that researchers can create more 'head room' or separation between work and home life. Examples include taking time while commuting to and from work, travelling to and from data collection sites, taking a break from the subject area by engaging in other activities (see also escapism).
2   Rituals. In particular our researchers engaged in shedding rituals. These rituals often incorporated elements of self-care, escapism and space creation.
3   'Doing justice'. As mentioned above and interconnected throughout, our researchers had a desire to 'do right' by their participants. Examples of this included capturing participant's voices, writing and presenting their data, and activism.

Overall, our research has explored the experiences of thirty criminological researchers in terms of the emotional labour they perform as part of their empirical qualitative research activities, the consequences of that performance, and their coping strategies. Feelings of guilt, gratitude, humility, responsibility, sadness, grief, depression, anger, frustration, disgust and imposter syndrome were all felt by our researchers. The emotional labour of empathy and suppression was also keenly articulated by our researchers. The consequences of these performances were increased resilience and responsibility, emotional overload, and feeling unsupported and isolated. In response to this, our researchers exhibited a number of coping strategies including self-care, escapism, space creation, rituals, 'doing justice' and communities of coping. Going forward, our researchers felt that more training and support to deal with the emotional labour of research was needed, especially for doctoral students and early career researchers.

Conclusion and recommendations

There are a number of cross-cutting themes evident from both the review of the literature and the case study around power, gender, reflexivity, training and support which highlight the particular issues that arise from conducting *criminological* research. Issues around power and the power dynamic amongst researchers themselves and between researchers and their participants are evident across both the extant literature and the case study. Amongst the researchers, there are noted power issues between doctoral students and supervisory teams, between principal investigators (PIs) and the rest of the research team, and between more junior and more senior researchers. This power dynamic manifests itself in feelings of inadequacy, imposter syndrome and emotional suppression, which in turn lead to feeling unsupported and isolated, and experiencing emotional overload. Many researchers dealt with this by establishing communities of coping and engaging in escapism. Between researchers and participants this is reflected in the huge feeling of guilt and worries about taking advantage of their participants. This leads to an increased sense of responsibility to their participants; many researchers discussed 'doing justice' for their participants as a way of coping and alleviating some of the guilt and perceived power differential. Gender was seen to exacerbate the above power dynamic, particularly as female researchers tend to hold more junior positions (student, early careers, research assistant, etc.) and male researchers tend to hold more senior positions (PI, reader, professor, etc.).

The need for greater reflexivity during the research process was also identified as a cross-cutting theme. This is reflexivity *in situ* to use emotional responses as analytical data, to monitor the influence of your own emotional responses in the research and for self-care to recognise the emotional cost of the research experience; moreover, after some distance from the research to make sense of the experience for methodological insight. In training, institutions should pay attention to the performance of emotional labour by researchers facilitating discussions about what emotions might be displayed by researchers and to what degree they should be used in research. Further to this, the researchers should be encouraged to reflect on their own knowledge and experiences, how this influences their approach to the research, their coping strategies and the emotional cost of the research (to themselves, the gatekeepers and the participants).

The lack of adequate training and support for criminological researchers, particularly for those in the early stages of their careers, was universally noted. This was in relation to both formal or institutional training and support, as well as more informal training and support. It is not an exaggeration to say that all the criminological researchers who participated in our study at some point during their interview discussed the lack of emotional support provided by their institutions. For those of our participants who then found themselves in the position of 'supervisor' or 'PI', many made the explicit effort to put support mechanisms in place for those researchers they were responsible for. Our participants spoke about how they learned through their own primary research experiences the importance of being able to access proper emotional support throughout the research process. For them there was no need to 'learn the hard way'.

From the existing literature and our research we would make five recommendations to help researchers cope with the consequences of performing emotional labour and therefore improve their research experience.

1   Address and improve the culture within the criminology community to allow for emotions and emotional labour and their consequences to be openly and critically discussed. Of the key issues raised by our researchers is why the same formal and informal support systems that exist for other professions who perform 'emotional labour', such as psychology or counselling (Brannen, 1988), do not exist within criminological research practice (Letherby, 2003: 113). While the vicarious trauma that psychological professionals can suffer has been widely recognised (McCann and Pearlman, 1990), social researchers also experience vicarious trauma. Yet there is an eerie silence in the social sciences about this, as well as about ways of managing the emotional labour necessary to ensure qualitative data collection with participants is successful. Adeptly put by Trina, 'how important it would be for PhD students but also for research teams to have institutional support and that there should be built a culture around that, where it should not be seen as a weakness'.

2   There needs to be more training provided at all levels around emotions and emotional labour. This training should be aimed not only at doctoral students and early career researchers but also supervisors and PIs so that they are better able to support researchers who they are responsible for. Areas for training should include planning emotional wellbeing into research projects, the acknowledgment and mechanisms of self-care, asking for help and accessing support, acknowledging and performing emotional labour, understanding how are emotions used in research, etc. Academic institutions should also learn from the third sector, where training around the use of emotion and emotional labour are employed to a greater degree.

3   Institutional ethical approval forms should have a section for reflecting on the potential emotional impact of the research on the researcher(s). The emotional wellbeing of the researcher(s) conducting research should be considered of equal importance to their physical safety and to the physical and psychological safety of their participants. Equally this should not become an administrative burden nor be used as a way to prevent certain types of research or researchers.

4   Clinical supervision should be recommended in emotionally high-risk pieces of research, and encouraged to any researcher(s) who may benefit

from it. Research might be considered to be emotionally high risk due to either the research subject, environment or participants, or the needs of the researcher themselves.

5   The creation of formal and informal support networks and communities of coping. As different researchers will need different types and levels of support at different times it is important that a variety of support options are available. Potential support networks could include mentoring schemes or 'buddy' programmes, social media groups, walking groups, pub nights, etc.

Acknowledging and starting to address these recommendations is a good first step in improving the quality of criminological research and the quality of life for criminological researchers. These recommendations will have a more substantial impact on our students and early career researchers, making for better doctoral experiences and a better introduction to the academy more generally.

References

Bellas, M.L. (1999). Emotional labor in academia: The case of professors. *Annals of the American Academy of Political and Social Science*, 561, 91–110. https://www.jstor.org/stable/1049284?seq=1#metadata_info_tab_contents.

Bergman Blix, S. & Wettergren, A. (2015). The emotional labour of gaining and maintaining access to the field. *Qualitative Research*, 15(6), 688–704. doi:10.1177/1468794114561348.

Blagden, N. & Pemberton, S. (2010). The challenge in conducting qualitative research with convicted sex offenders. *The Howard Journal*, 49(3), 269–281. doi:10.1111/j.1468-2311.2010.00615.x.

Brannen J. (1988). The study of sensitive subjects. *The Sociological Review*, 36(3), 552–563. doi: 10.1111/j.1467-954X.1988.tb02929.x.

Braun, V. & Clarke, V. (2006). Using thematic analysis in psychology. *Qualitative Research in Psychology*, 3(2), 77–101. https://www.tandfonline.com/doi/abs/10.1191/1478088706qp063oa.

Burgess, R.G. (1984). *In the Field: An Introduction to Field Research*, London, Allen & Unwin.

Calvey, D. (2018). Covert ethnography in criminal justice and criminology: The controversial tradition of doing undercover fieldwork. *Oxford Research Encyclopedia of Criminology and Criminal Justice*. doi:10.1093/acrefore/9780190264079.013.296.

Copes, H. (2018). "Did i just get caught being stupid?" Experiencing and managing the emotional labor of fieldwork. In S.K. Rice & M.D. Maltz (Eds.), *Doing Ethnography in Criminology: Discovery through Fieldwork*, pp. 75–81. doi:10.1007/978-3-319-96316-7_7.

Copes, H., Brown, A., & Tewksbury, R. (2011). A content analysis of ethnographic research published in top criminology and criminal justice journals from 2000 to 2009. *Journal of Criminal Justice Education*, 22(3), 341–359. doi:10.1080/10511253.2010.519714.

Cowburn, M. (2005). Confidentiality and public protection: Ethical dilemmas in qualitative research with adult male sex offenders. *Journal of Sexual Aggression*, 11(1), 49–63. doi:10.1080/13552600512331298284.

Dickson-Swift, V., James, E.L., Kippen, S., & Liamputtong, P. (2009). Researching sensitive topics: Qualitative research as emotion work. *Qualitative Research*, 9(1), 61–79. https://journals.sagepub.com/doi/abs/10.1177/1468794108098031.

Drake, D. H. & Harvey, J. (2014). Performing the role of ethnographer: Processing and managing the emotional dimensions of prison research. *International Journal of Social Research Methodology*, 17(5), 489–501. doi:10.1080/13645579.2013.769702.

Emerald, E. & Carpenter, L. (2015). Vulnerability and emotions in research: Risks, dilemmas and doubts. *Qualitative Enquiry*, 21(8), 741–750. doi:10.1177/1077800414566688.

Ellis, A. (2016). *Men, Masculinities and Violence an Ethnographic Study* (1st ed.), New York, Routledge.

Fitzpatrick, P. & Olsen, R.E. (2015). A rough road map to reflexivity in qualitative research into emotions. *Emotion Review*, 7(1), 49–54. doi:10.1177/1754073914544710.

Glesne, C. & Peshkin, A. (1992). *Becoming Qualitative Researchers: An Introduction*, White Plains, Longman.

Gobo, G. & Molle, A. (2017). *Doing Ethnography* (2nd ed.), London, Sage.

Harding, N. (2018). Places on probation: An auto-ethnography of co-produced research with women with criminal biographies. In A. Plows (Ed.), *Messy Ethnographies in Action*, Malaga, Vernon Press, pp. 91–100.

Hochschild, A.R. (1983). *The Managed Heart: The Commercialisation of Human Feeling*, Berkeley, University of California Press.

Hoffman, E.A. (2007). Open-ended interviews, power and emotional labor. *Journal of Contemporary Ethnography*, 36(3), 318–346. doi:10.1177/0891241606293134.

Hubbard, G., Backett-Milburn, K., & Kemmer, D. (2001). Working with emotions: Issues for the researcher in fieldwork and teamwork. *International Journal of Social Research Methodology*, 4(2), 119–137. www.tandfonline.com/doi/abs/10.1080/13645570116992.

James, T. & Platzer, H. (1999). Ethical considerations in qualitative research with vulnerable groups: Exploring lesbian and gay men's expressions of healthcare-a personal perspective. *Nursing Ethics*, 6(1), 73–81. doi:10.1177/096973309900600108.

Jewkes, Y. (2012). Autoethnography and emotion as intellectual resources: Doing prison research differently. *Qualitative Inquiry*, 18(1), 63–75. doi:10.1177/1077800411428942.

King, R.D. & Liebling, A. (2008) 'Doing Research in Prisons'. In R.D. King & E. Wincup (Eds.), *Doing Research on Crime and Justice*, 2nd ed., Oxford, Oxford University Press, pp. 431–451.

Kleinman, S. (1991). Fieldworkers' feelings: What we felt, who we are, how we analyze. In W.B. Shaffir & R.A. Stebbins (Eds.), *Experiencing Fieldwork: An Inside View of Qualitative Research*, Newbury Park, CA, Sage, pp. 184–95. doi:10.4135/9781483325514.n15.

Korczynski, M. (2003). Communities of coping: Collective emotional labour in service work. *Organization*, 10(1), 55–79. doi:10.1177/1350508403010001479.

Lee-Treweek, G. (2000). The insight of emotional danger. Research experiences in a home for older people. In L. Treweek & S. Linkogle (Ed.), *Danger in the Field. Risk and Ethics in Social Research*, London, Routledge, pp. 114–131.

Letherby G. (2003). *Feminist Research in Theory and Practice*. Buckingham, Open University.

Liebling, A. (2014). Postscript: Integrity and emotion in prisons research. *Qualitative Enquiry*, 20(4), 481–486. doi:10.1177/1077800413516273.

Lumsden, K. (2009). 'Don't ask a woman to do another woman's job': Gendered interactions and the emotional ethnographer. *Sociology*, 43(3), 497–513. doi:10.1177/0038038509103205.

McCann, I.L. & Pearlman, L.A. (1990). Vicarious traumatization: A framework for understanding the psychological effects of working with victims. *Journal of Traumatic Stress,* 3(1), 131–149. doi.org/10.1007/BF00975140.

Morris, J. & Feldman, D. (1996). The dimensions, antecedents, and consequences of emotional labor. *The Academy of Management Review*, 21(4), 986–1010. doi:10.2307/259161.

Okomus, F., Atinay, & Roper, A. (2007). Gaining access into organizations for qualitative research. *Annals of Tourism Research*, 34(1), 4–26. http://epubs.surrey.ac.uk/216662/3/FINAL_31147_OKUMUS_ALTINAY_ROPER_JULY2-2006__2_.pdf.

Patton, M.Q. (2002). *Qualitative Research and Evaluation Methods* (3rd ed.), Thousand Oaks, CA, Sage.

Phillips, C. & Earle, R. (2010). Reading difference differently? Identity, epistemology and prison ethnography. *The British Journal of Criminology*, 50(2), 360–378. doi:10.1093/bjc/azp081.

Poulton, E. (2012). 'If you had balls, you'd be one of us!' doing gendered research: Methodological reflections on being a female academic researcher in the hypermasculine subculture of 'football hooliganism.' *Sociological Research Online*, 17(4), 1–13. doi:10.5153/sro.2717.

Poulton, E. (2014). Having the balls: Reflections on doing gendered research with football hooligans. In K. Lumsden & A. Winter (Eds.), *Reflexivity in Criminological Research: Experiences with the Powerful and the Powerless*, pp. 77–89. doi:10.1057/9781137379405_6.

Rice, S. & Maltz, D. (2018) (Eds.), *Doing Ethnography in Criminology: Discovery through Fieldwork*. Basingstoke, Palgrave Macmillan.

Seear, K.L. & McLean, K.E. (2008). Breaking the silence: The role of emotional labour in qualitative research. In T. Majoribanks, Australian Sociological Association, & University of Melbourne. (Eds.) The annual conference of The Australian Sociological Association 2008. *Re-imagining Sociology: Conference Publication Proceedings*, Melbourne, The Australian Sociological Association, pp. 1–16.

Shenton, A.K. & Hayter, S. (2004). Strategies for gaining access to organisations and informants in qualitative studies. *Education for Information*, 22, 223–231. https://pdfs.semanticscholar.org/3c43/ace735b06e5b2407f33f2c7e4441b19d562f.pdf.

Sloan, J. (2016). *Masculinities and the Adult Male Prison Experience*, Basingstoke, Palgrave Macmillan.

Treadwell, J. (2019). Criminological Ethnography: An Introduction. London, Sage.

Van Maanen, J. & Kolb, D. (1985). The professional apprentice: Observations on fieldwork role into organisational settings. *Research in Sociology of Organisations*, 4, 1–3.

Wakeman, S. (2014). Fieldwork, biography and emotion doing criminological autoethnography. *The British Journal of Criminology*, 54(5), 705–721. doi:10.1093/bjc/azu039.

Waters, J. (2016a). Editorial: Entering the field of criminological research. *British Journal of Community Justice*, 14(2), 1–6. www.mmuperu.co.uk/bjcj/articles/editorial-entering-the-field-of-criminological-research.

Waters, J. (2016b). Editorial: How biography influences research: An autoethnography. *British Journal of Community Justice*, 14(2), 45–60. www.mmuperu.co.uk/bjcj/articles/editorial-entering-the-field-of-criminological-research.

Watts, J. H. (2008). Emotion, empathy and exit: Reflections on doing ethnographic qualitative research on sensitive topics. *Medical Sociology Online*, 3, 3–14. www.medicalsociology online.org/current/jhwatts.html.

Westaby, C., Fowler, A., & Phillips, J. (2019). Managing emotion in probation practice: Display rules, values and the performance of emotional labour. *International Journal of Law, Crime and Justice*, in press. doi:10.1016/j.ijlcj.2019.100362.

Wincup, E. (2001). Feminist research with women awaiting trial: The effects on participation in the qualitative research process. In Gilbert, K.R. (Ed.), *The Emotional Nature of Qualitative Research*, Boca Raton, FL, CRC Press LCC, pp. 17–35.

Wray, N., Markovic, M., & Manderson, L. (2007). "Researcher saturation": The impact of data triangulation and intensive research practices on the researcher and qualitative research process. *Qualitative Health Journal*, 17(10), 1392–1402. doi:10.1177/1049732307308308.

Wykes, M. & Welsh, K. (2008). Gendering criminology? In *Violence, Gender and Justice*, London, Sage, pp. 49–69. doi: 10.4135/9781446213896.n4.

Part Two

Chapter 8

Prison officers

Emotional labour and dying prisoners

Carol Robinson

Introduction

Prisons are accepted to be emotional places (Crawley, 2004b; Nylander et. al., 2011) and as a consequence it is recognised that prison officers undertake considerable emotional labour (Arnold, 2016; Crawley, 2004a,b; Lemmergaard and Muhr, 2012; Nylander and Bruhn, this volume; Nylander et. al., 2011; Tracy, 2004, 2005). However, no studies to date have considered the specific forms of emotional labour performed by prison officers working with terminally ill prisoners or those prisoners who die from natural causes. This is a significant omission given that in recent years the rate of deaths in prison custody in England and Wales from natural causes has increased steadily, from 1.11 per 1,000 prisoners in 2007 to 2.23 per 1,000 in 2017, resulting in more prison officers working with dying prisoners.[1] Prison population projections from the Ministry of Justice suggest that this trend will persist.[2]

Emotional labour is recognised as crucial to the functioning of the prison (Crawley, 2004b) and as 'an embedded activity that facilitates provision of services' (Tracy, 2005, p. 263). Better appreciating the emotional labour of prison officers working with dying prisoners is therefore important in understanding the care provided to this group, as well as the wellbeing of officers whose work brings them into regular contact with the highly emotional and sensitive topics of death and dying. Furthermore, if the 'feeling rules' for prison officers differ between contrasting functions in the prison, as Nylander et al. (2011) describe, then the emotional labour of prison officers working with dying prisoners needs to be considered separately from that of officers engaged in other roles or tasks.

Recognising the considerable similarities to the emotional labour of prison officers in other roles, this chapter highlights how working with dying prisoners involves officers drawing on different personal resources to inform the emotional labour required by their specific situation. Whereas surface acting is used to meet organisational expectations, deep acting helps meet the needs of the prisoner and the officer. This chapter highlights three main aspects of prison officers' emotional labour in work with dying prisoners, starting with the surface acting required by 'feeling rules' – the acceptable and expected emotions associated with their occupational culture. It then considers how prison officers are changed by the emotional labour necessitated by their roles, including becoming desensitised, and the effect this has on their home life. Lastly, it explores four protective emotional labour strategies of deep acting deployed by prison officers, including trying to keep an emotional distance, seeking to reassure themselves, defining what they do in ways that support more positive emotions and, sometimes in contradiction with other strategies, seeking to humanise the prisoner.

Methods

This chapter uses data from interviews with prison officers with experience of working with dying prisoners to illuminate key aspects of the emotional labour they undertake. The participants, from a high security prison in the north of England, had all worked either in the prison's healthcare centre or as Family Liaison Officers or had escorted prisoners receiving medical treatment in a hospital outside of the prison (known as a 'bedwatch'). Five participants were recruited using snowball sampling and interviewed in the summer of 2016. The interviews were semi-structured, using an interview guide which included asking them to provide an account of an experience of working with a dying prisoner. Interviews typically lasted between 40 minutes and an hour and with the Governor's permission were conducted in work time. Transcription was undertaken by the researcher to ensure participant confidentiality and meet concerns about security in a culture where information about who works or is imprisoned in a particular prison is regarded as a security risk. Participants' names have been changed for this chapter.

'Feeling rules' around dying prisoners

Learning what emotions not to express is often claimed to be key to the emotional labour of prison officers (Arnold, 2016; Tracy, 2005). Several writers (Arnold, 2005; Crawley, 2004b; Lemmergaard and Muhr, 2012; Nylander et al., 2011) emphasise the importance of prison officers learning the 'feeling rules' – formal and informal – of their function. Writing from a US context, Tracy (2005) gives the example of a female officer feeling sadness after the death of an inmate on her shift but needing to hide her emotions to avoid colleagues condemning her as unsuitable for the job. In contrast, interviewees in this study reported feeling a range of emotions when working with dying prisoners, including frustration, boredom, satisfaction, sympathy and pride, but also sadness. However, their expressions of sadness at a prisoner's death were typically qualified by reminders of the prisoner's crime or statements that suggested their emotional response was not specific to the prisoner:

> You've got to be, you've got to be sad when somebody dies. You wouldn't be human if you weren't sad when somebody dies. But (sigh) I wouldn't have shed any tears for his death because he was a despicable human being in his crimes.
>
> (Eric)

Similarly, Denise regarded sadness as appropriate after any death:

> I'm so sad when somebody dies. But you always get that moment of sadness, no matter what they've done or where they are, it's still well, I still find it sad. Even if I hear of people that I don't really know that have died, I have that moment of sadness.
>
> (Denise)

Sadness was thus regarded as an expected and acceptable emotion within the occupational culture of prison officers but to be expressed with qualifications that did not afford the prisoner any special status. However, a distinction was made with the unacceptable, stronger emotional responses of being 'upset' or 'traumatised' by a prisoner's death. Denise, an officer in the prison's healthcare centre, feared showing she was upset by a death would have consequences for her employment:

> If I say this death has upset me, will they think 'well, you're a liability; we'll move you out back on to the wings.'? Or if you did, you went off, y'know, if you got upset, you had a couple of days off because you've got upset, will they then start looking at you and thinking 'well, you're maybe not suitable then because you're too emotional.'? It is strange how the prison service works.
>
> (Denise)

There were deaths Denise felt upset about, particularly when the prisoner had not accepted they were dying, but she kept these emotions to herself because she did not want to be moved from her role. Eric, who had been with a prisoner when he died in hospital, found that the death reminded him of the trauma of his wife's death, but was clear the prisoner's death did not 'traumatise' him. Other officers were also wary of the consequences of talking about their feelings after a death, even when they felt the need to 'offload'. They had concerns about sharing their emotions with the official staff care team or their line managers, preferring to talk to trusted colleagues, who formed 'an unseen support network', as one said.

Officers' awareness of the operational needs of the prison also informed emotional labour to maintain a display of emotion judged to be acceptable in their working environment. One officer who frequently undertook 'bed-watches' spoke about lacking time to reflect on his feelings after he had escorted prisoners receiving medical treatment outside of the prison:

> things have gone pear-shaped and somebody could have died, and the next thing you know it's 'you need to be down in the workshops, why are you not down there, you're holding up the workshop, we need to get it open, we need to get this, that and the other'.
>
> (Bruce)

The importance of controlling his emotional display derived from the organisation's need for him to be available for the next task.

Being changed by the work

Hochschild (1983) finds that emotional labour, whether surface or deep acting, has a human cost. Several interviewees acknowledged working as prison officers had changed them emotionally as Crawley (2004b), Tait (2011) and Arnold (2005) suggest is common. In this study, these changes could happen both quickly and gradually and be either temporary or lasting. They were sometimes linked to specific roles. For example, Adrian reported needing to adjust quickly to the different emotional demands of working in the healthcare centre after being on a wing. Other officers spoke about experiencing particular emotions in the immediate aftermath of a death, but of the effects being transitory. There were two key respects in which officers reported being changed by their work: becoming desensitised and experiencing emotions from work impacting on their home life.

Exhaustion and emotional dissonance are commonly acknowledged to potentially arise from emotional labour in any work setting, including prisons (Johnson et al., 2005; Nylander et al., 2011; Tracy, 2005). Within the prison studied, participants frequently associated emotional desensitisation with the emotional labour undertaken. However, this was not solely a result of their work with dying prisoners, but attributed to more general experiences as prison officers. Bruce talked about desensitisation as a common experience for prison officers and described becoming gradually desensitised. He saw this as problematic but also potentially useful:

> I've been told it's quite heartless, but I think working here that many years, and dealing with that many things it just becomes part of you without even realising, creeps up on you without realising. And, er, maybe it's a bad thing, but then it helps you with the job.
>
> (Bruce)

Similarly, Clive found his emotional responses were dulled by having worked in the prison: 'I think, having been a prisoner officer and dealt with so many things in 18 years, I think you become pretty numb to it really' (Clive). This is in keeping with Arnold (2016): most prison officers in her study 'described themselves as having become hardened, cynical and detached' (p. 274) as a defence mechanism against potentially traumatising events. Becoming de-sensitised was the result of the emotional labour undertaken by prison of-ficers, but also a conscious tool that helped them to cope, especially around the sensitive subject of death and dying.

Unsurprisingly, the data supports the idea that working with dying prisoners could affect interviewees' home life. This was not the experience of all the in-terviewees and the impact of working as a prison officer on home life was not necessarily limited to the experience of working with dying prisoners. Clive reported that few issues from the prison troubled him at home. He coped with any difficult emotions by taking his dogs for a run, but he was also clear that this was his strategy for coping with any day in the prison, not just one that had involved working with a dying prisoner. However, most participants reported that their feelings from their work with dying prisoners did 'spill-over' into their home lives, as Crawley (2004b) finds for work with generic prisoners. For example, Adrian spoke fondly about a prisoner who he had liked, saying that after his death 'I must admit I went home the next day and I was thinking about him'. Working with dying prisoners could also stir memories which had an emotional impact beyond the prison. Eric had recognised the breathing pattern of the prisoner on a 'bedwatch' as an indicator that death was approaching be-cause of his memories of when his wife was dying. Whilst he did not feel strong emotions about the prisoner who had died, the death did affect him:

> I did for, not that I ever forget my wife, but I did, for a couple of days, I was thinking more, I think of her every day, but I did think more of the time when I lost her because it reminded me of her, it reminded me of the shallow breathing and the last breath.
>
> (Eric)

Participants were also engaged in a form of emotional labour at home, pro-tecting family members from their experiences. Crawley (2004b) reports a reluctance amongst prison officers to discuss their work at home because of concerns their partners would worry. This was the case for both Denise, who would rarely discuss work at home, and Bruce:

> Erm, unfortunately I just do the usual and keep it to myself. Because I don't really want to be, if my missus knew everything about what hap-pened in the prison I don't think she'd ever want me to come to work. It's a problem.
>
> (Bruce)

Although Bruce acknowledged it was problematic, his response also revealed an assumption it was normal for prison officers in any role to keep occupational concerns separate from home life.

Strategies for doing emotional labour

Some participants made deliberate attempts to manage their feelings to lessen the impact of the emotions they were experiencing. Four protective emotional labour strategies were employed to achieve 'deep acting' (Hochschild, 1983): trying to keep an emotional distance; seeking to reassure themselves; defining what they do in ways that support more positive emotions and, sometimes in contradiction with other strategies, seeking to humanise the prisoner. This was 'deep acting' in that it sought to make feigning feelings unnecessary, and to self-induce a real feeling deemed appropriate to the work undertaken (Hochschild, 1983). Some strategies relied on previous life experiences. Most participants attributed their ability to deal with the harder aspects of emotional labour when working with dying prisoners to having experienced several deaths in their personal lives.

Some participants sought to protect themselves from difficult emotions by keeping emotionally distant from the situation of the dying prisoner. Nylander et al. (2011) found that prison officers in general roles tried not to get emotionally involved as a form of self-protection. Similarly, in this context, Adrian said he tried not to get too emotionally involved, recognising that if he did so 'it will play on my mind' and wishing to avoid this happening. In this respect, Adrian was performing what Hochschild (1983) describes as the deep acting required in everyday life, where actors 'must dwell on what it is we want to feel and on what we must do to induce the feeling' (p. 47). This was not always successful for him, as discussed above. Other participants described strategies for coping with feelings after a prisoner had died as being 'like flicking a switch' (Bruce) or knowing 'which little boxes you put things when it happens' (Denise). Their focus was on 'switching from different modes' (Bruce) in order to concentrate on the next task and thus meet the operational requirements of their role. Denise had learned to do this whilst working as a nurse. Bruce made overt comparisons with nurses and police officers, seeing it as something that was shared by these occupational cultures. Officers were thus actively trying not to feel emotions before or after a prisoner's death because of the impact it would have on them personally and on their ability to meet organisational expectations.

Another common strategy was to seek something positive in the circumstances of a prisoner's death. Working in the healthcare centre, Denise and Adrian had experienced several deaths. For Denise, who had a deep Christian faith, her strategies included telling herself that the deceased was now with his family in heaven and free, in a better place than when he was alive. These 'positive' outcomes lessened her sadness that the death had occurred in prison, in circumstances she regarded as less than optimal. Similarly, Adrian gave an account of a conversation with a prisoner the day before he died. He had taken the prisoner into the exercise yard and they had had a lengthy conversation. Adrian had known and liked the prisoner for a long time. His death in prison caused Adrian some sadness, which Adrian sought to manage:

> He said to me "I think this will be my last day out here" and he knew. And so I think, well maybe he got his wish and that sort of puts a closure on it for me. So I try to look through things and see, y'know, what good can come out of that. And I tend to sit on them a little bit rather than dwell on the negatives.
>
> (Adrian)

Adrian thus deliberately looked for a positive interpretation of events. He subsequently drew comparisons between the prisoner's last day, his own father's death and an imagined ideal last day. In doing so he sought ways to reassure himself that few deaths were ideal.

For officers in roles which meant they regularly worked with dying prisoners, Denise, Adrian and Clive, their emotional labour was also facilitated by self-conceptions of being special. By defining their role as requiring skills and abilities not all their colleagues possessed, they seemingly protected themselves from potential criticism by reconstructing 'spoiled' work as special (Tracy, 2005). For example, as a Family Liaison Officer, Clive had worked with dying prisoners to make end of life plans, liaising between the prisoners, their families and the prison. He felt that not every officer could do his job:

> I think a lot of people say, "I couldn't do what you do", or "wouldn't want to do what you do", but I guess that's individual choice really. And if you're not trained to do it then I wouldn't expect anybody to do it. It's not the kind of role that I think would be appropriate to push anybody into either.
>
> (Clive)

Following Tracy (2005), by framing themselves as able to work beyond the abilities of other people, these prison officers may have found the emotional labour necessary for the nurturing aspects of their role easier. Tracy suggests that performances of self-respect are especially hard for prison officers during service activities, such as giving prisoners their food. Whilst some officers, she argues, may respond by seeking alternative sources of power based on aggression, she finds others will, as the interviewees in this study, derive power and this study suggests, self-respect, through framing their role as needing expert skills and specialist knowledge. As 'specialists', when it came to working with dying prisoners, the prison officers interviewed found their work matched their values and preferred skills and provided reward. This was not achieved by Bruce or Eric, in non-specialist roles, whose work with dying prisoners was limited to escorting 'bedwatches'.

In comparison with medical staff and rescue workers, 'prison officers' emotional work… is likely to be more problematic, since it emerges in interactions with individuals who are often perceived as *unworthy* of such emotion' (Crawley, 2004a, p. 418). The implication is that the caring roles prison officers undertake are for undeserving clients, and officers are essentially 'scum serving scum' (Tracy, 2005, p. 272). Prison officers in roles that require a human-services orientation can thus find themselves facing difficult emotional labour, since service is usually provided by low status individuals for high status individuals (Tracy, 2005). The prison officers interviewed addressed the challenging emotional labour this required of them by humanising the dying prisoners they worked with, granting them a valued status. As a consequence, they were able to provide better care. Humanising the prisoner was however in direct contrast to keeping a distance, and as such officers risked being more affected by a death.

One key approach was, as Sykes (1958) describes, to see the man beyond the crime. This was done by the participants who regularly worked with dying prisoners, who actively avoided looking up the prisoner's record or made attempts to treat them 'as decent and as dignified as we possibly can, irrespective of what crimes they've committed' (Clive). Prisoners were also humanised through the formation of 'normal' relationships. Adrian reported getting tips from one dying prisoner on how to grow better tomatoes, and on chatting with another about their shared interest in classic cars. He and Clive each recounted sitting with prisoners approaching the end of their lives, watching game shows on television together. One of the things Bruce appreciated about doing 'bedwatches' was the chance for the prisoner to 'talk to you just as a normal person'. These interactions all helped humanise the dying prisoners and ease the emotional labour required of the officers.

As Crawley (2004a) argues, there is inevitably a degree of intimacy between prison officers and prisoners, especially when the prison officer has worked with the same prisoner through a variety of difficult and disappointing experiences in their sentence. Arnold (2016) suggests that prison officers are trained to see relationships between staff and prisoners as instrumental, but in many cases the prison officer interviewed expressed a seemingly genuine sympathy for the prisoner in the situation of dying in prison. They mentally awarded the dying prisoner a valued status by drawing comparisons with deceased family members. In doing so, they were drawing on 'emotion memory' (Hochschild, 1983, p. 41), using feelings around other deaths to inform their work with a dying prisoner. For Adrian, this was his grandparents and his father. For Eric, as previously discussed, the death of a prisoner on a 'bedwatch' reminded him of his wife's death. For Denise, the memory of her daughter's sudden death encouraged her to talk to prisoners about their end of life preparations. Furthermore, some prison officers made direct comparisons between themselves and the prisoner, imagining the possibility of themselves dying in prison.

Seeing the prisoners as having equal value to themselves assisted the participants in performing the emotional labour and the tasks of caring required of them. They reported making toast for prisoners, cutting up their food, finding more comfortable chairs, helping order meals, filling water jugs and even in one case going to the hospital shop to buy the prisoner an ice-cream. These were small acts, redolent of care, unusual in the prison setting but occurring because when the prisoner was dying, the officers working with them became more aware of their humanity.

Conclusion

The emotional labour of prison officers working with dying prisoners shares many of the characteristics of the emotional labour undertaken by prison officers more generally (see Nylander and Bruhn, this volume). Considering their emotional labour in this specific context serves to highlight the mechanisms and motivations of more generic emotional labour amongst prison officers. As with officers in other roles, these officers are subject to 'feeling rules'. Expressing certain feelings, in this case sadness, is acceptable but other emotions, including being upset, are accompanied by a concern that the officer will be perceived to contradict occupational norms and be failing to meet organisational requirements. As with other roles undertaken by prison officers, those who have worked with dying prisoners need to perform surface acting not just to maintain 'face' but in order to keep the prison regime functioning. The pressures of the job mean there is little time for emotional responses. Whilst needing to adapt to the 'feeling rules' associated with roles in which officers work closely with dying prisoners, there is also a recognition that all work as a prison officer changes the individual. Becoming desensitised is expected and even recognised by some as useful, particularly when dealing with death and dying. Questions inevitably arise as to how far the surface acting required by a job leading to such desensitisation affects the long-term wellbeing of prison officers, with the potential commensurate impact on staff-retention rates within the prison service.

What is more specific to the emotional labour of prison officers working with dying prisoners is the impact these deaths have on them and the strategies for doing emotional labour they develop as a result. Officers who had worked with dying prisoners brought more of their personal lives to the relationships they formed, using memories of family bereavements to inform their work. Perhaps as a consequence, prisoner deaths could 'spill over' into their home life, into reflections about the deceased or memories of their own losses. The sympathy they felt for the individual facing death in prison informed the way in which officers sought to humanise prisoners, reducing the gap between them and the men they worked with until they were discussing shared interests and seeing parallels with loved ones and themselves. The specific ways in which prison officers tried to manage their feelings about a prisoner dying were linked to their conception of death in prison as far from optimal. They needed to find ways to reassure themselves after a death in order to lessen their negative emotions. One of the most important strategies for the emotional labour of prison officers working with dying prisoners was the ability to define themselves as being special, as undertaking tasks other colleagues could not do. This helped them with the more difficult nurturing aspects of their roles, and as such arguably did the most to enhance the care of the dying prisoners.

Notes

1 Ministry of Justice and Her Majesty's Prison and Probation Service (2017). *Safety in custody quarterly: update to September 2018.* [Online]. Ministry of Justice and Her Majesty's Prison and Probation Service, UK. Available at: www.gov.uk/government/statistics/safety-in-custody-quarterly-update-to-september-2018 [Accessed 5 March 2019].
2 Ministry of Justice. *Prison population projections.* [Online]. Ministry of Justice, UK. Available at: www.gov.uk/government/statistics/prison-population-projections-ns [Accessed 17 November 2017].

Bibliography

Arnold, H. (2005). The effects of prison work. In A. Liebling and S. Maruna, (Eds). *The Effects of Imprisonment.* Abingdon: Routledge, pp. 391–420.
Arnold, H. (2016). The prison officer. In Y. Jewkes, B. Crewe and J. Bennett, (Eds). *Handbook on Prisons.* 2nd edn. Abingdon: Routledge, pp. 265–283.
Crawley, E. (2004a). Emotion and performance: Prison officers and the presentation of self in prisons. *Punishment & Society,* 6(4), 411–427.
Crawley, E. (2004b). *Doing Prison Work: The Public and Private Lives of Prison Officers.* Cullompton: Routledge.
Hochschild, A. R. (1983). *The Managed Heart: Commercialization of Human Feeling.* Berkeley: University of California Press.
Johnson, S., Cooper, C., Cartwright, S., Donald, I., Taylor, P. and Millet, C. (2005). The experience of work-related stress across occupations. *Journal of Managerial Psychology,* 20(2), 178–187.
Lemmergaard, J. and Muhr, S.L. (2012). Golfing with a murderer—Professional indifference and identity work in a Danish prison. *Scandinavian Journal of Management,* 28(2), 185–195.
Nylander, P.-Å., Lindberg, O. and Bruhn, A. (2011). Emotional labour and emotional strain among Swedish prison officers. *European Journal of Criminology,* 8(6), 469–483.
Sykes, G. M. (1958). *Society of Captives: A Study of a Maximum Security Prison.* Princeton: Princeton University Press.

Tait, S. (2011). A typology of prison officer approaches to care. *European Journal of Criminology*, 8(6), 440–454.

Tracy, S. J. (2004). The construction of correctional officers: Layers of emotionality behind bars. *Qualitative Inquiry*, 10(4), 509–533.

Tracy, S. J. (2005). Locking up emotion: Moving beyond dissonance for understanding emotion labor discomfort. *Communication Monographs*, 72(3), 261–283.

Chapter 9

Gendering emotional labour
Independent domestic violence advisors

Marian Duggan

Introduction

In 2019, the number of women killed as a result of domestic abuse reached its highest level in five years (BBC News, 2019). On average, two women are killed by a partner or ex-partner every week in England and Wales; 82% (*n* = 239) of all domestic homicides recorded between 2014 and 2017 involved women killed by male current or former partners (Office for National Statistics, 2018). Domestic homicide reviews have highlighted that previous or recent experiences of domestic abuse are a significant risk factor to determining women's safety (Aldridge & Browne, 2003; Monckton Smith et al., 2014). Contrary to some media headlines which suggest that killers 'snapped' or the fatal violence came 'out of the blue', many domestic homicides could have been predicted on the basis of the perpetrator's attitudes and behaviours towards his partner (Dobash et al., 2009; Sheehan et al., 2015). Despite decades of research, theory and policy development, domestically abusive (male) partners remain one of the most dangerous threats to women's safety. Therefore, keeping women alive means recognising this threat early on.

To this end, Clare's Law (the *Domestic Violence Disclosure Scheme*) forms part of ongoing attempts to reduce domestic abuse deaths in England and Wales. Clare's Law is not a law, but rather an information sharing mechanism which operates along two access routes. The *right to ask* permits members of the public (who might be at risk of harm) to apply for information from the police about whether their partner has a history of abusive behaviour. It supplements the pre-existing *right to know* which permits statutory sector workers to apply for permission to pro-actively share (otherwise confidential) information with a member of the public on safeguarding grounds. The public *right to ask* route was implemented in 2014 and named 'Clare's Law' after Clare Wood, a domestic abuse victim who was prevented from finding out about her ex-partner's documented history of violence against women before he killed her in 2009. Clare's Law has proven to be a popular approach despite little evidence to suggest that sharing such information actually *prevents* domestic homicide. Variations of the scheme have emerged elsewhere in the UK, as well as in some states in Australia, Canada and South Africa.

Independent Domestic Violence Advisors (IDVAs) play an important role in relation to Clare's Law and information sharing. The need for a specialist IDVA role emerged from recommendations set out in *Domestic Violence: A National Report* (Home Office, 2005). IDVAs undertake accredited professional training before working in partnership with a range of statutory and voluntary agencies, funded by both the Home Office and non-governmental sector. IDVAs are usually assigned to domestic abuse victims assessed as 'high risk' by the police to safeguard them against further serious or fatal harm. Alternatively, they may work with victims on an ad hoc basis through the courts or domestic abuse service providers. They serve as the victim's primary point of contact, working with them (and any dependents) from the crisis incident onwards to ensure the implementation of suitable and tailored safeguarding plans (Safe Lives, 2016). This intensive short- to medium-term support ranges from safety planning (which may include target hardening at their domestic dwelling or facilitating access to sanctuary schemes or refuge accommodation) through to providing support in relation to criminal court cases, civil justice remedies, housing issues, benefits, immigration issues, and counselling and mental health services.

This chapter explores how emotional labour features in IDVAs' engagement with Clare's Law as a domestic abuse prevention mechanism. It draws on findings from an empirical study which evaluated the scheme's efficacy alongside how risk and responsibility affected its operation (Duggan & Grace, 2018). Initial information on the scheme was obtained via Freedom of Information (FOI) requests to 42 police forces, of which 39 replied. These replies formed the basis for semi-structured interviews in one policing area with eight key stakeholders who had direct responsibility for implementing Clare's Law in the local community. The purposive sample included: two domestic violence 'single point of contact' police officers; a police and community support domestic violence 'single point of contact' officer; a domestic violence organisation manager; a domestic violence perpetrator prevention programme facilitator; and three IDVAs (two affiliated with the police and one with the domestic violence organisation). The project received full ethical approval from the author's institution and was part-funded by a Socio-Legal Studies Association research grant. The data collection took place in two stages (FOIs 2015–2016 and interviews 2016–2017). The researcher thematically analysed and coded the transcribed data using NVivo.

The data for this chapter was analysed within a framework which foregrounds IDVAs and emotional labour. An IDVA's involvement with Clare's Law – and domestic violence victims – differs between the *right to ask* or the *right to know* routes. Therefore, the chapter begins with an overview of these two routes, showcasing their differences in terms of public and IDVA engagement. The discussion then explores the nature and impact of emotional labour by drawing on excerpts from the interviews with IDVA's Tanya, Eleanor and Alice (pseudonyms). The chapter concludes with recommendations for how to improve the nature and impact of Clare's Law with enhanced IDVA engagement in light of ongoing discussions to consolidate and strengthen legislation and policy relating to domestic abuse.

Accessing Clare's Law: the *right to ask* v the *right to know*

Members of the public in England and Wales were given the *right to ask* for otherwise confidential information about an individual's background under Clare's Law, part of the Domestic Violence Disclosure Scheme. Prior to this, such information could only be shared by statutory professionals for safeguarding reasons if they demonstrated that the person at risk had a *right to know*. The two different routes are outlined in the flow chart given in Figure 9.1.

Important discrepancies exist between these two routes which affect the nature and extent of IDVA involvement. Under the *right to ask*, members of the public instigate a Clare's Law application, often upon recognising their partner's behaviour to be of concern. At this point they will undergo a risk assessment.exercise. Those deemed to be at medium or high risk will usually be referred for more immediate specialist support, including access to an IDVA. Applicants deemed as being at standard risk will have their application assessed at a Multi-Agency Risk Assessment Conference (MARAC), comprising of a police officer, a duty IDVA and any other relevant safeguarding representatives. If the MARAC decides to grant a disclosure, the wording is

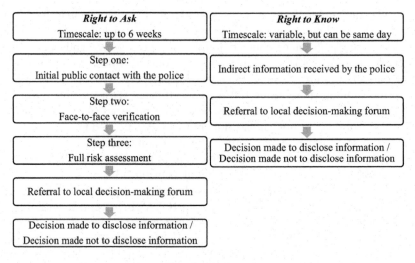

Figure 9.1 The *right to ask* v the *right to know*.

drafted there and then, where the attendant IDVA plays a key role in ensuring the accuracy and relevance of advice for recipients. This is an important responsibility as recipients may choose to subsequently remain in the relationship; therefore, not receiving correct, useful or full information could increase their risk of harm. If the MARAC decision is *not* to grant a disclosure, the IDVA's involvement officially ends there. Contrastingly, under the *right to know* route the IDVA assigned to the high-risk domestic violence victim (or 'client') may have access to information on the perpetrator, so can instigate an immediate disclosure request as part of the client's safeguarding package. The IDVA will call for an urgent MARAC (as permission must be granted), attend on their client's behalf, present their case and convey the information directly afterwards. The process is more immediate and involves IDVA engagement throughout. Of interest to this chapter is how the two routes encompass very different levels of emotion and experiences of emotional labour.

IDVAs, crisis management and emotional labour

> Emotional labour can be as exhausting as physical labour. Sitting with a distressed person (child, friend, relative), listening to someone when they are angry, courageous, resentful or sad, and acquiring the ability just to 'be' with someone who is lonely, frightened or in pain, is taxing and requires an appropriate response. Comfort, confrontation, humour, empathy or action may each be appropriate in different circumstances.
>
> (James, 1989, p. 27)

Safeguarding domestic abuse victims (both generally and using Clare's Law) requires IDVAs to variably engage with emotional labour depending on the nature or circumstances of the situation, and the victim. To better understand this, the following section addresses the IDVAs' emotion work with domestic violence victims through three key areas: managing risk, managing expectations and managing involvement.

Managing risk

IDVAs recognise that the complexity of domestic abuse means freeing oneself from a harmful relationship is not necessarily a simple or linear process. Many people fail to recognise the reality of their situation until it has escalated to a point where seeking help is difficult or dangerous, rendering risk categorisations dynamic rather than static. IDVAs noted that a victim could move from standard to medium or high risk very quickly without being aware of it:

> [U]nfortunately... [victims] do wait 'til they're physically assaulted before they [apply]. When it's the emotional stuff, they find it harder to

recognise that it's [abuse] so, you know, it is the physical stuff when they do then think *'actually, I can have this'*.

(Tanya, her emphasis)

IDVAs welcomed Clare's Law but displayed frustration around the risks affiliated to the *right to ask* route, such as the length of time the process took (in light of the dynamic nature of risk status) and the lack of detail provided in some of the disclosures. Applying to Clare's Law or receiving a disclosure may increase a recipient's risk level; Tanya indicated that several of her clients had graduated to high risk after receiving a Clare's Law disclosure under the *right to ask* route, seemingly as a result of the vague or generalised nature of the information provided by the MARAC. IDVAs also cited concerns around the requirement for these recipients to sign the Data Protection Act 1998 (DPA) before receiving the information, which prohibits them from sharing it with anyone else:

> [Y]ou do have to be mindful that some [victims] *may* share information if they're still with their partner or they're going to be going back to them so it's not always necessarily just as straight forward as, *'Yes, there's this information'*.

(Eleanor, her emphasis)

These feelings must be masked through 'surface acting' (where emotional expressions are regulated), creating displays that affect others in desired ways in order to do the job (Hochschild, 1983). This is important as Howarth et al. (2009) evidenced the positive impact IDVAs were having on risk management and victim safety, despite having to navigate very difficult and dangerous terrain. The majority (86%) of the IDVA clients in their study were experiencing multiple and ongoing forms of abuse, despite 66% being separated from the abusive partner at the time (Howarth et al., 2009). Victims require practical and emotional support regardless as to whether they continue with or leave the relationship, particularly if the person fears that separating may further antagonise the perpetrator (as it did in Clare Woods' case). Walby and Allen (2004) demonstrated that over a third (37%) of women had experienced continued violence *after* they had separated from their abusive partner. In 18% of cases the nature of the violence altered as a result, sometimes becoming worse than before; 7% of women who left their domestically violent partner were subjected to the worst incident *after* they had separated (Walby & Allen, 2004). Despite this knowledge, separating from a partner was grounds to withhold disclosure information from potential recipients until 2016 (when the guidance was updated) (Home Office, 2016).

As well as citing feelings of responsibility for their clients' safety, IDVAs expressed fears of being blamed if that safety was compromised, which in turn 'may psychologically bind one to the role such that one's well-being becomes more or less yoked to perceived successes and failures in the role' (Ashforth & Humphrey, 1993, p. 107). In terms of domestic abuse, what counts as a 'success' or 'failure' can be complex; ensuring a person's safety and freedom from abuse may count as a procedural success, yet be considered (in the short term, perhaps) a personal failure by the victim/client, leaving the IDVA to deal with the emotional (and practical) fallout. This links to Hochschild's (1983) dramaturgical notion of 'over-identification', which often arises from deep acting (where feelings are consciously modified to express the desired emotion). Recognising that there is a high risk of fatal harm regardless of safety planning means instilling difficult professional boundaries to ensure emotional self-protection.

Managing expectations

Most domestic abuse evades police attention thus remains undocumented, but in other cases may be categorised in a way that omits the 'domestic' element (Walby & Towers, 2017). Examining background factors to domestic abuse, Howarth et al. (2009, p. 8) noted that 50% (n = 1,296) of the perpetrators in their study had a criminal record, 26% (n = 669) of which involved domestic violence related crimes. The importance of full and accurate police data on incidents impacts on the usefulness of the disclosure information which can be shared:

> Most of my clients have asked for a Clare's Law disclosure. When it's offered to them the thing with managing their expectations is hard; just because something isn't disclosed doesn't mean that it hasn't happened and just because, you know, we can't share information that isn't relevant to their safety so, you know, it's only things that are deemed relevant to keep that person safe and sometimes it can have different effects ... but if there isn't any information to share then they might think that there isn't anything wrong, it just means that that person hasn't been convicted so that's something you have to manage that as well.
>
> (Eleanor)

By contrast, the information might be so robust that the disclosure causes recipients to 'switch off', go into denial, or refuse to hear it, necessitating that the IDVA carefully considers any immediate and ongoing emotional impacts:

> ...if I can see it's getting too much I'll say, "Do you want to take five minutes?" And they're like, "Yes please." I mean I know [the disclosures] are quite short but, you know, some of them when they are a little bit lengthy and the first sentence is quite horrific, you know, you can tell by their face that the rest of it – they're not going to take in – so we just say, "Do you want to take a couple of seconds to...? Do you want to talk

about that bit?" So we can sort of break the disclosure down which works quite well sometimes.

(Tanya)

Dealing intensively with cases of sexual and domestic abuse can desensitise police over time, impacting on their communications with victims (Martin, 1999, p. 119). Having IDVAs accompany police officers to *right to ask* disclosures is important to provide both specialist *and* emotional support, yet the latter has traditionally been conceptualised as (low-status) women's work (Hunt, 1984). In *right to know* disclosures, the absence of a police officer (as the IDVA discloses) creates a different dynamic:

What I love about my job is the fact that I can sort of do that [rapport building], that's what we're there to do and that's what we try and do. And then… You know, it sort of shows the client as well that actually they're not just… it's not just about *there's the information, blurt out to you; there you go, you deal with that.* It's about everything else.

(Tanya)

Most clients remain assigned to an IDVA for around three months (Howarth et al., 2009); therefore, ongoing interaction means building trust. This can result in greater client engagement with investigations and trials but carries disappointment when an IDVA's efforts appeared to be thwarted by legal processes:

… you do sometimes feel a bit let down by the system when these women have finally come forward, get themselves up to the state of '*yes, we're going to give a statement, yes, we're going to support it*' and months later it goes to court and they're still having to live with the consequences when he's out so that's sometimes quite difficult.

(Alice)

Middleton's (1989) notion of 'emotional dissonance' can prove beneficial if repressing emotion enhances production (i.e. allows for getting on with the job). In some cases, this can blend into 'impression management' whereby emotional labour as an act of displaying appropriate emotions requires less conscious effort in order to become routine and effortless over time (Ashforth & Humphrey, 1993). Conversely, the IDVAs' narratives suggested experiences more in line with Hochschild's in terms of internalisation, responsibility and personalisation. In other words, there were high levels of identification and investment which renewed with each case. However, this may impact on the ability to set boundaries, particularly if clients are estranged from family or friends or have become emotionally dependent on the IDVA as their only source of support.

Managing involvement

The IDVA role is inherently gendered, with the vast majority involving women assisting other women. In doing so, they 'simultaneously construct, or do, gender through their work, and the culturally shaped gender designations of work activities are reinterpreted in ways that support the jobholders' gender identities' (Martin, 1999, p. 114). This has implications for IDVAs' emotional labour in terms of setting boundaries with clients while working to ensure that relevant safeguarding processes are implemented, adhered to and function in the desired manner. For example, the IDVAs expressed a desire to be able to interact or follow up with a *right to ask* applicants at an earlier stage in the Clare's Law process, as they recognised the missed opportunity to provide specialist advice:

> [A]t that point when that person has taken it upon themselves to actually go to the police and ask for a Clare's Law, if at that point they could be referred to the IDVA service equivalent... it would be amazing because you would have that person getting that support.
>
> (Tanya)

Earlier IDVA intervention without adequate resourcing, however, could be detrimental to existing clients (reducing IDVAs' time for serious cases) and the IDVAs themselves (through exhaustion). IDVAs acknowledged that they and their colleagues were working increasingly longer hours due to higher caseloads and extended duties, often with no extra provision:

> We could always do with more [IDVAs]. We could always do with more; it would be lovely. Obviously, I came into the IDVA service a couple of years ago and some of my colleagues who were in there before me, they know the old days where their client caseload was a lot smaller so they could meet with clients in the community and could do a lot more work. Unfortunately, because of our higher caseload now we can't always do that.
>
> (Tanya)

Additionally, changes and reductions in legal aid provision also meant more IDVAs were accompanying clients to court:

> Yeah, definitely more work for us IDVAs as obviously we're trained to go into court but shouldn't be, we should be just sort of like signposting [victims] and everything but I have taken [victims] to court and have taken cases on their behalf because they can't get legal aid. ... We haven't got the time for that because it takes the whole day out, you know, time out of our working day because you've got to be at court in the morning.
>
> (Alice)

Feelings of duty and responsibility meant they would put the extra hours in, but were mindful of the possible impact additional work could have on their productivity. There was no bitterness about going above and beyond their contracted hours, but a sense of fear that when exhausted they may miss something in a case, or not give a client the correct assistance. This has also been noted in IDVA research:

> IDVAs were having to prioritise access to specific interventions and concentrated support within an already 'high risk' case load, suggesting that there may be a lack of capacity to work at the highest level with all high-risk victims.
>
> (Howarth et al., 2009, p. 11)

Working in such a high-pressured environment can mean IDVAs expend more emotional resources than they can replenish, leading to 'emotional exhaustion, depersonalization and reduced personal accomplishment' (Grandey, 2000, p. 104). Research on occupational burnout often focuses on issues related to the frequency, quantity and/or quality of interactions; the demands of emotional work as effective predictors of burnout are rarely considered (Brotheridge & Grandey, 2002, p. 18). Maslach (1982) found that 'individuals with high initial job involvement, professional commitment, idealism, and empathy for others are most susceptible to burnout, presumably because they invest more emotion in the enactment of their helping role' (cited in Ashforth & Humphrey, 1993, p. 106). As this is highly applicable to IDVAs, the potential for burnout is a significant risk.

However, warning signs of burnout may go unnoticed as 'the supposed "naturalness" of women's caring role is central to the significance, value and invisibility of emotional labour and its development through gender identity and work roles' (James, 1989, p. 22). Despite a growing awareness of the links between high levels of emotional intelligence and strong social and interpersonal skills (Goleman, 1995), the additional emotional work undertaken by IDVAs may be less recognised or rewarded because it is expected. James (1989, p. 15) suggests that such oversight may be because 'the norms emotional labour takes and the skills it involves leave women subordinated as unskilled and stigmatised as emotional'. In other words, the supposedly unskilled nature of 'women's work' is, in fact, highly skilled but those skills are often not acknowledged or duly accounted for, leaving IDVAs vulnerable to emotional exhaustion and potentially unable to separate work and home life.

Conclusion and recommendations

An IDVA's task – keeping clients safe – is hugely complex, fraught with difficulties and becoming increasingly necessary. To encourage recruitment, more needs to be known about the nature and impact of this responsibility, particularly how IDVAs separate their personal and professional lives, how they deal with vicarious victimisation, how they manage their own well-being and the impact of performing emotional labour. To remain effective, IDVAs must regularly negotiate their emotions during their engagement with victims (and criminal justice professionals), yet often their expressions require careful concealment, indicating how 'even the apparent *absence* of emotion may be the produce of emotional labor' (Ashforth & Humphrey, 1993, p. 93). A failure to pay due care and attention to this additional work not only disadvantages the IDVA but can be detrimental to their clients.

Although they are part of wider support networks, IDVAs spend a large portion of their time working on a one-to-one basis with different clients in order to meet their needs, and less time engaging with colleagues. However, while the role can be considered an individualised one to some degree, there are shared elements to the occupation which lend themselves to a form of 'collective emotional labour' (Hochschild, 1983, p. 114). This in turn may allow for individualised workers to form communities of support and resilience in the face of external adversities (such as cuts to funding, increased workloads, and fewer prosecutions). It may also be important to differentiate between IDVAs who work with domestic abuse organisations and those who work in an independent capacity while affiliated to the statutory sector in order to discern any patterns or trends in how their environment and working practices may impact on emotional labour. Domestic abuse is a highly emotive issue and one that, to be effectively addressed, requires a more nuanced approach in terms of support for service providers as well as service users.

The proposed Domestic Abuse Bill may be a key resource here. Despite still being under review, Nicola Jacobs was appointed the new Domestic Abuse Commissioner in October 2019. While she has no formal powers until the Bill passes through Parliament and becomes law, she can be considered a national figurehead for IDVAs, and should therefore have their best interests at heart. One of her roles as Commissioner will be to review the provision and impact of domestic abuse services, of which IDVAs play a key part. The impact of these services on those working to provide them is an important area for inclusion in such reviews. While the government recognises the increasing importance of IDVAs, particularly when acting in a representative capacity for victims in court as a result of cuts to legal aid, there has – as yet – been no mention of planned pastoral or tailored support for them. It is important to ensure that the heavy emotional toll of working with people in crisis, and at a potential risk to the IDVA's own personal safety, is better recognised alongside logistical efforts to establish more posts, greater funding and wider investment.

It is envisaged that the proposed Bill will also place Clare's Law on a statutory footing in order to increase the scheme's visibility, uptake and impact (Duggan & Grace, 2018). This would be of great benefit to IDVAs in clarifying their engagement with the scheme and outlining their responsibilities to clients more clearly in relation to Clare's Law disclosure information. Currently, the vague guidelines mean some IDVAs may be unsure about whether or not they can share information; this in turn can cause additional mental stress on top of an already stressful role. While not directly seeking to address issues of emotional labour, clearer guidance and evident legal perimeters may provide greater assurance to IDVAs seeking to navigate (increasingly complicated) bureaucratic systems on behalf of domestic abuse victims. In light of this, and the aforementioned increasing IDVA caseload, it is more important than ever to consider the ramifications of this work on those seeking to keep victims alive.

References

Aldridge, M. L. & Browne, K. D., 2003. Perpetrators of spousal homicide: A review. *Trauma, Violence & Abuse*, 4(3), pp. 265–276.

Ashforth, B. E. & Humphrey, R. H., 1993. Emotional labor in service roles: The influence of identity. *Academy of Management. The Academy of Management Review*, 18(1), pp. 88–115.

BBC News, 2019. *Domestic Violence Killings Reach Five-Year High.* [Online] Available at: www.bbc.co.uk/news/uk-49459674 [Accessed 6 September 2019].

Brotheridge, C. & Grandey, A., 2002. Emotional labor and burnout: Comparing two perspectives of "people work". *Journal of Vocational Behaviour*, 60, pp. 17–32.

Dobash, R., Dobash, R. & Cavanagh, K., 2009. "Out of the blue": Men who murder an intimate partner. *Feminist Criminology*, 4(3), pp. 194–225.

Duggan, M. & Grace, J., 2018. Assessing vulnerabilities in the domnestic violence disclosure scheme. *Child and Family Law Quarterly*, 30(2), pp. 145–166.

Goleman, D., 1995. *Emotional Intelligence: Why It Can Matter More Than IQ.* New York: Bantum Books.

Grandey, A., 2000. Emotion regulation in the workplace: A new way to conceptualise emotional labour. *Journal of Occupational Health Psychology*, 5(1), pp. 95–110.

Hochschild, A., 1983. *The Managed Heart: Commercialization of Human Feeling.* Berkeley: University of California Press.

Home Office, 2005. *Domestic Violence: A National Report.* [Online] Available at: https://webarchive.nationalarchives.gov.uk/+/http:/www.crimereduction.homeoffice.gov.uk/domesticviolence/domesticviolence51.pdf [Accessed 6 October 2019].

Home Office, 2016. *Domestic Violence Disclosure Scheme (DVDS) Guidance.* [Online] Available at: www.gov.uk/government/uploads/system/uploads/attachment_data/file/575361/DVDS_guidance_FINAL_v3.pdf [Accessed 6 October 2019].

Howarth, E., Stimpson, L., Barran, D. & Robinson, A., 2009. *Safety in Numbers: A Multi-Site Evaluation of Independent Domestic Violence Services.* London: Sigrid Rausing Trust/The Henry Smith Charity.

Hunt, J., 1984. The development of rapport through the negotiation of gender in field work among police. *Human Organization*, 43, pp. 283–296.

James, N., 1989. Emotional labour: Skill and work in the social regulation of feelings. *The Sociological Review*, 37(1), pp. 15–42.

Martin, S., 1999. Police force or police service? Gender and emotional labour. *Annals of the American Academy of Political and Social Science*, 561, pp. 111–126.

Maslach, C., 1982. *Burnout: The Cost of Caring*. Englewood Cliffs, NJ: Prentice Hall.

Middleton, D. R., 1989. Emotional style: The cultural ordering of emotions. *Ethos*, 17(2), pp. 187–201.

Monckton Smith, J., Williams, A. & Mullane, F., 2014. *Domestic Abuse, Homicide and Gender*. London: Palgrave Macmillan.

Office for National Statistics, 2018. *Domestic Abuse in England and Wales: Year Ending March 2018*. [Online] Available at: www.ons.gov.uk/peoplepopulationandcommunity/ crimeandjustice/bulletins/domesticabuseinenglandandwales/yearendingmarch 2018 [Accessed 6 October 2019].

Safe Lives, 2016. *Safelives' 2016 Survey of Independent Domestic Violence Advisor Provision in England & Wales*. [Online] Available at: www.safelives.org.uk/sites/default/ files/resources/SafeLives%20Idva%20survey%20report%202016.pdf.

Sheehan, B., Murphy, S., Moynihan, M., Dudley-Fennessey, E., & Stapleton, J. 2015. Intimate partner homicide: New insights for understanding lethality and risks. *Violence Against Women*, 21(2), pp. 269–288.

Walby, S. & Allen, J., 2004. *Domestic Violence, Sexual Assault and Stalking: Findings from the British Crime Survey*. London: Home Office Research, Development and Statistics Directorate.

Walby, S. & Towers, J. S., 2017. Measuring violence to end violence: Mainstreaming gender. *Journal of Gender-Based Violence*, 1(1), pp. 11–31.

Chapter 10

"And you didn't tell them that they were getting robbed!?" emotional labour, ethnography and danger

Anthony Ellis

Introduction

The effects of the afternoon's alcohol consumption are now starting to fade, giving way to an incipient hangover. My throat feels dry, the hazy feeling in my head begins to dissipate, replaced with the first flashes of what will eventually become a headache. My partner talks to me from across the table as we eat. I try to listen and follow the conversation, but I struggle to give it my full attention. Knowing that she will be concerned if she detects my thoughts are elsewhere, I glance up at her more regularly from my plate of food in an attempt to avoid this; but my head is filled with memories of the fieldwork completed only hours ago with Tommy.[1] The nauseating smell of alcohol on Tommy's breath still feels palpable; his face, contorted with anger and anguish; his words, shouted in my ear amid the noise and chatter around us, and the image those words now conjure of his dad retrieving the belt from *"the cupboard"*:

"My dad wouldn't hit me with the belt if I pissed myself in fright first".

As the words and images keep replaying in my mind I watch my own 18-month-old son for a moment while he plays on the floor with his toys. He happily pushes his toy car along and I feel really overwhelmed suddenly by his innocence and vulnerability. I feel a tightness start to develop in my stomach and I have to look away for a moment, blinking as I feel the sharp prick of tears developing in my eyes.

(Reflective notes after a period of fieldwork)

In an article addressing the emotive aspects of prison ethnography, Jewkes (2011) suggested that criminology has tended to minimise the significance of researchers' emotional experiences during their fieldwork (see also Chapter 8, this volume). As a result, Jewkes (2011: 66) argues, 'there have been few attempts by criminologists to account for…how they *feel* both while carrying out the research and afterwards'.

Jewkes raises a number of important points in this article, but very often with reference to the context of prison ethnography. In this short chapter, I seek to address the significant absence of emotion in criminological research that Jewkes identifies, with a particular focus upon emotional labour during ethnography. To illuminate the discussion offered here, I draw specifically upon my experiences of several years spent conducting in-depth fieldwork in de-industrialised communities in the north of England with men who possess reputations for violence and who were also involved in other forms of illicit activity (see Ellis, 2016; Ellis et al., 2017). My emphasis here then is upon emotional labour in field research outside of organisational settings and their inherent demands – the context in which the concept of emotional labour has most often been applied and which is the focus in most contributions to this volume (see Chapter 1, this volume, and Hochschild, 1983). Emotional labour in the case of my ethnographic research, as others have found (McQueeney and Lavelle, 2017), has been influenced to some extent by participants and the specific demands of the field sites, with some personal autonomy involved too. Quite often, given the nature of the environment and those present, this regularly consisted of the need to present what Mastracci et al. (2006: 125) refer to as 'hard', traditionally masculine, emotions, alongside the suppression of fear.

As the reflective notes that open this chapter attest, ethnographies of violence evidently generate immediate and lasting emotions that can be deeply troubling and may demand ongoing management in, and out of, the field. Hochschild's (1983) concept of 'emotional labour', which ties together the various contributions to this volume, considers the ways in which emotions feature in various forms of work. Emotional labour, as Hochschild conceived it, involves the instrumental management of one's feelings in return for payment, in a similar way that one's capacity to engage in physical labour is sold. Just as workers must utilise their physical bodies to perform labour tasks, Hochschild recognised the increased demands in advanced economies that are placed upon workers to utilise their emotions in various ways. Emotional labour frequently involves the inducement or suppression of certain feelings depending upon the type of work the individual engages in. This raises important questions about the implications for, in this case, how criminological researchers carry out their fieldwork, the emotional impact of this, and how this is managed, particularly when entering environments that contain various possible dangers. However, criminologists tend to 'share few of these experiences and when we do so, we do it privately' (Liebling and Stanko, 2001: 424).

In response, this short chapter aims to make some of that private emotional labour public and is divided into two substantive sections. The first considers briefly how emotive experience is relevant to doing 'dangerous' ethnography. Specifically, this first section highlights some issues common in dangerous ethnographic studies to set the context for the second section. The second section focuses upon my own emotive experience and resultant emotional labour during and after research encounters in potentially dangerous settings.

A brief conclusion follows the second section to draw together the main points I raise in this chapter.

Emotional labour and 'dangerous' ethnography

Offline ethnographies of the human world require an established physical presence and a period of immersion over time in the field that is being studied. Ethnography represents a deeply embodied practice. Ethnographers must place themselves within the everyday physical locations of those they seek to understand and will have to, in all likelihood, partake to varying degrees in the activities that are performed routinely by the individuals or group being researched (Pearson, 1993). The ethnographer will inevitably have to fulfil a variety of roles during this period. Rarely can an ethnographer simply 'sit and watch' what is going on, nor will participants always be able, or willing, to sit and talk about themselves and their lives (Pearson, 1993). It may not always be appropriate or safe to openly ask questions. Some of the roles that will have to be adopted, as well as the typical demands of the field site, will be known by the researcher in advance. Although some demands and pressures will only become clear as relationships with participants and gatekeepers develop. The inevitably unpredictable demands placed upon the researcher by the field and those individuals within it, means that roles may have to be adopted immediately, and decisions made instantly, with little forethought, time to plan, nor fully consider the possible implications (Lee, 1995).

Emotional labour is fundamental to these predictable and more serendipitous aspects of the ethnographic method. Drawing upon insights from interactionist sociology, Hochschild (1983) identifies 'surface' acting to describe occasions when individuals feign emotions in an attempt to disguise how they really feel. This is contrasted with 'deep' acting when the individual exhibits the particular emotion or attempts to experience it. Both methods of 'acting' are relevant in the context of dangerous ethnography. Researchers may have to feign particular feelings depending upon the circumstance; amusement or happiness, surprise or anger may be required at those times where these emotions are socially expected. Similarly, an ethnographer's role is to immerse themselves, as much as is practically and ethically possible, in order to 'tell it like it is' (Pearson, 1993: viii), part of which will entail attempting to some degree to experience the emotional lives of those being researched. In such instances though, the ethnographer may not have to 'act', but might experience and display 'genuine' emotions that are expected in such social encounters (Ashforth and Humphrey, 1993). During immersive encounters within the field it is possible, as the reflective notes that introduce this chapter indicate, for the researcher to genuinely feel emotions as they seek to understand their participants' lived experiences. These feelings may be managed through surface acting, but outside of the social expectations and constraints of the field, researchers of dangerous places may be left with what will likely be negative feelings that may have consequences for personal well-being.

These elements of serendipity and unpredictability characteristic of immersive ethnographies, that examine sensitive issues, arguably make it the most emotionally demanding and challenging method available to criminologists. For such emotive experiences to be routinely extracted from research and not subjected to subsequent reflection is then, as Jewkes (2011) has suggested, an issue for the discipline. This is especially so given the potential impact these experiences can have upon researchers' psychological well-being (Liebling and Stanko, 2001). However, this is to be expected within a disciplinary environment that tends to 'train researchers to be rational and objective to...not disclose feelings of anxiety, confusion, vulnerability or anything else of their selves' (Jewkes, 2011: 64). Likewise, ethnographer Steve Wakeman (2014) points to the inevitable but often unacknowledged synthesis between ethnographic encounters and the researcher's own emotional and biographical experience. Wakeman describes this aptly as an 'absent-presence' in which physical, rather than emotional, selves are present in accounts of research:

> ...instrumental researchers seeing and recording things rather than emotive beings feeling things... the self is and always has been present in criminological research, but it is infrequently acknowledged and rarely if ever prioritized to the extent that it can be considered virtually absent.
>
> (2014: 706–707)

Methodological literature often reflects this absent-presence, affording little concern for the emotive although, there is a, albeit small, body of work within that methodological literature which critically engages with practical, empirical and ethical issues and highlights some of the important emotive dimensions of ethnographic fieldwork in dangerous settings (see for instance Ancrum, 2013; Calvey, 2008; Jacobs, 1998; Liebling and Stanko, 2001; Wakeman, 2014; Winlow et al., 2001).

It is perhaps worth re-iterating the very simple and obvious point that exposure to danger will likely take a considerable emotional toll upon the researcher. Liebling and Stanko (2001) offer a pretty exhaustive list of the potential emotional impacts of researching a difficult topic like violence. Their discussion considers the potential difficulties researchers may experience with academic colleagues, the media and wider society after fieldwork has taken place. This may also induce difficult emotive experiences as researchers encounter and must navigate the nuances of 'feeling rules' (Hochschild, 1983) often specific to these various contexts. I will consider examples of this from my own research later.

On the issue of working directly with potentially violent individuals, Bruce Jacobs (1998: 162) rightly points out that the threat of 'danger, it must be remembered, is "inherent" in fieldwork with active offenders'. Jacobs himself provides a frightening but important example when he describes being robbed at gunpoint by an individual participant that he trusted and who had also acted as an initial gatekeeper. Management of danger represents a central aspect of such ethnographic work and a reason why it is perhaps sometimes regarded as ethically unpalatable by some sections of the wider research community. On the subject of ethics and ethnographic work with active criminals, Ancrum (2013: 113) perceptively notes that:

> In unpredictable research environments the engaged ethnographer has no choice but to marginalise the formal world of ethics committees and methodological guidelines and proceed under the somatic guidance of his or her own ethical code as it interacts with the ethics and values of the researched community.

Ancrum continues by suggesting that such an approach is not necessarily ethically 'wrong', but is rather grounded in 'an emotional concern with what is right' (2013: 113). What is significant here is Ancrum's allusion to the role of 'emotional concern' in deciding what is, and what is not, ethical while in the field. The key point being that an emotive 'feeling' for what is right or wrong while present in that community should inform the researcher's conduct, rather than the well-intentioned, but often naïve and idealistic instructions of social science ethics committees. This suggests an individualistic, more instinctual approach based on the need to act as 'ethically' as possible. However, as Ancrum points out, this is highly context-bound and means researchers may have to, for the benefit of the research, engage in or bear witness to practices they find ethically and morally repugnant. The opposite consequence is that some researchers may be unwilling to cross such boundaries, which in itself can have potential issues for them and the research.

Calvey (2008) identifies the necessity to practice what he terms 'situated ethics' – a process of managing ethical issues as they arise within what is an unpredictable and potentially dangerous research field. What is crucial to acknowledge here is that depending upon the particular situation the ethnographer is confronted with, the situated practice(s) they ultimately engage in may not necessarily reflect what is routinely defined as a rational and 'ethical' course of action endorsed by University ethics committees or that would necessarily be accepted by non-academics located outside the field. Rather, it is highly probable that practices will be, as Ancrum (2013) has suggested, instinctual, habitual, spontaneous and, crucially, highly emotive. They may involve little forethought or planning, reflecting what the researcher judged to be 'right' at the time. This may require a resort to surface acting (Hochschild, 1983), as researchers may know that what is 'right at the time' does not necessarily fit with their organisation's expectations, nor perhaps even their own emotive sense of what is ethically and morally right. Yet, the social pressures or expectations (Rafaeli and Sutton, 1987) of the specific ethnographic encounter and immediate setting may require particular emotional responses and surface acting to effectively disguise this. In addition, Ashforth and Humphrey suggest that social identity may be relevant here and work to mitigate against the negative impacts of intense emotional labour through the individual's level of 'identification with the role in question'. They contend this can reduce the negative effects on well-being through the use of 'various behavioural and cognitive defense mechanisms' (1993: 89). What this suggests is that some researchers, who by virtue of their biographical experience and ability to identify with the field under study, may be more appropriately equipped to manage the negative impacts of emotional labour in particular types of research settings – an issue which I return to below.

While these points are important, what must also be considered are the consequences of such an individualised, autonomous, and sometimes highly reactive, mode of emotional labour that is, nevertheless, largely unavoidable if one is to successfully gain and maintain access. Indeed, as Liebling and Stanko (2001) have rightly outlined, those conducting research in potentially violent places often have little choice but to rely on their instincts, displaying courage and fortitude in the face of various dangers. However, they also highlight the potential for harm from engaging in these practices, which will likely result in emotional exhaustion.

Wakeman's (2014) ethnographic research with substance users on a housing estate in the North West of England provides a useful illustration of some of these points. Wakeman's 'biographical congruence' with this community furnished him with an important emotional awareness of its inherent dangers that served him well throughout the fieldwork process. Wakeman comments upon the positive aspect of this congruence, which enabled him to avoid being victimised as his keenly honed emotional sensibilities provided early warnings of danger that enabled him to better identify with the pressures of this research and the roles he had to fulfil. In this sense, Wakeman's experience seems to confirm some of the points raised by Ashforth and Humphrey (1993) in regard to identity and emotional labour. However, previous connection to the community under study can provide an ambivalent experience, which Wakeman also acknowledges. The negative underside to the positivity of biographical congruence was the return of difficult memories from Wakeman's past, as well as re-awakening a desire to consume the substances he observed his participants using on a daily basis. As the research progressed, Wakeman's emotional labour appears to have increasingly involved suppression of these feelings and desires, or what Hochschild (1983) called surface acting – pretending he was 'okay' to colleagues and family in order to complete the fieldwork. However, as he candidly acknowledges, Wakeman eventually reached a point at which he felt:

> no longer able to face the constant effort required to maintain an outward appearance of control, of being 'ok', no longer able to face the fear that my present circumstances were harming me to the extent they were.
> (2014: 714)

The brief insights provided in this section demonstrate how emotional labour is inherent to potentially dangerous criminological research that is undertaken outside of organisational contexts.

Giving 'them' the 'time of day'

During the initial stages of my own ethnographic research on male violence, I was mostly concerned with how best to act and manage potential ethical issues: what should I do if I am made aware of something ethically problematic? What should I do if I am being threatened? Will participants accept my presence? It was these practical and ethical issues that were at the forefront of my mind. The role of emotion in potentially guiding my engagement with matters of ethics and practice, as well as the immediate and subsequent emotional impact of decisions I would have to make, were not issues I considered much, if at all, at the outset. I began to realise, however, that I was fairly adept at managing practical difficulties. It also became quite clear – as I ventured further into the field – that my adeptness came not so much from research training, nor simply from an ability to surface act, but from a deeper emotional intuition acquired through a specific gendered and class-based socialisation. Aspects of social identity, grounded in biographical experience, were significant in this respect then, as they provided some of the behavioural and cognitive defence mechanisms that Ashforth and Humphrey (1993) suggest are crucial for mitigating against negative emotional impacts and to operate competently within a given setting.

Despite initial reservations concerning my abilities as an ethnographer, I instinctively knew how to act, how to talk, when to keep quiet, when I could ask questions. I was able to engage in such surface acting (Hochschild, 1983), with a particular emphasis on the display of certain 'hard' emotions (Mastracci et al., 2006) expected amongst the individual men I encountered (Rafaeli and Sutton, 1987). I do not possess a violent or criminal history, but I knew enough about violence and crime to be able to act competently, even if I was not always comfortable doing so. I found that I could effectively suppress the regular feelings of fear and trepidation, something I had learned to do in my formative years while in the company of potentially violent young men. I could induce amusement at inappropriate or offensive jokes and could summon the emotional energy required to engage in various bodily performances typical amongst this group of men. My upbringing and experiences had also taught me how to walk in a particular way and formulate physical appearance to look like I was capable of taking care of myself, but not in a manner that would appear contrived or over-exaggerated. Outwardly obvious displays of physical 'hardness' and masculine credibility – walking with a swagger, boasting about one's physical prowess, taking the 'piss' out of others – can, and does, attract attention from individuals who may seek to test these credentials or perceive threat that requires a reaction. An intuitive awareness of these complexities was vital, but emotionally burdensome to engage in and manage.

When one participant became involved in a confrontation with a group of young men in a nightclub during fieldwork, I felt deeply conflicted over how to react. Given he was outnumbered as well as my positive relationship with him, I felt obliged to back him up, and did so, standing by his side trying my best to look and act 'hard'. My decision did no harm to my relationship with him, especially when the three young men backed down. However, the experience was uncomfortable given that I am not someone who considers himself to be a competent fighter. This raised some significant questions about the extent to which I could act in particular ways while in the field. As I have discussed in more detail elsewhere (see Ellis, 2016), this research re-opened memories of past experiences of some confrontations that I had tried very hard to suppress because they are humiliating. The words and actions of participants, who stressed the importance of never backing down from physical confrontation, compounded my existing feelings of guilt and humiliation from those times when I did. My decision to back up my participant seems, upon reflection, to be partly related to my ability to act, manage or summon emotional displays that accord with the feeling rules of this milieu and that were necessary to maintain a credible presence. Yet, genuine emotion (Ashforth and Humphrey, 1993) was felt during this incident too, which I suspect partly motivated a response deemed appropriate and in accordance with, particularly masculine and working class, cultural injunctions that shape those specific emotional displays (see Ellis et al., 2017; Hochschild, 1983). Perhaps as a result of this kind of emotional labour, participants evidently liked me: I was invited into their homes; introduced to their family members and friends; invited to social events; offered illicit substances (which I always politely declined); and, via gatekeepers, regularly received informal 'feedback' from participants who reported I was a 'sound lad' or a 'good kid'. One particular participant became visibly concerned when I, rather naively in hindsight, confided in him about a personal issue I was experiencing. I had to quickly diffuse the developing situation as the participant indicated a preparedness to help me, insinuating that violence would be a suitable means of resolving the issue.

Despite the rigorous and lengthy research training I had undertaken within my discipline that emphasised, as Jewkes (2011) has suggested, the qualities of objectivity and rationality, I could not view these personal connections that I formed with participants and the experiences I had with them in such an instrumental and objective manner. In truth, I developed emotional connections to some individuals I worked with, I formed relationships with them that were friendly, and, as controversial as this may sound, I found myself caring, and still do, about them and their welfare despite the horrific things some of them had done to others. When I reflect back on the years I spent collecting data, I remain genuinely elated that I had formed positive relationships with my participants. I am proud of the detailed data that I gathered from these individuals, and of the fact that I had been able to enter the spaces they occupied and acted appropriately. Ethnographer of crime Hobbs (1993) referred to the 'muck' that ethnographers often bring back from their time spent in the field. This 'muck' offers the possibility of an academic career and an accompanying celebrity-like status for 'the ethnographer, who was nearly arrested, almost beaten up, and didn't quite go crazy' (Hobbs, 1993: 62) during their dangerous fieldwork. Upon his return from the field, Hobbs confessed that:

> …audiences assumed…I had actually been involved in the crimes that I described…for a period of about six months I wallowed in this minor celebrity and did nothing to disabuse my audiences of the darkness of my soul.
>
> (1993: 50)

I too accepted and even enjoyed the plaudits I received from some academic colleagues, particularly my status as an individual that had earned the trust of a notoriously hard to research group and had the emotional strength and resilience to research them. However, this 'muck' from the field has not always generated a positive emotional experience. Like Wakeman (2014), I too have found it ambivalent in several respects, particularly when my research has intersected with aspects of my life outside of that setting.

My partner, in particular, has always found this aspect of my vocation challenging. The title of this chapter are her shocked words when I explained that I once witnessed a robbery take place during the course of research and did not intervene. Upon learning I had spent time with an individual who had been involved in the torture of a rival criminal, she did not hesitate to express her moral repugnance at him, while also making clear her bemusement at my ability to, as she put it, "give him the time of day". Her bemusement related to my aforementioned ability to 'act' and conceal the emotions that feeling rules dictate I should feel about an individual who has inflicted extreme suffering upon others. In particular, it was my ability to put aside feelings of repugnance and disgust and give to participants other emotions, like empathy, that their behaviour and lifestyle are felt to not deserve, that was the issue. And my abilities of emotional suppression, management and presentation have generated conflict and difficulties on other occasions since completing fieldwork. As I approached the end of a live interview on national radio, the presenter asked me: 'Did you like the guys?'. The truth was I actually did quite like them; after all they had been kind enough to allow me a considerable insight into their lives, and, as highlighted previously, I was obviously prepared to put myself in harm's way for one of them. What immediately crossed my mind was whether I could openly admit in a public forum to feeling that way? Could I publicly air those private feelings? What should I 'feel' about my participants, who, despite their kindness towards me, still engaged in very harmful behaviour towards others? To tell the truth in response to the interviewer's question would risk incurring the wrath of a society that affords little understanding to such in-dividuals. As the encounters with my partner discussed already demonstrate, it would in effect have breached the societal feeling rules that broadly pattern emotional engagement on matters of crime and justice. Under these feeling rules, criminals are clearly felt to not be 'owed' some of those private emotions that I was feeling. To surface act in this case would betray my own feelings and to an extent I felt this would constitute a betrayal of the men who were actually kind enough to share so much with me and help me to forge a career as an aca-demic. It was difficult to just conveniently forget, upon exiting the field, that it was my time spent with them, their stories, as well as their various misfortunes that became the 'data' that was the springboard for the – relatively – secure and well-remunerated academic career I now have. The fumbled response that I eventually gave perhaps indicated that despite my evident ability to act, this was a performance that, on this occasion, I could not fully deliver.

Conclusion

It is evident when studying highly emotive issues like violence that there are 'inherent uncertainties in the way we choose our allegiances in the field' (Liebling and Stanko, 2001: 424) and also in the decisions that criminologists make, sometimes in considerably pressurised circumstances. However, as I have hopefully begun to demonstrate in this chapter, and in following the general point raised by Jewkes (2011: 72), 'the extracting out of emotion... from the research process...at the very least, represents a missed opportu-nity' for the discipline. The emotional labour undertaken in the course of ethnographic research on issues of crime requires a willingness to 'induce or suppress feelings in order to sustain...the proper state of mind in others' (Hochschild, 1983: 7). In my experience, this regularly necessitated engage-ment in surface or deep acting to enable not only effective and continued access to participants, but the maintenance of my own personal safety. And those acts have to, and had to in my case, be cognizant of the specific social expectations that govern the expression of emotions in those spaces. Bio-graphical experience, or congruence, and an ability to identify with the field, are relevant and evidently provide a basis from which to act in ways that con-form to these requirements and that aid the, at times arduous, demands of the emotional labour involved. As the field notes that open this chapter, and some of the other examples provided, indicate, exiting the field does not conclude this labour process. Researchers encounter further nuances and complexities, particularly in regard to what Hochschild (1983) identified as societal feeling rules, around how and which emotions are expressed or suppressed. Manag-ing these often-competing demands effectively requires that labour continues long after vacating the field. Importantly, this chapter brings into focus the immense and sometimes conflicting emotional pressures that researchers who study sensitive issues up-close must face and manage.

Note

1 Pseudonym.

References

Ancrum, C. (2013) Stalking the margins of legality: Ethnography, participant observation and the post-modern 'underworld'. In Winlow, S. & Atkinson, R. (eds.) *New Directions in Crime and Deviancy*. London: Routledge, 113–126.

Ashforth, B.E. & Humphrey, R.H. (1993) Emotional labor in service roles: The influence of identity. *The Academy of Management Review*. 18 (1) 88–115.

Calvey, D. (2008) The art and politics of covert research: Doing 'situated ethics' in the field. *Sociology*. 42 (5) 905–918.

Ellis, A. (2016) *Men, Masculinities and Violence: An Ethnographic Study*. Oxon: Routledge.

Ellis, A., Winlow, S. & Hall, S. (2017) 'Throughout my life I've had people walk all over me': Trauma in the lives of violent men. *Sociological Review*. 65 (4) 699–713.

Hobbs, D. (1993) Peers, careers, and academic fears: Writing as field-work. In Hobbs, D. & May, T. (eds.) *Interpreting the Field: Accounts of Ethnography*. Oxford: Clarendon Press, 45–66.

Hochschild, A.R. (1983) *The Managed Heart. Commercialization of Human Feeling*. Berkeley. University of California Press.

Jacobs, B.A. (1998) Researching crack dealers: Dilemmas and contradictions. In Ferrell, J. & Hamm, M.S. (eds.) *Ethnography at the Edge: Crime, Deviance and Field Research*. Boston: Northeastern University Press, 160–177.

Jewkes, Y. (2011) Autoethnography and emotion as intellectual resources: Doing prison research differently. *Qualitative Inquiry*. 18 (1) 63–75.

Lee, R.M. (1995) *Dangerous Fieldwork*. London: Sage.

Liebling, A. & Stanko, E. (2001) Allegiance and ambivalence: Some dilemmas in researching disorder and violence. *British Journal of Criminology*. 41 421–430.

Mastracci, S., Newman, M.A. & Guy, M.E. (2006) Appraising emotion work: Determining whether emotional labour is valued in government jobs. *American Review of Public Administration*. 36 (2) 139–155.

McQueeney, K. & Lavelle, K.M. (2017) Emotional labor in critical ethnographic fieldwork: In the field and behind the desk. *Journal of Contemporary Ethnography*. 46 (1) 81–107.

Pearson, G. (1993) Talking a good fight: Authenticity and distance in the ethnographer's craft. In Hobbs, D. & May, T. (eds.) *Interpreting the Field: Accounts of Ethnography*. Oxford: Clarendon Press.

Rafaeli, A. & Sutton, R.I. (1987) Expression of emotion as part of the work role. *Academy of Management Review*. 12 23–37.

Wakeman, S. (2014) Fieldwork, biography and emotion: Doing criminological autoethnography. *British Journal of Criminology*. 54 (5) 705–721.

Winlow, S., Hobbs, D., Lister, S. & Hadfield, P. (2001) Get ready to duck: Bouncers and the realities of ethnographic research on violent groups. *British Journal of Criminology*. 41, 536–548.

Chapter 11

Emotions at the prevention end of youth justice

Anne Robinson

Introduction

This volume underlines the reality that penal practices are imbued with emotion. That this is only now being recognised and articulated does not diminish the important part that the emotions of practitioners have long played in their vocational commitments (Crawley, 2004; Mawby and Worrall, 2013), ability to make connections with others (Knight et al., 2016; Fowler et al., 2018) and resilience in the face of constant organisational change (Robinson et al., 2016; see also Souhami, 2007, on the creation of youth offending teams).

This chapter turns attention to the emotional work of an occupational group marginal to criminal justice and indeed, with a history largely antagonistic to criminal processes and potential injustices to young people (de St Croix, 2016). Youth workers have stepped late – and reluctantly – onto the criminal justice merry-go-round, torn between deeply held beliefs in voluntary engagement and the empowerment of young people (Davies, 2005, 2015; Jeffs and Smith, 2008; Nicholls, 2012) and the harsh realities of existence in austerity Britain (Davies and Merton, 2010; Bradford and Cullen, 2014). Especially vulnerable as a non-statutory service, youth work organisations have become drawn into a network of children's services targeted on particular groups and 'at risk' young people (de St Croix, 2016, 2018) in order to survive and for their unique contribution to be recognised (however compromised within the current configuration of early intervention and prevention services).

My comments here are based on narrative interviews with five youth work practitioners involved in the youth work settings for my PhD research. The focus of that study was young people and their transitions to adulthood and, as I made contact with participants through two youth work organisations, naturally my analysis included observations on the ways that young people were agentic in using youth work and youth work relationships as a resource. At the end of the fieldwork I conducted these interviews and have since reflected on the nature of youth work as a pro-fession (a status that is not a given (Davies R, 2016)). The willingness of youth workers to reach out to young people and to start from 'where they are at' (Davies B, 2015) stands in stark contrast to the – undoubtedly well meaning, but also undoubtedly power-laden – relationships between young people and workers in my own professional territory of youth jus-tice. The professional aim of youth work is to 'tip balances of power' in young people's favour, empowering at a collective and political, as well as individual, level (Davies B, 2015: 103).

The five youth workers were of varied ages from late twenties upwards and of mixed ethnicities. One was in a management position but through choice and out of necessity in a hard pressed voluntary agency, and was still involved in work with young people. I will therefore use the term practitioner or youth worker throughout to include all the interviewees. Their length of time in youth work ranged from seven years to more than 30 but, despite entering the field at different points in its history, they each echoed the core values of youth work centred on young people, with social education and empowerment at its heart. In a difficult climate, this is re-affirmed by the *In Defence of Youth Work* campaign as an aspiration 'to a special relationship with young people'. It wants to meet young women and men on their own terms. It claims to be 'on their side; and to start from their concerns and interests' (IDYW, 2011, cited in Nicholls, 2012: 37).

Involving the personal in practice

Social learning within relationships is at the heart of youth work, with trust and intimacy as key ingredients. However,

> Youth workers need to be friendly but understand the friendship offered in the context of their work and friendships in their personal lives. This is especially important because of the informality of the approach to practice, including the negotiation of relationship.
>
> (Batsleer, 2013: 106)

The boundaries around youth work relationships are different, and often more tricky, than for other workers with young people. Murphy and Ord ar-gue that 'part of the emotionality of youth work involves self-disclosure, the making of ourselves "present" in our role. Self-disclosure is therefore essen-tial to the practice of youth work' (2013: 330). This establishes the mutuality and the equality that youth work thrives upon, but entails careful judgement about when, what and how much to reveal of self – in contemporary practice, online as well as in face-to-face encounters (Jaynes, 2019). The latter was illustrated in one interview in relation to the specialist area of 'boys work' (Harland, 2001):

YW 3: When I work with boys.... I now present my heart on my sleeve and not in a way that sounds overly wishy washy, I am what I am so I take my whole part of me......you can prod and poke wherever you want, it's out there and those are the things that help people to link up, especially angry boys .... It's about being brave and that brave is not about you in that macho brave thing, it's about taking that risk [with] your own emotions.

ANNE I: Was going to say, doesn't that mean leaving yourself a bit -?

YW 3: There's no vulnerability because you have to be – You won't do that unless you're an assured human being but there are points of vulnerabilities. Like you use our life experiences to help guide others and hopefully learn ourselves but within that there are points for appropriate collusion and sharing.

(Youth worker 3, male, White)

In criminal justice contexts collusion would be seen as wholly negative but here it is reframed as helpful in relating to young people experiencing difficulties. This is skilled work and two points are worth noting. The first is about the degree of openness that elicits a response from young people. As Harland advocates,

if those working with young men learn to disclose their feelings in a more open and appropriate way, then this in itself will enable young men to believe that disclosing certain feelings and emotions they are not compromising their emotions or masculine identity.

(2001: 293)

He acknowledges, however, that male workers relating in this way need to have the sort of security in their own masculine identity and awareness of emotions suggested by my interviewee. And I would add that this might include talking frankly about feelings, impulses and, on occasions, actions that are not entirely pro-social, to show points of weakness and fragility that young people might be able to see as comparable to their own.

The second point is about the authenticity of the feelings expressed and how that engenders empathic relations with young people. Here perhaps Farrugia et al.'s (2018) term 'affective labour' might be nearer to capturing what is happening than Hochschild's (1983) 'emotional labour'. 'Affective work' is not characterised by either deep or surface acting in emotional display because of the closer correspondence it implies between the feelings of the worker and, in this case, young people. The nature of relational work between practitioners and young people means this is necessarily in the interests of forging a much deeper human connection than in the leisure industry that was Farrugia et al.'s (2018) concern. Even so, practitioners still engage in the sorts of emotional and impression management identified by Ashforth and Humphrey (1993) in the service sector.

Human connections may be present in fleeting encounters between practitioners and young people, but many youth work relationships develop over months and years, needing careful maintenance. In one-to-one work, another interviewee stressed how important it is to stand alongside a young person particularly where other agencies are involved in intervention, saying that

> Just that language says a lot about what that experience is like for a young person. This intervention, it will come in here and then it will come back out and then this thing will happen and it will come back out and often what kids need is somebody to walk that path with them while they're having all this stuff done to them, that's just giving them that support and that care.
>
> (Youth worker 4, female, White)

Some young people have a confusing array of professionals and agencies in their lives and appreciate youth workers being at their side (and on their side too). Whereas policy discourse often suggests that troubled young men would benefit from the sorts of role models offered by footballers and celebrities, Robb et al.'s (2015) research with young men involved with support services indicates that what they appreciate more are older males who can be present in their lives as guides and mentors. It is telling that

> It was not just what was done (for example, a worker making them a cup of tea or helping them fill out a benefit form), although that was important and appreciated, but it was also how and why. The 'how' referred to the conveying of respect and this could be tangible or intangible. Tangibles included workers doing what they said they would do.
>
> (Robb et al., 2015: 21)

The intangible qualities of trust and trustworthiness are communicated via tangible behaviours, because it is through their words and actions that workers demonstrate their trustworthiness and the values that they hold. As an illustration, young people in one study of youth clubs indicated that they were reluctant to open up to workers that they did not know, who were, as one young person said, 'basically a stranger'. The youth workers themselves felt that 'both respect and trust have to be earned and this was a process that developed over time' (Mason, 2015: 62). The sense of 'being in for the long haul' resonated through my interviews with youth workers too. There is, then, emotional connection in the moment that enables youth workers to reach out to young people, and emotional commitment that keeps young people involved over time.

Passion and commitment

In essence, practitioners working with young people are seeking to 'befriend them but not *be* their friend' (interviewee cited in Jaynes, 2019: 2, emphasis in original). The pride and pleasure that youth workers experience in their relationships with young people, and their genuine interest, shone through all of the interviews. For example,

> That's one of the core principles of youth work, being able to establish and maintain a relationship based on trust and that's something youth workers thrive off and that's what we are the best at, engaging young people because of that skill that we've got. Its person centred.
>
> (Youth worker 1, male, Asian)

In a similar way to the part time and volunteer youth workers in de St Croix (2013, 2016), these youth workers freely expressed their passion for their work. One envisaged always working with young people, 'until I'm too old to do it!' Another appreciated the political aspects of the work and the space that had been allowed to challenge the existing power structures (Nicholls, 2012):

> When I first came into it that was the passion that was there, that people really enjoyed working with young people. Like I said, it was like a political thing. It wasn't just play some table tennis with them. It was about shaping them, that's what it was.
>
> (Youth worker 2, male, Black)

This same youth worker also said that his previous practice was a '24 hour job', echoing Batsleer's observation that 'youth work is, among other things, a form of emotional labour. And emotional labour does not run along clock time' (2013: 103). He was motivated by the way that

> Young people would be active, doing stuff. Young people would be waiting for you outside the club before you came, you know what I'm saying? Because they enjoyed the type of engagement, the energy that you gave them as a worker. It wasn't just knocking on their door and them hiding from you.
>
> (Youth worker 2, male, Black)

He described entering youth work through a life-changing initiative to recruit from local minority ethnic communities but was not the only one who spoke of youth work and youth work training as transformational. One interviewee explained how her ability to move beyond the gendered expectations of her working class community 'all kind of stemmed from that year, that year that just opened up all these doors in my head and made me realise I was clever' (youth worker, 4, female, White). For another, attachment to youth work went back to his experience of being a member of a youth club:

> I actually get up on days that I work and I enjoy what I do, I'm excited to get in to the car, I'm excited to go to my place of work. I do enjoy it. I enjoy working with young people and the organisation I work for has given me that opportunity, they've invested in me as a young person, they've brought me to this point.
>
> (Youth worker 1, male, Asian)

The sense of youth work as potentially transformational for both workers and young people harks back to the underpinnings of youth work education in the emancipatory philosophy of Paulo Friere (1988) and Friere and Shor (1987): see also Nicholls (2012). The potency of this vision is central to the passion with which youth workers view their work. The personal gains and self-knowledge they find there make the emotional and other demands worth their while. Of course, the reality of youth work practice has inevitably always been somewhat less than this potential, given the exigencies of local politics, pressures on provision and the ambiguous professional status of youth workers. However, the gulf between what practice could be, and what practice is in too many contexts, is widening (Garasia et al., 2015). The rest of this chapter considers the multiple challenges that face 21st-century youth work and the conflicting emotions that surround.

Negotiating tensions

For many of its advocates, the precarious position of youth work has altered and, in many respects, worsened in the past two decades (Nicholls, 2012; Davies, B, 2015; de St Croix, 2016), constraining its ability to engage in these types of emotion work. In these interviews, the positive feelings as youth workers talked about the satisfactions and the 'buzz' of working with young people were balanced by a mixture of emotions about the direction that contemporary youth work is taking and its closer relationship with other children's services. On the one hand, there are benefits in working in conjunction with other services and being recognised for a unique skill set and approach to work with 'hard to reach' young people. On the other, in the wake of New Labour's Every Child Matters agenda and the Children's Workforce Development Council, integrated children's services and a broad early intervention agenda threatened to subsume the identity of youth work in a generic 'youth professional role' (Davies and Merton, 2009, 2010). That threat has lessened since, but the years of Coalition and now Conservative governments, austerity and the continued impact of managerialism have in themselves had a deleterious effect (Mason, 2015; de St Croix, 2016, 2018).

In the early 2000s in fact, youth work found itself in a paradoxical situation as new Labour heralded a new era for work with young people. The attention of policy-makers was double-edged as Bernard Davies explains in his clarion call, *Youth Work: A Manifesto for Our Times – Revisited*:

> What the new youth work enthusiasts seemed to be demanding was a cherry-picked, if not a de-rooted, version of youth work practice, re-engineered largely to stop young people from dropping out of school, of-fending, taking drugs or displaying other kinds of 'anti-social behaviour'.
>
> (2015: 96)

He caustically observes that 'within this refiguring, only incidentally (if at all) was youth work's core educational commitment to tapping into young people's personal potential being endorsed or even recognised' (2015: 96). The implications of this are felt in terms of increased accountability, a push for targeted work with young people and a radically different set of relations with other agencies.

Taking the latter of these implications first, youth work within local authorities or conducted on their behalf (by one of the organisations here, for example) has been co-opted into a range of prevention activities with youth justice and police. Involvement in overt surveillance and control is not comfortable for street-based youth workers used to relating to young people on their own terms (de St Croix, 2016). In the city where my research was conducted, 'rapid response' youth work teams are being deployed in 'hot spot' areas but not allowed sufficient time to embed themselves in one community before being moved on to the next. One interviewee commented on the frustration and embarrassment of seeing young people with whom they had previously been in contact through detached work entering the justice system simply because they had not been around long enough to build an effective relationship. While issues of trust as part of integrated children's services were mentioned – collateral damage from the loss of youth work autonomy – the strongest feelings arose in relation to the police. The greatest problem cited was the wariness of young people where they perceived youth workers to be in too close an association with police (see also Hall et al., 1999; Mason, 2015 on police presence in youth club spaces).

A distinction might be made here between collaborations with the police and being directed to work with them, because the latter involves pre-scribed rather than negotiated activities. De St Croix (2016) describes some of her interviewees expressing deep unhappiness about expectations that they accompany police officers on weekend evenings confiscating alcohol from young people, while others felt satisfied that they were able to foster better understandings between police and young people. As she comments,

Youth workers I interviewed were primarily concerned about policies that *required* them to work alongside the police, rather than being able to make this complex judgement together with young people and colleagues.

(de St Croix, 2016: 124)

This tension arose in my own interviews, with youth workers anxious about jeopardising credibility and keenly aware of the fragility of their hard-earned reputation with young people. However, just as in de St Croix's research, there was evidence of youth workers drawing a line in relation to particular practices and feeling vindicated where their position was supported by managers.

Resistance is more problematic in relation to the record-keeping and the accountability involved in integrated children's services. De St Croix (2016) recounts an instance where workers defended the anonymity of young people they met through detached work, successfully appealing against demands for names and details of young people to be entered on a shared database. This, however, is exceptional in situations where youth services are expected to produce increasing evidence of their contact with young people and measurable impacts (de St Croix, 2018). Managers have embraced the opportunity to 'prove' what youth work can achieve more than practitioners (Davies and Merton, 2010) who, on the evidence of my interviews, feel constrained by the emphasis on targeted one-to-one work and out of court disposals. One particular comment offers some explanation:

You've got to trust process for youth work to work and trust that the process will lead you to the right kind of outcome. I think lots of people are really uncomfortable with that because they need a target, they need an indicator and they need an output because they're easier things to measure.

(Youth worker 4, female, White)

There are two sides to a performance culture, which has its seductions when the figures seem impressive and stand up well against other services. Relatedly, one interviewee, whilst mourning the impacts on 'proper youth work' with groups, spoke with pride of being praised for his work supporting individual young people. However, poor performance against measures and negative comparisons can cause feelings of shame and disillusion, particularly when made public (de St Croix, 2016). The resulting demoralisation may lead to workers forming the sorts of 'communities of coping' described by Korcynski (2003) that allow them to subvert managerial dictates and let off steam about 'difficult' services users. That is perhaps indicative of some level of resilience but not a healthy atmosphere overall.

The crux of the matter for youth workers is the impingement on their principle of voluntarism, and what referrals and directed contact mean for the closeness and continuity of their relationships with young people. There are, of course, differing views about the sanctity of the voluntary principle which represents a red line for some. Ord, in contrast, argues that the way that young people have historically come to open access youth provision of their own volition is unique among children's services, but that voluntarism *per se* is neither a necessary nor a sufficient condition for youth work. He distinguishes between attendance and participation, suggesting that it is not the latter in itself that is important

> It is what it 'enables'. It is after all a means to an end, not an end in itself. Voluntary participation allows the formation of an authentic youth work relationship. One based on honesty, respect, mutuality and a concern for the well-being of the young person, as well as, importantly, a degree of power at the disposal of the young person.
>
> (Ord, 2009: 44)

Degrees of choice, then, and empowerment are critical and the possibility of 'working informally in formal settings' (Curran and Golding, 2013) such as schools and colleges is increasingly recognised, and indeed is often essential for the continued existence of voluntary sector youth organisations.

The precarity of youth work in the voluntary sector raises emotions across an alternative spectrum. In the interviews here, workers from the voluntary organisation expressed pleasure at the relative freedom that they had to respond to need, a prime example being the boys work now extending over multiple educational settings. They spoke of the creativity needed to find monies to pursue ideas as energising. The downside, however, was the burden of finding sufficient core finance to maintain the infrastructure of the organisation and jobs: the manager interviewed said that it was a standing joke among the staff team that they would all receive a 'pre-redundancy letter' every Christmas. The strain of living with that insecurity should not be under-estimated, albeit mitigated by close relations among the staff group and with an active Advisory Committee, who are involved in the difficult decisions made on occasions not to bid for funding for activities that would be antithetical to the aims and values of the organisation. Yet even with the funds that are accessed, there are compromises in paying attention both to young people and where they might want to take a project, and to reporting and other requirements:

> It becomes a tricky balance between fulfilling the outcomes that your funders have said you can work with a group around and then, obviously, how you want to work with the young people. So I think it's about being flexible a bit, sometimes maybe pushing the boundaries of what funders

have said money's for, or [what] you can use resources for, and being creative with how you think what you've been funded to do [matches] what the
group of young people actually need when you start working with them.

(Youth worker 5, female, White)

The consciousness of performance pervades the voluntary sector just as it
does the work of local authorities and allied organisations, but perhaps with
staff teams who feel more empowered and resilient in the face of the particular difficulties they face.

Conclusion

What we see here is emotional labour as an inherent part of youth work,
enabling practitioners to reach out to young people and to be allowed into
their space. However, a new and more varied range of emotions attach to
the contemporary context of youth work which has lost much of its historic
autonomy just as it is becoming recognised for its particular set of skills.
Experienced youth workers are, of necessity, highly emotionally intelligent
which research suggests may protect against the worst effects of occupational stresses (Mikolajczek et al., 2007). Nevertheless, it evident that youth
workers are increasingly managing emotions in two significant respects that
make demands upon them. First in terms of displaying 'appropriate' behaviours and attitudes within their employing organisations, whatever they may
be feeling about ethical compromises and de-professionalisation. Second,
managing what they say and what they show of their feelings to young
people, for example, when their ability to engage meaningfully is affected
by the burdens of record-keeping and having to accredit young people's
activities, as well as more dramatic instances where services are under threat
(de St Croix, 2016). This raises a question for me about whether the longer
term cultural effects of managerialism and austerity on youth workers might
be similar to those noted for social workers, namely coping with 'ethical
stress' and inability to provide constructive help by emotional distancing and
judgements of whether service users are 'deserving' or otherwise (Grootegoed and Smith, 2018). This is worthy of further investigation. I end by
simply noting that this small piece of research suggests that youth work can
still thrive where organisations nurture the passion that binds youth workers
to their profession and work nimbly around the pressures the external environment presents.

References

Ashforth, B E and Humphrey, R H (1993) 'Emotional labor in service roles: the influence of identity' in *The Academy of Management Review* Vol 18(1): 88–115.

Batsleer, J (2013) 'Informal learning in youth work: times, people and places' in S Curran, R Harrison and D Mackinnon (eds) *Working with Young People 2nd Edition* London: Sage, 99–115.

Bradford, S and Cullen, F (2014) 'Positive for youth work? Contested terrains of professional youth work in austerity England' in *International Journal of Adolescence and Youth* Vol 19(1): 93–106. doi:10.1080/02673843.2013.863733.

Crawley, E (2004) *Doing Prison Work: The Public and Private Lives of Prison Officers* Cullompton: Willan.

Curran, S and Golding, T (2013) 'Crossing the boundaries? Working informally in formal settings' in S Curran, R Harrison and D Mackinnon (eds) *Working with Young People 2nd Edition* London: Sage, 125–136.

Davies, B (2005) *Youth Work: A Manifesto for Our Times* Leicester: NYA.

Davies, B (2015) 'Youth work: a manifesto for our times – revisited' in *Youth & Policy* Vol 114: 96–117.

Davies, B and Merton, B (2009) *Squaring the Circle: Findings of a 'Modest' Inquiry into the State of Youth Work Practice in a Changing Policy Environment* Leicester: De Montfort University.

Davies, B and Merton, B (2010) *Straws in the Wind: The State of Youth Work Practice in a Changing Policy Environment (Phase 2)* Leicester: De Montfort University.

Davies, R (2016) 'Youth work and ethics: why the 'professional turn' won't do' in *Ethics & Education* Vol 11(2): 186–196. doi:10.1080/17449642.2016.1182309.

de St Croix, T (2013) ''I just love youth work!' Emotional labour, passion and resistance' in *Youth & Policy* Vol 110: 33–51.

de St Croix, T (2016) *Grassroots Youth Work: Policy, Passion and Resistance in Practice* Bristol: Policy Press.

de St Croix, T (2018) 'Youth work, performativity and the new youth impact agenda: getting paid for numbers?' in *Journal of Education Policy* Vol 33(3): 414–438. doi: 10.1080/02680939.2017.1372637.

Farrugia, D, Threadgold, S and Coffey, J (2018) 'Young subjectivities and affective labour in the service economy' in *Journal of Youth Studies* Vol 21(3): 272–287. doi: 10.1080/13676261.2017.1366015.

Fowler, A, Phillips, J and Westaby, C (2018) 'Understanding emotions as effective practice, The performance of emotional labour in building relationships' in P Ugwudike, P Raynor and J Annison (eds) *Evidence-Based Skills in Community Justice: International Research on Supporting Rehabilitation and Desistance* Bristol: Policy Press, 243–262.

Friere, P (1988) *Pedagogy of the Oppressed* New York: Continuum.

Friere, P and Shor, I (1987) *A Pedagogy for Liberation* Basingstoke: Macmillan.

Garasia, H, Begum-Ali, S and Farthing, R (2015) ''Youth club is made to get children off the streets': some young people's thoughts about opportunities to be political in youth clubs' in *Youth & Policy* Vol 115. Available online www.youthandpolicy.org

Grootegoed, E and Smith, M (2018) 'The emotional labour of austerity: how social workers reflect and work on their feelings towards reducing support to needy children and families' in *British Journal of Social Work* Vol 48(7): 1929–1947. doi:10.1093/bjsw/bcx151.

Hall, T, Coffey, A and Williamson, H (1999) 'Self, space and place: youth identities and citizenship' in *British Journal of Sociology of Education* Vol 20(4): 501–513. doi:10.1080/1425699995236.

Harland, K (2001) 'The challenges and potential of developing a more effective youth work curriculum with young men' in *Child Care in Practice* Vol 7(4): 288–300. doi:10.1080/13575270108415337.

Jaynes, V (2019) '"Befriend them but not *be* their friend': negotiations of youth practice in a digital age' in *Journal of Youth Studies* Online access. doi:10.1080/13676261. 2019.1592131.

Hochschild, A R (1983) *The Managed Heart: Commercialization of Human Feeling* USA: University of California Press.

Jeffs, T and Smith, M (2008) 'Valuing youth work' in *Youth and Policy* Vol 100: 277–299.

Knight C, Phillips, J and Chapman, T (2016) 'Bringing the feeling back: returning emotions to criminal justice practice' in *British Journal of Community Justice* Vol 14(1): 45–58.

Korcynski, M (2003) 'Communities of coping: emotional labour in service work' in *Organisation* Vol 10(1): 55–79. doi:10.1177/1350508403010001479.

Mason, W (2015) 'Austerity youth policy: exploring the distinctions between youth work in principle and youth work in practice' in *Youth and Policy* Vol 144: 55–74.

Mawby, R and Worrall, A (2013) *Doing Probation Work: Identity in a Criminal Justice Occupation* Abingdon: Routledge.

Mikolajczek, M, Menil, C and Luminet, O (2007) 'Explaining the protective effect of trait emotional intelligence regarding occupational stress: exploration of emotional labour processes' in *Journal of Research in Personality* Vol 41: 1107–1117. doi:10.1016/j.jrp.2007.01.003.

Murphy, C and Ord, J (2013) 'Youth work, self-disclosure and professionalism' in *Ethics & Social Welfare* Vol 7(4): 326–341. doi:10.1080/17496535.2012.760639.

Nicholls, D (2012) *For Youth Workers and Youth Work: Speaking Out for a Better Future* Bristol: Policy Press.

Ord, J (2009) 'Thinking the unthinkable: youth work without voluntary participation?' in *Youth & Policy* Vol 103: 39–48.

Robb, M, Featherstone, B, Ruxton, S and Ward, M (2015) *Beyond Male Role Models: Gender Identities and Work with Young Men* Milton Keynes: OUP.

Robinson, G, Burke, L and Millings, M (2016) 'Criminal justice identities in transition: the case of devolved services in England and Wales' in *British Journal of Criminology* Vol 56(1): 161–178.

Souhami, A (2007) *Transforming Youth Justice: Occupational Identity and Cultural Change* Cullompton: Willan.

Chapter 12

Emotional labour, cooling the client out and lawyer face

Lisa Flower

Introduction

In this chapter, I show the emotional labour used by defence lawyers in Sweden in order to perform their role, a performance which is centred on conveying professionalism and accomplishing the legal principle of loyalty. It draws on material gathered from my doctoral research including interviews with 18 lawyers and ethnographic observations of over 50 criminal trials. I begin by presenting defence lawyers' emotion talk – how they talk about emotions – along with which emotions are presented as in need of management and the strategies used to accomplish this.

As the Swedish courtroom is a relatively informal place – devoid of ceremonial robes and gowns – there are interactional demands placed on defence lawyers to perform professionalism. This chapter will therefore move on to show the ways in which defence lawyers sustain professional lawyer face in a context where sacred props are absent.

The unique role of the defence lawyer in a Swedish criminal trial also means that they are not only expected to manage their own performance, but also that of the defendant – their client. This is particularly demanding as defence lawyers have direct contact with their clients even in the courtroom, in contrast to countries where an intermediary buffer takes this role, such as a solicitor in England or a paralegal in the United States. Additionally, as defendants may be uninitiated into the ritual of a criminal trial, the defence lawyer must manage any emotional and interactional disruptions that may occur. This chapter will finish with an exploration of how this is accomplished pre-emptively on the backstage, and during the frontstage performance of the trial.

Methodology

As already mentioned, this chapter draws on material gathered for a doctoral research project which explored the emotions of defence lawyers and the interactional strategies they use to defend their clients in Swedish criminal trials. I collected ethnographic observations over a period of four years, beginning in late 2013 at four district courts. The trials I observed were randomly chosen, although I endeavoured to include a range of crimes from petty theft to murder. My subsequent analysis shows that the same performances and strategies are used in all of these trials.

In addition to these observations, I interviewed 18 lawyers – 8 women and 10 men – from 14 different law firms. The level of experience ranged from 1.5 to over 40 years working as lawyers. The interviews were conducted in Swedish and then transcribed verbatim and all respondents have been given a pseudonym. As the interviews and fieldwork were conducted concurrently, it enabled me to pose questions to my respondents regarding gestures, interactions and exchanges that I had observed. I thus used an 'analytical abduction' (Atkinson, 2014) approach – returning to the field to gather more data in order to test my emotion sociological and interactionist interpretation of the material and drawing out themes which will be presented in the following sections.

The emotions behind loyalty

Defence lawyers comprise a professional group that may face moral suspicion, distressed clients, unforeseeable situations, disturbing evidence and emotional plaintiffs, all of which should be managed in a proper and appropriate manner, suitable to an overarching framework which outlines appropriate emotions – the emotional regime of law (Flower, 2018). This regime partly ensures that the execution of law is protected from emotional influence by rationalising and subduing emotions and partly assists the smooth flow of justice by providing the rules of interaction (cf. Bandes, 1999, Maroney, 2011).

Defence lawyers' emotion talk separates professional emotions from those personal emotions which are deemed inappropriate for their legal role. Unprofessional emotions are thus presented as those which deviate from the emotional regime of law. Defence lawyers present themselves as having a 'circuit breaker' in their heads as Andrew, a defence lawyer I interviewed, described it. Similarly, defence lawyer Daniel talked about being able to 'switch off' his emotions whilst Perry – another defence lawyer I interviewed – 'smothered' his when he goes to work. As I explore in more detail in the next section, the emotion talk of defence lawyers thus upholds the emotional regime which continues to silence the importance of emotions in legal professionals' performances and is learned in law school (Flower, 2014).

However, a closer analysis of defence lawyers' emotion talk shows that inappropriate everyday emotions such as disgust, irritation and sadness are not smothered. Rather, they are engaged with and transformed into appropriate professional emotions which, in turn, are presented as instrumental tools. Defence lawyers thus use emotion management strategies in order for inappropriate emotions to become appropriate. For instance, defence lawyers may be required to look at evidence such as graphic photos of child por-nography. Such images may provoke disgust – stemming from their moral reprehensibility (Nussbaum and Kahan, 1996). Many of the defence lawyers I interviewed talked about viewing such images 'clinically' akin to the way in which medical doctors talk about performing autopsies (cf. Smith and Klein-man, 1989). However, they simultaneously talked about how such images are 'not pleasant' and not anything they would want to look at, as defence lawyer Kate told me in an interview. They are therefore saying that they have emo-tionally engaged in the images in order to recognise that they are unpleasant and thus disgusting. My analysis shows that this disgust is then transformed into a professional tool – searching for evidential clues, for instance, classify-ing the colouring of bruises in order to search for evidence that can support the client's version of events. In this way the inappropriate emotion of disgust is transformed into professional curiosity; however, other emotions such as pride and sadness may need to be managed in a different way as demonstrated in the following section.

Which emotions are inappropriate?

It is the particular situation and the defence lawyers' role within that decides which emotions are in need of management and how. For instance, in many situations where we have successfully attained a goal, feelings of pride may arise. This may be the case for defence lawyers who have succeeded in mak-ing a witness seem uncertain during a cross-examination. Having accom-plished this tactical goal, the defence lawyer may inadvertently display their pride in the form of a smile; however, more overt displays are taboo – not once did I observe a triumphant fist-pump. In the court itself explicit displays of pride would be an inappropriate emotion to display, yet it would be per-mitted in the backstage of the law offices where performance rules are more relaxed and where successes (and indeed mistakes) can be re-lived and future performances prepared (Goffman, 1959).

Sadness may also be an emotion in need of management at certain times during a trial. For instance, if one's client denies charges of rape then, as the defence lawyer, it would be unfitting to start crying when the plaintiff de-scribes the attack. The inappropriateness of this emotion stems from the de-fence lawyer's professional role to loyally represent his or her client. Implicit to this is the representation of the client's version of events and therefore, in some cases, the client's innocence. In such instances, a defence lawyer's tears could risk conveying doubt in their own clients' version of events, and thus risk conveying disloyalty. In the section on 'American expectations meet stonefaced loyalty' I return to this idea, and reveal the strategy defence law-yers use in order to follow this display rule.

Interestingly, sadness is not always inappropriate for the defence lawyer to show. For instance, the final stage of a criminal trial in Sweden entails the presentation of the defendant's personal circumstances. Here any economic, mental and physical problems are presented to the court along with previous convictions and contacts with social services for example. It is during this stage of proceedings that the defendant's personal tragedies and hardships can be presented to the court and it is during this part of the trial, that the defence lawyer may seek to produce emotions in himself or herself such as a display of sympathy for the defendant's life situation in order to, in turn, evoke sympathy in the judiciary.

Anger is another emotion in need of management, either to be produced or reduced, depending on the situation. Defence lawyers' emotion talk presents anger as an inappropriate emotion, something to be handled with care or avoided (cf. Lerner et al., 1998, Lerner and Tiedens, 2006, Litvak et al., 2010, Feigenson, 2016). Angry defence lawyers are perceived as risking being viewed by the court as acting on their personal feelings – their everyday emotions – or worse still, the emotions of the client – as though you were the client's 'twin' as Peter, a criminal defence lawyer told me. In showing anger one risks one's performance as being perceived as over-involved, as losing self-control and thus unprofessional (Goffman, 1957). Instead, defence lawyers' emotion talk presents themselves as becoming indignant, annoyed or worked-up in court – not angry. Indignation and annoyance are consequently talked about as acceptable forms of anger, sparked by a rule violation and the ensuing injustice – for example, if a prosecutor is perceived to be non-objective or a witness is suspected of perjury – but, importantly, without the defence lawyer being personally affronted (cf. Flam, 1990, s. 232). In short, good lawyers don't get angry, they get annoyed.

Displays of anger, or indeed, annoyance, should be subtle (see also Bergman Blix and Wettergren, 2018). In my interviews with defence lawyers, a clear contrast to the 'Rambo litigators' (Pierce, 1995) as depicted in the U.S. courtroom became apparent. Such Rambo, extravagant displays of aggression and hardness were discussed by the lawyers I interviewed as inappropriate in many Swedish courtrooms. For instance, Lo, a defence lawyer said:

> You don't have anything to gain from being cocky and unpleasant towards a witness – even if it's the prosecution's witness – you don't gain anything so it's better to try and create as good a relationship as possible, like a straight and honest communication.
>
> (Lo)

Kate also told me that she thinks that lawyers 'are often considerate. Then there are those who are very feisty and call everything into question and speak quickly and loudly and forced', but she is not one of those, she was quick to note. Andrew, another of the defence lawyers I interviewed, told me:

> There was a colleague – everyone is your colleague – a colleague in Stockholm who went a bit too far in his interrogation of a rape victim

and there are undoubtedly more who have done this, where you try and make the plaintiff look loose (…) I go quite far in my cross-examination in order to show whatever it is that I want to show (…) but I would never go over the line where you can say that I have been unpleasant and like, disgusting – yes but you were wearing a thong so that speaks for itself – because I know there are lawyers who do that. No. Forget it.

(Andrew)

Here we see Kate and then Andrew doing two things – distancing himself from Rambo lawyers who have a hard style of interrogating plaintiffs and witnesses, particularly in rape cases. We also see that Andrew is distancing himself from a colleague in Stockholm – the capital city of Sweden. None of the lawyers I interviewed work in Stockholm and very few of them had actually seen Stockholm lawyers in action; however, the majority of respondents recounted stories of Stockholm lawyers as Rambo litigators. This intrigued me and so I went to Stockholm to observe these aggressive performances which, I soon discovered, were no more Rambo-like than almost all the other performances I had observed. An explanation from this is that the lawyers I interviewed were doing 'boundary work' (Gieryn, 1983) by socially constructing their performance as distinct from characteristics that they deemed inappropriate: Stockholm lawyers are Rambo lawyers; we are not.

My ethnographic observations of criminal trials supported this shared understanding as I observed that overt and strong displays of anger led to emotion rule reminders from the judge or opposing counsel – either implicitly in the form of a frown or a headshake, or an explicit, spoken reminder (Hochschild, 1983, Flower, 2018). It should however be noted that these deviations were few and far between, such is the strength of the emotional regime of law.

Anger should instead be shown in a softer, less threatening manner more akin to the Disney cartoon character Bambi rather than the hard, aggressive Rambo – a film character known for his aggression, strength and determination. However, I argue that Rambo is hiding beneath the Bambi displays in Swedish criminal courts. I therefore present this performance as 'Rambo-Bambi'; defence lawyers' emotional displays are adjusted to the emotional regime and the defence lawyer's position within. Anger can therefore be shown by raised eyebrows, a shake of the head or a quiet exclamation such as 'what!?' For instance, Daniel told me that rather than treating a plaintiff aggressively, he prefers a calmer approach:

There are those who ask questions like this [speaks louder and more abruptly] "don't sit there and lie!" and like, use a more aggressive tone but I believe that you can get the exact same answer, exactly the same reaction even though you don't provoke [the plaintiff].

(Daniel)

Daniel also told me that he thinks that he can show that someone is lying without being 'hard' as he described in the excerpt above. Daniel is thus saying that he hides his Rambo approach – which has the goal of showing that someone is lying – behind a softer, non-provocative, Bambi façade.

Rambo-Bambi is consequently a professional expectation which risks clashing with the social 'Rambo' expectation of clients as I explore in more detail below.

Lawyer face

Defence lawyers' performance on the 'personal front' (Goffman, 1959) encompasses not only their emotions, but also includes *sounding* the part – for instance, not raising one's voice – and *looking* the part using clothing, gestures and props in order to convey the appropriate impression in a context devoid of distinct ceremonial equipment. As already noted at the start of this chapter, legal professionals in Sweden do not wear gowns or wigs – clothing which immediately symbolises the gravity of a criminal trial (Rock, 1993). Nevertheless, clothing is seen as an important aspect in making a good impression by defence lawyers in Sweden and is used in order to convey respect for the court and for one's role within. Suits are the norm, for men and women, for prosecutors, lawyers and judges.[1] Suits are used to go into one's role – putting on one's suit means putting on one's legal professional role. Clothes can thus not only convey a trial's gravity they can also serve as a reminder for all those involved as to the roles and rules at play.

Other aspects of the personal front performance include being well-groomed and remaining alert throughout proceedings (although on occasion glimpses of boredom or tiredness can be seen, for instance when a cross-examination becomes drawn out). Props can also be used to convey professionalism, for instance, well-ordered paperwork is carried in a briefcase or similar in order to communicate that one is well-prepared.

All of this is done in order for the defence lawyer to uphold his or her 'lawyer face' which is the public image we claim for ourselves in certain situations in accordance with the norms and values of the group, setting or local culture (Goffman, 1967). Defence lawyers thus use different strategies to stay in role – to uphold lawyer-face thereby conveying professionalism and loyalty.

---

1 Although all legal professionals dress similarly, professional roles are easily distinguishable from the positioning in the courtroom: the judges (often three lay judges and one legally trained judge) along with the notary, sit at the front of the court behind one long table which is often slightly raised from the rest of the courtroom. The defence lawyer shares a table with the defendant on one side of the courtroom and on the opposite side the prosecutor, the injured party (strictly speaking it is the prosecutor who is the plaintiff as it is the prosecutor who presses charges, not the injured party), and counsel for the plaintiff (when relevant) all sit behind another table.

Upholding lawyer face also means following the rules of interaction, for instance, standing up means standing out – it is a deviation from the expected way of presenting oneself and is talked about as a way of inappropriately drawing attention to one's performance. Thus, although there is no explicit rule that defence lawyers may not stand up, for instance, when holding their closing argument, there is an unwritten rule that doing so is strange. For example, Perry told me about a colleague who was branded as deviant for doing so, whilst Daniel said that if he stood up during a trial his colleagues would think 'What is he doing?!'

Defence lawyers' courtroom performances thus uphold lawyer face by displaying emotions subtly and courteously and by conveying a loyal and professional impression. This is made more complex due to the criminal trial being a scene of predictable unpredictability. The defence lawyer can never know with certainty what will happen next: an expert witness may change his or her testimony, the plaintiff may come with new details or one's own client may react angrily to evidence presented.

American expectations meet stonefaced lawyers

Many of the defence lawyers I interviewed talked about their clients having American expectations, hinting at the role of the media in forming understandings of the legal world. Although Sweden has seen a boom in Nordic Noir over the past decade with fictional crime TV shows such as *The Bridge* drawing massive viewing audiences, the focus in such shows tends to be on police work, rather than on legal proceedings. Instead, American TV shows such as *Perry Mason* and, more recently, *Suits* may play a part in forming the courtroom expectations of defendants. Expectations of a trial can thus be associated with medialised depictions (see also Adelswärd, 1989, Greenfield and Osborn, 1995, Machura and Ulbrich, 2001, Thelin, 2001, Fielding, 2006). Connected to this, the general public may receive inaccurate descriptions of trials via the media, and such mediated descriptions may be misleading, biased or sensationalised (cf. Heider, 1958).

This clash between clients' expectations and the reality of the Swedish defence lawyer finds its roots in dissonant expectations regarding 'display rules' (Hochschild, 2003). The client is expecting a performance that lies outside the permitted intensity and form of emotional expressions available to the defence lawyer. George talked about the risks associated with attempting to please the client's wishes by using a more Rambo-like approach:

> No-one is going to reward you for a good effort if it doesn't work in this context. It's like coming second in a race. It's a good effort but you didn't get more than second place. And it's the same thing – a good effort but you didn't go all the way and if you haven't reached all the way, when it comes to this – then the effect can be the complete opposite. So, you have to be careful.
>
> (George)

Defence lawyers therefore engage in expectation management – preparing the client for the coming trial. A central aspect of this entails explaining the underlying meaning of doing nothing. With this I am referring to one of the tools in the defence lawyer's professional toolbox, namely 'stoneface'. Stoneface is an impression management strategy used in an attempt to convey certain information about the situation at hand and their role within it using body language and facial expressions (Goffman, 1959). Stoneface looks exactly as it sounds – the defence lawyer sits stony-faced, with immobile facial features and body. This is also the strategy that is used when defence lawyers wish to hide inappropriate sadness or pride as I introduced previously. We see an example of this in the following extract from my fieldnotes from a criminal trial for assault. We join proceedings as the plaintiff is describing an occasion when the defendant attacked her, choking her so that she could not breathe:

> The plaintiff states that the defendant cried afterwards and said 'what have I done?!' The defence lawyer sits facing her, looking straight at her. The plaintiff goes on to talk about another instance when the defendant choked her. The plaintiff says, 'I couldn't breathe, I panicked'. The defence lawyer sits very still, not making any notes but not looking up either.
>
> (Fieldnote)

For those uninitiated in the ritual of the criminal trial, it appears as though the defence lawyer is doing nothing in the above fieldnote. There is no visible reaction but rather a retraction of otherwise expected responses – such as eye contact or displays of sympathy. However, this reductive performance is simultaneously the production of something else. The defence lawyer is actively pulling attention away from facts presented by the plaintiff in the courtroom, a strategy I have named 'factwork' (cf. Potter, 1996, pp. 107, 121) in an attempt to undermine the evidence presented. Stoneface can thus be used to build up or undermine facts. It is a strategy I observed in trials – ranging from petty crimes to murder –during similar situations, when evidence that is damaging to the defence has been presented, as in the above example. It is a strategy that is talked about by all of the defence lawyers I interviewed as being a vital trick of the trade. It is simultaneously also a way of conveying loyalty and accomplishing the defence team: the defence lawyer is communicating that he or she supports the client and the client's version of events by not visibly responding. Emotional labour is thus used in order to produce the appropriate outer countenance (Hochschild, 1983).

Stoneface can also be used when something unexpected has happened in order to convey an impression of control, composure and professionalism. For instance, it can be used to hide surprise or irritation if one's client says something damaging; again this is a way of drawing attention away from damaging information; nothing to see here (Emerson, 1970).

Accomplishing stoneface can thus be used both as a form of face work to uphold team face and lawyer face. However, if the client does not know the underlying meanings being conveyed, doing nothing risks being taken to be just that. We see this in the following fieldnote which begins with a policeman testifying as to what happened when the defendant was detained:

> The prosecutor looks at the policeman whilst he testifies, as does everyone else in the room – the judges, the prosecutor, the plaintiff, the counsel for the injured party, the defendant and those sitting in the gallery including myself. It is only the defence lawyer who does not watch him. When the policeman talks about chasing the defendant, the defence lawyer leans forwards, hand on chin with thumb on his cheek, elbow on desk, underlining some of the papers on the desk in front of him, eyes down, facial expression neutral. After about five minutes he has still not looked up from his papers, not even when the policeman describes drawing his service weapon when the defendant resisted arrest. The policeman goes on to say that he deemed the situation to be very dangerous as he was aware that the suspect had a weapon and had inflicted a serious injury on the plaintiff. Still the defence lawyer does not look up. He stays in the same position – hand on chin, fingers on cheek, leaning forwards, checking in his papers.
>
> The first time the defence lawyer looks up is about eight minutes into the policeman's testimony when he recounts what the defendant said upon his arrest (when they finally caught up with him).
>
> When the policeman has finished testifying, there is a great deal of whispering between the defence lawyer and his client. The defence lawyer doesn't answer to start with, it's more that the client has said something to which he doesn't really respond. He leans over towards the client, but doesn't reply and continues flicking through his paperwork. The client is trying to engage the defence lawyer in interaction but the lawyer is not interested.
>
> (Fieldnote)

We see the defence lawyer using stoneface in the first part of this extract in order to reduce the impact of the policeman's testimony, then towards the end we see that there is whispering in the defence team. This can reasonably be assumed to be the client wanting the defence lawyer to ask more questions of the policeman, something that all of the defence lawyers I spoke to say that their clients say during trials – they want the plaintiff or witness to be questioned more harshly or more comprehensively that is, they want a Rambo lawyer, not the Rambo-Bambi we see above.

Expectation management is thus an important aspect of the defence lawyer's role as many of the defence lawyers I interviewed perceived defendants as being unsure not only of what their role as defendant in a trial entails, but also, what their defence lawyer will actually do. Defence lawyers should therefore prepare the client in the backstage of the law offices or waiting room of the court to ensure that clients have reasonable expectations regarding the defence lawyer's performance. This expectation management also involves describing what the various legal professionals in the courtroom will do and, importantly, how they will do it. It is a practice of cooling the client out – preparing him or her for the imminent face-threat that is a criminal trial (Goffman, 1959).

Cooling the client out can be pre-emptively done by using expectation management. This is aimed at reducing the risk of the client 'flooding out' (Goffman, 1961, pp. 50–57) during proceedings which may have adverse consequences – for instance, revealing something regarding the client's character that the defence team would have preferred to stay hidden. It is therefore a way of managing future, inappropriate or unwanted emotions. We see a client 'flooding out' in the following extract:

> The defendant reacts to something that has been read out from one of the reports. He lashes out with his hand and raises his voice: "It wasn't like that!" he says loudly. His lawyer immediately reacts with his whole body, turning towards his client and saying "shh, shh, shh", holding his hand in front of his client's face. The client quietens down and the defence lawyer leans in so that they can talk. The lawyer then says to the judge that he wants to point out that his client was reacting to an error in the translation and that this is what his client is reacting to.
>
> (Fieldnote)

In this extract we can see the frontstage direction of the client with the defence lawyer attempting to calm him down. The close proximity makes it is easier for the defence lawyer – the director – to immediately manage their client's and thus the defence team performance if the client is on the verge of flooding out. In Sweden, the defence lawyer and client sit next to each other behind a table which shields any interaction between defence lawyer and client from the eyes of the judges and prosecutor. This means that defence lawyers can place a calming hand on their client's leg if the client's temper starts to flare, a mollification of particular importance in situations where such an outbreak is the tactical goal of the prosecutor.[2] After all, a criminal trial is, in part, a chess game of emotions.

---

2 Whilst the emotion rules for lay participants may differ to those for legal professionals, there are still zones within which lay participants are expected to stay – too much emotion may lead to a break in proceedings and thus a disruption in the flow of the trial.

Closing argument

This chapter extends our knowledge of emotional labour by highlighting the clash of emotional expectations between the legal profession and society which I present in the context of different display rules. Thus an important implication for policy is to ensure that the various performances in a criminal trial are explained to lay participants. All too often the focus is on practical information; however, interactional and emotional information is also necessary regarding who will do what, how and why.

There are also implications for legal education as the emotional labour of defence lawyers is often not discussed, nor strategies for managing inappropriate emotions; hence, law students and newly qualified legal professionals are expected to learn on the job (Flower, 2014). This can lead to increased levels of uncertainty regarding their role which may, in turn, have negative consequences, not least considering the high standards that tend to be held in the legal profession. Relatedly, spaces should be created where legal professionals and law students can receive support when their emotional labour fails and they display inappropriate emotions.

References

Adelswärd, V. 1989. Defendents' interpretations of encouragements in court: The construction of meaning in an institutionalized context. *Journal of Pragmatics*, 13, 741–749.

Atkinson, P. 2014. *For Ethnography*, London, SAGE Publications Ltd.

Bandes, S. (ed.) 1999. *The Passions of Law*, New York, New York University Press.

Bergman Blix, S. & Wettergren, Å. 2018. *Professional Emotions in Court*, Abingdon, Routledge.

Emerson, J. 1970. Nothing unusual is happening. *In*: Shibutani, T. (ed.) *Human Nature and Collective Behavior: Papers in Honor of Herbert Blumer*, Englewood Cliffs, NJ, Prentice-Hall, Inc., 208–223

Feigenson, N. R. 2016. Jurors' emotions and judgements of legal responsibility and blame: What does the experimental research tell us? *Emotion Review*, 8, 26–31.

Fielding, N. 2006. *Courting Violence: Offences Against the Person Cases in Court*, Oxford Scholarship Online, Oxford, Oxford University Press.

Flam, H. 1990. Emotional 'man': II. Corporate actors as emotion-motivated emotion managers. *International Sociology*, 5, 225–234.

Flower, L. 2014. The (un)emotional law student. *International Journal of Work Organisation and Emotion*, 6, 295–309.

Flower, L. 2018. *Loyalty Work: Emotional Interactions of Defence Lawyers in Swedish Courtrooms*, Doctorate, Lund, Lund University.

Gieryn, T. F. 1983. Boundary-work and the demarcation of science from non-science: Strains and interests in professional ideologies of scientists. *American Sociological Review*, 48, 781–795.

Goffman, E. 1957. Alienation from interaction. *Human Relations*, 10, 47–60.

Goffman, E. 1959. *The Presentation of Self in Everyday Life*, Harmondsworth, Penguin Books Ltd.

Goffman, E. 1961. *Asylums: Essays on the Social Situation of Mental Patients and Other Inmates*, Harmondsworth, Penguin.

Goffman, E. 1967. *Interaction Ritual: Essays on Face-to-Face Behavior*, New York, Anchor Books.

Greenfield, S. & Osborn, G. 1995. Where cultures collide: The characterization of law and lawyers in film. *International Journal of the Sociology of Law*, 23, 107–130.

Heider, F. 1958. *The Psychology of Interpersonal Relations*, New York, Wiley.

Hochschild, A. R. 1983. *The Managed Heart: The Commercialization of Human Feeling*, Berkeley, University of California Press.

Hochschild, A. R. 2003. *The Managed Heart - Commercialization of Human Feelings*, Los Angeles, University of California Press.

Lerner, J. S., Goldberg, J. H. & Tetlock, P. E. 1998. Sober second thought: The effects of accountability, anger, and authoritarianism on attributions of responsibility. *Personality and Social Psychology Bulletin*, 24, 563–574.

Lerner, J. S. & Tiedens, L. Z. 2006. Portrait of the angry decision maker: How appraisal tendencies shape anger's influence on cognition. *Journal of Behavioral Decision Making*, 19, 115–137.

Litvak, P. M., Lerner, J. S., Tiedens, L. Z. & Shonk, K. 2010. Fuel in the fire: How anger impacts judgement and decision-making. *In*: Potegal, M., Stemmler, G. & Spielburger, C. (eds.) *International Handbook of Anger: Constituent and Concomitant Biological, Psychological, and Social Processes*, New York, Springer, 287–310.

Machura, S. & Ulbrich, S. 2001. Law in film: Globalizing the hollywood courtroom drama. *Journal of Law and Society*, 28, 117–132.

Maroney, T. A. 2011. The persistent cultural script of judicial dispassion. *California Law Review*, 99, 629–681.

Nussbaum, M. C. & Kahan, D. M. 1996. Two conceptions of emotion in criminal law. *Columbia Law Review*, 96, 269–374.

Pierce, J. L. 1995. *Gender Trials*, Berkeley, University of California Press.

Potter, J. 1996. *Representing Reality: Discourse, Rhetoric and Social Construction*, London, SAGE Publications Ltd.

Rock, P. 1993. *The Social World of an English Crown Court*, Oxford, Oxford University Press.

Smith, A. C. & Kleinman, S. 1989. Managing emotions in medical school: Student's contacts with the living and the dead. *Social Psychological Quarterly*, 52, 56–69.

Thelin, K. 2001. *Sverige som rättsstat*, Stockholm, AB Timbro.

Chapter 13

Hidden in plain sight

Contrasting emotional labor and burnout in civilian and sworn law enforcement employees

Ian T. Adams and Sharon H. Mastracci

Introduction

Beginning in the late 1960s and continuing into the 1970s, police agencies in the United States were called upon to increase their numbers of civilians. The ensuing civilianization of US law enforcement has been pronounced, though little academic energy has been devoted to understanding how those employees shape, and are shaped by, the police agencies that employ them. In the modern era, civilians represent up to 46% of law enforcement employees (Reaves, 2011). Concerningly, despite extensive research on the emotional burnout of sworn officers, only one study has compared the civilian employee experience (McCarty & Skogan, 2013).

This chapter reports the results of a dual test on the subscales of burnout – emotional exhaustion and depersonalization – for civilian and sworn employees in a large US correctional agency. The lone previous study to compare burnout in civilian and sworn law enforcement employees (McCarty & Skogan, 2013) found the levels and predictors of burnout were invariant across the two groups. The chapter takes that finding as a departure point, extending both its scope and findings by including burnout via depersonalization, with essential differences noted across employee type. The chapter concludes with suggestions for law enforcement managers tasked with supervising both civilian and sworn employees, with a focus on understanding the differing burnout paths for each.

Literature review

Burnout is a psychological construct first labeled by Bradley (1969), but specific measurement of the phenomenon and construction of a gold-standard scale was led by Christina Maslach and colleagues (Maslach & Jackson, 1981, 1982; Maslach et al., 1986). Early burnout research centered on public service workers, including police officers (Burke & Deszca, 1986), and is defined as "a syndrome of emotional exhaustion and cynicism that frequently occurs among individuals who do 'people-work' of some kind" (Maslach &

Jackson, 1981, p. 99). Burnout does not occur in a vacuum, and researchers have established the role of emotional labor in driving burnout, particularly in people-service professions (Guy et al., 2008; Jeung et al., 2018). The Maslach Burnout Inventory (MBI) identified three subcomponents of burnout: emotional exhaustion, depersonalization, and personal accomplishment.

Meta-analysis of burnout research finds that emotional exhaustion and depersonalization are the consistent heart of burnout (Lee & Ashforth, 1996). Burnout is "one of the most frequently-studied phenomena" in organisational research (Swider & Zimmerman, 2010, p. 487), and ample research links burnout to adverse organisational, professional, emotional, and physical health outcomes (Jeung et al., 2018). Police-focused studies confirm that law enforcement employees experience some of the highest levels of burnout (Burke & Deszca, 1986; Kop et al., 1999; Schaible & Six, 2016; Kwak et al., 2018; Adams & Mastracci, 2019). However, these studies all focus on sworn officers in law enforcement. Despite comprising upwards of half of the total employees in law enforcement (Reaves, 2011), only one study examines civilian workers specifically.

McCarty and Skogan (2013) tackle the question of what precipitates burnout in sworn and civilian employees. The authors find the two groups experience the phenomenon identically, as "the burnout process is a universal one, driven by virtually the same factors among both civilian and sworn officers" (McCarty & Skogan, 2013, p. 66). However, the authors operationalize 'burnout' as emotional exhaustion only. This presents an incomplete picture of how burnout may be experienced differently in two different job roles – one male-dominated, and the other female-dominated – given the meta-analytic finding (Purvanova & Muros, 2010) that women tend to experience higher rates of emotional exhaustion, while men report higher levels of depersonalization.

Depersonalization is the "cynicism" initially identified and defined by Maslach and Jackson (1981, p. 99). Depersonalization is a phenomenon wherein the individual becomes more callous, leading them to see colleagues and clients as problems, numbers, and otherwise less than fully human. Moreover, depersonalization and emotional exhaustion can have different outcomes, particularly in law enforcement. For example, Ellrich (2016) reports that in her study of German officers ($n = 1,742$), higher levels of depersonalization were linked to higher rates of being victimized while working. Relatedly, Kop and colleagues (1999) link depersonalization to higher rates of Dutch police using force. Taken together with the close links between emotional labor, burnout, and workplace violence (Jeung et al., 2018), depersonalization plays an important, and perhaps gender-differentiated, role in overall burnout. In this chapter, we test emotional exhaustion and depersonalization across both civilian and sworn employees to investigate crucial theoretical and empirical differences in the components of burnout.

We situate emotional labor correlates as the primary independent variables of interest. Emotional labor is the effort to comply with display rules, which are often unwritten codes of conduct instructing employees on how to comport their physical and emotional responses. First brought to scholarly attention in 1983's *The Managed Heart* (Hochschild, 2012), emotional labor was theorized to cause emotional harm to the practitioner and alienate the worker (Mastracci & Adams, 2018b) from her own emotions (Grandey & Melloy, 2017). Scholars have since expanded the scope of emotional labor research to include public service workers (Guy et al., 2008), and now recognize that there are both benefits and harms to the practice of emotional labor.

Suppression display rules are used to control often negatively construed emotional responses, such as anger, disgust, pity, and inappropriate humor. On the other hand, pretending display rules instruct the employee on how to express an unfelt emotion, such as smiling when unhappy, or projecting calm when upset. Surface acting is the employee's attempt to comply with display rules through the management of their emotive state, facial expression, and demeanor. All three correlates – suppression display rules, pretending display rules, and the resulting surface acting – are linked to burnout. This path forms part of the well-established framework for emotional labor research (see Grandey & Melloy, 2017, fig. 1, p. 409).

In addition, we consider the role of perceived organizational support (POS), a perception by employees that the employer values their contributions and cares about their well-being (Eisenberger et al., 1986). The POS literature is robust, and its measurement scale is well-validated by meta-analyses (Rhoades & Eisenberger, 2002; Riggle et al., 2009). In the law enforcement context, a marked distrust exists between front-line personnel and management (Crank, 2014), and studies have verified the negative relationship between POS and burnout (Jawahar et al., 2007; Adams & Mastracci, 2019). We posit three linked hypotheses:

Hypothesis One: Civilian and sworn employees experience invariant levels of emotional exhaustion and depersonalization.
Hypothesis Two: Pretending display rules, suppression display rules, and surface acting are positively related, and POS is negatively related, to depersonalization and emotional exhaustion in sworn employees.
Hypothesis Three: Pretending display rules, suppression display rules, and surface acting are positively related, and POS is negatively related, to depersonalization and emotional exhaustion in civilian employees.

Methods

Procedure

As part of a more extensive study of law enforcement employee wellness, the participating agency was contacted in late Spring 2018. Following administrative approval, we worked with an agency representative to develop supplemental questions specific to the agency's interests. The survey was distributed simultaneously to all employees of the agency. After removing non-valid emails, a total of 2,178 anonymous URL links were emailed to employees in July 2018 and remained open for 30 days. A total of 945 valid responses were received, resulting in a 43.48% response rate. Of that, 934 employees (703 sworn, 231 civilian) were retained in the final sample. Due to item non–response, regression outputs report a slightly smaller sample size.

Respondents

The agency is a sizeable correctional organisation in the Western United States. It is a large, modern agency, and employees work across a range of environments to supervise and care for many thousands of inmates, parolees, and probationers. Sworn employees include correctional officers who work behind prison walls and parole agents with full law enforcement authority whose work is mostly indistinguishable from investigators in more traditional policing agencies. Civilian employees tasked with providing medical, dental, and psychiatric services work alongside locksmiths, furniture construction managers, and drug rehabilitation specialists. To the degree that a correctional facility is a city, civilian employees work alongside sworn officers to manage the city and its residents. Though their work activities and stressors may appear separate, civilian and sworn employees generally inhabit the same environment.

Because we investigate differences between civilian and sworn employees, it is useful to understand how the two groups differ along demographic lines. Descriptive statistics are found in Table 3.1. The starkest difference is sex, with women comprising 77.4% of the civilian group, while fully 85.1% of sworn employees are men. The civilian and sworn 'sides of the house' are sex-linked, with far more women on the civilian side and far more men with sworn status.

Measures

Emotional labor research has established the "robust sequence from surface acting to burnout" (Allen et al., 2014, p. 21), and the inclusion of surface acting in burnout studies is particularly salient for US-based samples. This robust sequence may be subject to measurement variance when used across cultural boundaries (Mastracci & Adams, 2018a; Yang et al., 2018), but is generally accepted within Western and Individualistic cultures (Minkov & Hofstede, 2011).

Seven-point Likert-type scales are used to construct latent independent variables of pretending ($\alpha = 0.6623$) and suppression ($\alpha = 0.8864$) display rules, surface acting ($\alpha = 0.7870$), and POS ($\alpha = 0.9576$). With one exception, Cronbach's alpha scores for all constructs are well above the accepted cutoff of 0.70 (Cronbach, 1951; Nunnally & Bernstein, 1967). In the case of

Table 13.1 Descriptive Statistics

Variable	Civilian Employees					Sworn Employees				
	N	Mean	Std. Dev.	Min	Max	N	Mean	Std. Dev.	Min	Max
Emotional exhaustion	175	3.84	1.47	1	7	566	4.49	1.43	1	7
Depersonalization	172	4.34	1.55	1	7	563	5.30	1.21	1	7
Pretend display rules	195	5.28	0.92	1	7	614	5.57	0.84	2	7
Surface acting	175	4.21	1.36	1	7	570	4.57	1.33	1	7
Suppress display rules	184	4.92	1.22	1	7	593	5.30	1.12	1	7
Perceived organisational support	170	3.93	1.67	1	7	561	3.50	1.53	1	7
Sleep 7+ hours/ night	166	0.40	0.49	0	1	559	0.30	0.46	0	1
College graduate	165	0.56	0.50	0	1	557	0.52	0.50	0	1
Female	159	0.77	0.42	0	1	538	0.15	0.36	0	1
White	231	0.62	0.48	0	1	703	0.72	0.45	0	1
Years in profession	200	13.93	9.89	0	39	667	13.68	8.60	0	40

Bolded variables indicate a group-level mean difference, 95% confidence level.

pretending display rules, it is only slightly below 0.70. Given the vulnerability of constructs with only three or four items (Santos, 1999) and that the construct is relied upon throughout emotional labor research, it is retained for modeling.

Control Variables: In addition to the independent variables defined above, we model several demographic controls, including years of service and respondent race/ethnicity, sex, and education level. Mastracci, Guy, and Newman (2012) find that both new and tenured public employees engage in emotional labor, and suggest that as employees gain consistent experience engaging in emotional labor, they increase capacity. However, other research finds that length of service predicts higher levels of burnout and lower levels of POS (Adams & Mastracci, 2019). Meta-analysis of age and years-of-experience studies (Brewer & Shapard, 2004) found no conclusive effects across all professions, though differences in occupations are likely confounders of overall effects. Given the majority of police-specific burnout literature appears to view years-of-service as an essential predictor of burnout, it is included as a control variable, operationalized as a continuous measure of a respondent's total years in law enforcement.

Sleep deprivation and fatigue are recent concerns in burnout research. Police and other first responders are long known to suffer from sleep disorders at higher rates than other professions. Sleep deprivation is related to increased burnout and work error, poorer physical health, and decreased job satisfaction in police-specific studies (Rajaratnam et al., 2011; Basinska & Wiciak, 2012). We operationalize sleep with a dichotomous variable where '1' represents respondents' self-reports that they usually get at least seven hours of sleep during their typical sleep cycle.

Sex differences in emotional labor are inconsistent across studies, though the literature is clear that both sexes engage in emotional labor. Particularly salient for this study is the meta-analysis by Purvanova and Muros (2010), which finds that women tend to experience more emotional exhaustion, while men tend to experience higher levels of depersonalization. This is relevant to our study of differences between a male-dominated group (sworn officers) and a group comprised mostly of women (civilian employees).

Table 13.2 Burnout in Corrections Agency by Employee Group

	(Sworn)	(Civilian)	(Sworn)	(Civilian)
	Emotional Exhaustion	Emotional Exhaustion	Depersonalization	Depersonalization
Control variables				
Years in service	0.004	−0.076	**0.132*****	0.066
	(0.00624)	(0.0104)	(0.00517)	(0.0115)
White	0.048	0.000	0.053	0.054
	(0.201)	(0.306)	(0.166)	(0.339)
Female	0.039	0.042	−0.056	0.067
	(0.151)	(0.246)	(0.125)	(0.272)
College	−0.008	0.080	**0.081***	0.053
education (any)	(0.108)	(0.211)	(0.0896)	(0.234)
Sleep7plus	**−0.106****	0.052	−0.060	0.128
	(0.119)	(0.207)	(0.0985)	(0.230)
Independent variables				
Pretend display	**0.124***	−0.042	**0.126****	0.048
rules	(0.0824)	(0.150)	(0.0684)	(0.167)
Surface acting	**0.190*****	**0.333*****	**0.155*****	**0.314*****
	(0.0506)	(0.0943)	(0.0419)	(0.105)
Suppression	**0.121***	0.189	**0.223*****	0.078
display rules	(0.0716)	(0.123)	(0.0594)	(0.136)
Perceived	**−0.254*****	**−0.302*****	**−0.199*****	**−0.309*****
organisational	(0.0379)	(0.0685)	(0.0315)	(0.0760)
support				
Observations	507	142	507	142
Adjusted R^2	0.280	0.365	0.305	0.313

Standardized beta coefficients; standard errors in parentheses; significant results in bold, at levels * $p < 0.05$, ** $p < 0.01$, *** $p < 0.001$.

Results

Table 13.2 reports the regression results with standardized coefficients, which allow for a comparison of the relative strength of association between each independent variable and the two burnout components. Results from regression analysis allow us to reject Hypotheses One and Three, while accepting Hypothesis Two. Overall, and building on the findings of McCarty and Skogan (2013), we find sworn and civilian employees experience differing levels of burnout and for different reasons. Important similarities and differences between the groups of civilians and sworn officers emerge. Even among correlates that are significant for both groups, differences in magnitude offer insights into how the two groups experience burnout differently.

T-tests of both emotional exhaustion and depersonalization reject Hypothesis One, which predicts sworn and civilian employees experience the same levels of both measures. This test replicates and extends McCarty and Skogan's (2013) original finding for the emotional exhaustion subscale. We find significant differences in emotional exhaustion for sworn ($\bar{x}$ = 4.49, σ = 1.43) and civilian ($\bar{x}$ = 3.84, σ = 1.47) employees; t (739) = −5.17, p = 0.000. We further find a significant difference in the depersonalization score for sworn ($\bar{x}$ = 5.30, σ = 1.21) and civilian ($\bar{x}$ = 4.34, σ = 1.55) employees; t (733) = −8.51, p = 0.000. Results partially contradict gendered expectations of burnout (Purvanova & Muros, 2010), with sworn employees reporting higher levels of both depersonalization and emotional exhaustion.

Independent Variables: Important magnitude differences emerge for emotional labor–related independent variables. The role of surface acting on burnout is consistent across groups and outcomes, with statistically significant effects in the civilian group noted for both emotional exhaustion (β = 0.333, p = 0.000) and depersonalization (β = 0.314, p = 0.001). Surface acting has a similar significant positive relationship to burnout within the officer group for both emotional exhaustion (β = 0.190, p = 0.000) and depersonalization (β = 0.155, p = 0.001). While surface acting has a significant effect on both subcategories of burnout in both groups, the standardized effect in the civilian group is nearly twice as large.

The role of POS in protecting against emotional exhaustion and depersonalization is well supported in previous research (Jawahar et al., 2007; Adams & Mastracci, 2019). In the models tested here, we find a significant negative relationship between POS and both emotional exhaustion and depersonalization. For sworn employees, POS has a significant negative relationship with emotional exhaustion (β = −0.254, p = 0.000) and depersonalization (β = −0.198, p = 0.000). The civilian employee group shows a similar significant, negative relationship for emotional exhaustion (β = −0.301, p = 0.000) and depersonalization (β = −0.308, p = 0.000). The effect size is more consistent across employee groups compared to surface acting.

While invariant effects were found for surface acting and POS, the models show differing effects on burnout subscales for other independent variables of interest. The effect of display rules varies by employee group but is consistent by outcome. For officers, pretending display rules show a significant, positive relationship to both emotional exhaustion ($\beta = 0.124$, $p = 0.011$) and depersonalization ($\beta = 0.126$, $p = 0.008$), but is not significant in either of the civilian models. Suppress display rules also show a significant, positive relationship for officers in both the emotional exhaustion ($\beta = 0.121$, $p = 0.033$) and depersonalization ($\beta = 0.223$, $p = 0.000$) models, but is not significant in either civilian model.

Control Variables: We find mixed support for the role of sleep deprivation in burnout. Sworn employees who report sleeping at least seven hours in a sleep cycle experience significantly less emotional exhaustion ($\beta = -0.106$, $p = 0.006$). However, for officer depersonalization, no significant effect was detected, nor was any significant effect found for civilian employees on either burnout component. Sleep correlates were included to control for effects established in a previous study of burnout in law enforcement officers (Rajaratnam et al., 2011), and our results confirm a differential effect between civilian and sworn employees, as well as between emotional exhaustion and depersonalization. The intersection of sleep and work outcomes is a promising site of inquiry, and further research is warranted to explore the effect of sleep deprivation more purposively.

An interesting result for education level also arises. Officers with post-high school education levels report a significantly higher level of depersonalization. Demographic characteristics of race and sex do not have a significant effect on either emotional exhaustion or depersonalization for either group.

Discussion and implications

This study investigated the impact of emotional labor and POS correlates on both emotional exhaustion and depersonalization, with a focus on testing for invariant effects across civilian and sworn employee groups. Our results show the two groups experience burnout at different levels and for different reasons. We both extend and conflict findings from the only other research study to center civilian and sworn employees in the burnout literature.

Surface acting is a significant and consistent contributor to both subcomponents of burnout for both sworn and civilian employees. However, the effect size is not invariant as it has nearly double the standardized coefficient for the civilian group. All other factors held constant, surface acting is the single largest contributor to overall burnout for civilian employees.

Generally, a greater proportion of burnout in civilian employees can be explained with relatively fewer predictors compared to sworn personnel. In both the emotional exhaustion (adjusted $R^2 = 0.365$) and depersonalization (adjusted $R^2 = 0.313$) models, civilian burnout is significantly explained by only surface acting and POS. The officer models are more complex, yet less explanatory overall, with emotional exhaustion (adjusted $R^2 = 0.280$) and depersonalization (adjusted $R^2 = 0.305$) consistently predicted by surface acting, POS, and both pretend and suppression display rules. Interesting control variable significance is noted, with the emotional exhaustion model for officers significantly predicted by sleep health while depersonalization is significantly related to both education level and years in service.

Conclusion, limitations, and future research

This study differs in important ways from the sole previous research to look directly at burnout among both civilian and sworn personnel (McCarty & Skogan, 2013). While similar outcome variables are investigated in both, our research is focused on the emotional labor antecedents of emotional exhaustion and depersonalization within a single large agency, whereas McCarty and Skogan are primarily interested in organisational level explanations for only emotional exhaustion, across 12 different agencies. In this way, the two studies complement one another in pursuit of better understanding burnout in law enforcement.

While the research presented here advances the empirical base, there are important limitations to consider and future research directions to pursue. Crucially, this study locates its sample and findings in the US context. While extending our results to other Western/Individualistic cultures is likely appropriate (Minkov & Hofstede, 2011; Mastracci, 2017), there is reason to doubt the appropriateness of cross-cultural extension of the full model (Allen et al., 2014), particularly in Collectivist cultures. Though some studies have found the model is robust to cultural contexts (Mastracci & Adams, 2018a), caution is warranted, as even in similar cultural contexts such as the US and the UK, meta-analysis suggests differences exist in the gendered aspects of burnout (Purvanova & Muros, 2010). There are active research programs in the area of cross-cultural measurement of emotional labor, which presuppose differences in how emotional labor manifests between cultural groups, and caution must be used before assuming measurement and outcome invariance.

The consistently strong role of POS in decreasing burnout has been noted in previous work (Adams & Mastracci, 2019) and confirmed here. Previous research has established perceived organisational support as a mediating correlate for a host of job stressors and predictors, and intriguing differences in the US versus UK contexts have been noted (Jawahar et al., 2007). Given the lack of research focused on civilians in law enforcement, this is a viable research direction for scholars interested in extending and replicating the findings here. Law enforcement managers would do well to emphasize and POS to support both their civilian and sworn employees. Managers should support the vital role of sleep hygiene in relieving overall burnout levels in sworn personnel. Civilian employees appear particularly susceptible to the adverse outcomes associated with surface acting, so managers should seek to recognize that emotional labor is how much of the job is done, and compensate that effort.

References

Adams, I. T., & Mastracci, S. H. (2019). Police body-worn cameras: Effects on officers' burnout and perceived organizational support. *Police Quarterly, 22*(1), 5–30.

Allen, J. A., Diefendorff, J. M., & Ma, Y. (2014). Differences in emotional labor across cultures: A comparison of Chinese and US service workers. *Journal of Business and Psychology, 29*(1), 21–35.

Basinska, B. A., & Wiciak, I. (2012). Fatigue and professional burnout in police officers and firefighters. *Internal Security, 4*(2), 267.

Bradley, H. B. (1969). Community-based treatment for young adult offenders. *Crime & Delinquency, 15*(3), 359–370.

Brewer, E. W., & Shapard, L. (2004). Employee burnout: A meta-analysis of the relationship between age or years of experience. *Human Resource Development Review, 3*(2), 102–123.

Burke, R., & Deszca, E. (1986). Correlates of psychological burnout phases among police officers. *Human Relations, 39*(6), 487–501.

Crank, J. P. (2014). *Understanding Police Culture.* Abingdon: Routledge.

Cronbach, L. J. (1951). Coefficient alpha and the internal structure of tests. *Psychometrika, 16*(3), 297–334.

Eisenberger, R., Huntington, R., Hutchison, S., & Sowa, D. (1986). Perceived organizational support. *Journal of Applied Psychology, 71*(3), 500.

Ellrich, K. (2016). Burnout and violent victimization in police officers: A dual process model. *Policing: An International Journal of Police Strategies & Management, 39*(4), 652–666.

Grandey, A. A., & Melloy, R. C. (2017). The State of the Heart: Emotional Labor as Emotion Regulation Reviewed and Revised. *Journal of Occupational Health Psychology, 22*(3), 407–422.

Guy, M., Newman, M. A., & Mastracci, S. H. (2008). *Emotional Labor: Putting the Service in Public Service.* Abingdon: Routledge.

Hochschild, A. R. (2012). *The Managed Heart: Commercialization of Human Feeling.* Berkeley: University of California Press.

Jawahar, I. M., Stone, T. H., & Kisamore, J. L. (2007). Role conflict and burnout: The direct and moderating effects of political skill and perceived organizational support on burnout dimensions. *International Journal of Stress Management, 14*(2), 142.

Jeung, D.-Y., Kim, C., & Chang, S.-J. (2018). Emotional labor and burnout: A review of the literature. *Yonsei Medical Journal, 59*(2), 187–193. doi:10.3349/ymj.2018.59.2.187.

Kop, N., Euwema, M., & Schaufeli, W. (1999). Burnout, job stress and violent behaviour among Dutch police officers. *Work & Stress, 13*(4), 326–340.

Kwak, H., McNeeley, S., & Kim, S.-H. (2018). Emotional labor, role characteristics, and police officer burnout in South Korea: The mediating effect of emotional dissonance. *Police Quarterly, 21*(2), 223–249.

Lee, R. T., & Ashforth, B. E. (1996). A meta-analytic examination of the correlates of the three dimensions of job burnout. *Journal of Applied Psychology, 81*(2), 123.

Maslach, C., & Jackson, S. E. (1981). The measurement of experienced burnout. *Journal of Organizational Behavior, 2*(2), 99–113.

Maslach, C., & Jackson, S. E. (1982). *Burnout: The Cost of Caring.* Englewood Cliffs, NJ, PrenticeHall.

Maslach, C., Jackson, S. E., Leiter, M. P., Schaufeli, W. B., & Schwab, R. L. (1986). *Maslach Burnout Inventory* (Vol. 21). Palo Alto, CA, Consulting Psychologists Press.

Mastracci, S. H. (2017). Beginning nurses' perceptions of ethical leadership in the shadow of mid staffs. *Public Integrity, 19*(3), 250–264.

Mastracci, S., & Adams, I. (2018a). Is emotional labor easier in collectivist or individualist cultures? An east–west comparison. *Public Personnel Management.* doi:10.1177/0091026018814569.

Mastracci, S. H., & Adams, I. T. (2018b). "That's what the money's for": Alienation and emotional labor in public service. *Administrative Theory & Praxis, 40*(4), 304–319. doi:10.1080/10841806.2018.1485449.

Mastracci, S. H., Guy, M. E., & Newman, M. A. (2012). *Emotional Labor and Crisis Response: Working on the Razor's Edge.* Abingdon: Routledge.

McCarty, W. P., & Skogan, W. G. (2013). Job-related burnout among civilian and sworn police personnel. *Police Quarterly, 16*(1), 66–84.

Minkov, M., & Hofstede, G. (2011). The evolution of Hofstede's doctrine. *Cross Cultural Management: An International Journal, 18*(1), 10–20.

Nunnally, J. C., & Bernstein, I. H. (1967). *Psychometric Theory* (Vol. 226). New York, McGraw-Hill.

Purvanova, R. K., & Muros, J. P. (2010). Gender differences in burnout: A meta-analysis. *Journal of Vocational Behavior, 77*(2), 168–185.

Rajaratnam, S. M., Barger, L. K., Lockley, S. W., Shea, S. A., Wang, W., Landrigan, C. P., O'brien, C. S., Qadri, S., Sullivan, J. P., & Cade, B. E. (2011). Sleep disorders, health, and safety in police officers. *JAMA, 306*(23), 2567–2578.

Reaves, B. A. (2011). *Census of State and Local Law Enforcement Agencies, 2008* (NCJ 233982; pp. 1–20). Bureau of Justice Statistics. www.bjs.gov/index.cfm?ty=pbdetail&iid=2216.

Rhoades, L., & Eisenberger, R. (2002). Perceived organizational support: A review of the literature. *Journal of Applied Psychology, 87*(4), 698.

Riggle, R. J., Edmondson, D. R., & Hansen, J. D. (2009). A meta-analysis of the relationship between perceived organizational support and job outcomes: 20 years of research. *Journal of Business Research, 62*(10), 1027–1030.

Santos, J. R. A. (1999). Cronbach's alpha: A tool for assessing the reliability of scales. *Journal of Extension, 37*(2), 1–5.

Schaible, L. M., & Six, M. (2016). Emotional strategies of police and their varying consequences for burnout. *Police Quarterly, 19*(1), 3–31.

Swider, B. W., & Zimmerman, R. D. (2010). Born to burnout: A meta-analytic path model of personality, job burnout, and work outcomes. *Journal of Vocational Behavior, 76*(3), 487–506.

Yang, S.-B., Guy, M. E., Azhar, A., Hsieh, C.-W., Lee, H. J., Lu, X., & Mastracci, S. H. (2018). Comparing apples and manzanas: Instrument development for cross-national analysis of emotional labour in public service jobs. *International Journal of Work Organisation and Emotion, 9*(3), 264–282.

Chapter 14

Whom to punish? – Street-level dilemmas within the Swedish Border Police

Lisa Marie Borrelli[1]

Introduction

Practices of ostracism and exclusion enforced by 'Fortress Europe' onto the bodies of the migrant subject manifest, and are enacted through European and national laws. The arrival of migrant subjects on the shores of the Mediterranean has fuelled a new wave of restrictive laws and policies against the 'immigrant other' (Furman, Epps, and Lamphear 2016), but has also shown that law cannot be stripped from moral dimensions (Baudouin 2006, 297). Chauvin and Garcés-Mascareñas (2012) argue that especially 'undocumented migrants may make themselves "less illegal" [...] by avoiding crime' (Chauvin and Garcés-Mascareñas 2012, 426). Yet, recent policy shifts to target criminal migrants (Leerkes, Leach, and Bachmeier 2012) underline the differentiation and categorisation of migrants as more or less 'deserving', criminal or integrated, a bogus applicant or genuine refugee (c.f. Jilke and Tummers 2018 for a discussion on who deserves help within public administration). Further, research on the intersection of migration and crime has brought forward the term 'crimmigration', which argues that criminal categories are imported into immigration law (Stumpf 2006). This approach criticises the increased criminalisation of administrative characteristics of immigration control to the disadvantage of already marginalised individuals (Stumpf 2006; van der Woude and van der Leun 2017). These debates also highlight the growing interest to securitise migration and control potentially 'dangerous others', aiming to end their stay in national territories. On the political agenda we are thus able to find increasingly heated discussions about how to deport those individuals deemed 'illegal' and with no right to stay, whilst also making use of a rhetoric, which depicts asylum seekers as asylum abusers or bogus applicants.

Especially in this context, emotions play a significant role in the creation of moral views on migrants (Bernstein and Mertz 2011, 7; Hall 2010; Svašek 2010). They are intertwined with norms and laws and shape the implementation of migration policies, especially visible during migrant-bureaucrat encounters, in which personal opinions and organisational cultures become visible (Kalir 2019). Importantly, emotions are not only reflected in the sensational media coverage surrounding migration and rise in populist rhetoric (see e.g. Suarez-Krabbe,

Lindberg, and Arce 2018 on the openly violent policies implemented in Denmark). Rather, they also function to shape bureaucracy and subsequent encounters between migrants and street-level bureaucrats on the ground (Lipsky 2010). In spite of this, migration laws and policies and the emotional handling of their moral entanglements have been neglected by research, especially at the intersection of migration and criminal law.

This chapter presents ethnographic material collected during field stays at two Swedish Border Police Regional Offices. It focuses on mobile units, tasked with detecting irregularised migrants, processing their cases and, potentially, detaining them before deportation. In particular, the chapter focuses on bureaucratic handling of emotional encounters. This research expands work on moral dilemmas of so-called street-level bureaucrats (Eule et al. 2019; Lipsky 2010), which has extensively discussed coping mechanisms of bureaucrats (Borrelli and Lindberg 2018; Halliday et al. 2009; Tummers et al. 2015), discretionary practices in the migration regime (Eule et al. 2019) and the implementation of abstract policies in the everyday of public administration (Cheliotis 2006). By drawing on Hochschild's (2012) concept of 'emotional labour', it argues that in order to understand micro-translations of societal norms and broader discourses one needs to study street-level reactions to migrants with precarious legal status. Looking at how bureaucrats reflect and position themselves and their work visualises the way in which issues such as (gendered) discrimination or structural violence can come into being (Lavanchy 2013).

In the following, the chapter reflects on relevant work regarding emotion and emotional labour to show that emotions have a crucial role in the way that street-level bureaucrat-migrant encounters play out, thus shaping the lives of the excluded, such as alleged criminal migrants, by moralising their presence and actions. It concludes by critically discussing the implications such (at times ignored) emotions have on the 'migration regime' and migrants with precarious legal status.

Methodology

This chapter presents ethnographic material, collected during four months of full-time participant observation at one out of seven regional Swedish Border Police offices and a shorter stay of three weeks at a second one (2016–2017). In addition to these observations, 22 semi-structured interviews with legal decision-takers (representing the police in court and taking decisions on detention), the head of the office and sub-heads of units, as well as with police officers and civil caseworkers were collected. Further, plenty of informal talks evolved during administrative work, lunch or coffee breaks.

The Swedish Border Police has mobile units which act on reports from the public about potential irregular migrant individuals and conduct work controls in order to find people who are working without a valid work or residence

permit. They are allowed to patrol the streets, check train stations and har-
bours and actively seek to detect migrants with precarious legal status. This
means they end up doing migration-related work as well as dealing with other
non-migration–related cases. For example, they file the first cases when illicit
labour has been detected and conduct the interview with the employer and
employee. It is these mobile units on which this chapter focuses, presenting
two observed cases where the intersection between criminal and migration
law is especially visible, including illegal work and, as a specific sub-category,
sex work. The use of these cases demarcates how emotions bring forward
moralised ideas of migrant individuals. The material is anonymised, not disclosing the place, nor the name of the officers.

Emotions in practice

The concept of emotional labour (Hochschild 2012) has been used to map the
commodification of emotions and as such takes an interest in (1) the direct
contact and interaction between 'clients' and – in this example – bureaucrats;
(2) the production of emotional states in the other and (3) how the employer
can somehow exercise power over emotional activities, for example, by supporting certain practices and behaviour (Hochschild 2012, 147).

Emotions are created and redefined through interaction (Svašek 2010).
They are thus not a purely personal aspect of individual psychology
(Beatty 2014), but embedded in relations and structures of power, able to be
both consequences and causes. The following two sections present the way in
which emotions can be traced through bureaucrat-migrant interactions, il-
lustrating the kind of emotions that are invoked and considering how bureaucrats reflect on their work and broader discourses. Detailed fieldnote extracts
allow us to carefully study how an already marginalised group faces structural
violence and (gendered) discrimination within administrative processes. As
such, it is argued that emotions disclose moralising views of the street-level
officers (see also Beatty 2014). Closely connected to the emotional reactions
embedded in the political moral discourse is a discussion of deservingness,
within which so-called bogus applicants and asylum abusers, but also 'ter-
rorists' or 'criminal' individuals, are assessed. The need for differentiation
is enshrined in an idea of belonging. The nation state is presumed to be accountable for the welfare of its citizens and consequently partly refuses to take
on responsibility for 'outsiders' residing on the same national, territorial space
(Chauvin and Garcés-Mascareñas 2014; Gupta 2012) – something, which is
reflected on the street-level. By focusing on the emotional labour of bureaucrats, I argue that we see where emotions are manipulated and invoked by
the latter and where dilemmas arise due to conflicting emotional discourses.
This can be supported by identifying 'display rules' through the performance
of surface and deep acting. Display rules are socially internalised by individuals in order to know how emotions should be displayed (Ekman and Friesen

2003; Hochschild 2012). Further, individuals learn how to surface act and 'deceive others about what we really feel', but also are able of deep acting, which requires self-deception in order to realign feelings to the organisation or workplace (Hochschild 2012, 33).

Blue collar work – suspicion

The mobile border police unit has found some men sleeping on mattresses on the premises of a building in an industrial area. Their visas are expired. I am told that the situation during their apprehension was delicate, since one man had a pair of scissors in his hand. They are taken to the station for interrogation. I follow the interview of a Ukrainian man (Marek, M), who is questioned through a phone interpreter. The officer explains the situation and visa rules. He has a 90 days multiple entry visa (he can freely re-enter and stay 90 days within a period of 180 days) – but this has expired. Pelle, the officer, mentions they might be able to send him to Poland, which issued the visa. M. has not committed any crimes.

Pelle (P.): "Why are you in Sweden?" – M: "I am looking at the country, I am not working anywhere."

P: "Did you think about working here?" – M: "Maybe, I thought that I could maybe for a little extra, but I do not intend to stay long […]."

P: "Why were you at this place [where they found him]?" - […]

P: "Did you know before you arrived where you would stay?" – M: "No, I did not come in order to work."

P: "Do you work in Poland?" – M: "Yes, in Warsaw, as façade constructor."

P: "Because, where you live [where they found him], there is a painting enterprise…" – M: "No."

P: "You had a visa, but you have stayed longer than you were allowed to…" – M: "I am here as a tourist, for holidays."

Pelle asks about his position to be sent back to Ukraine. M: "I have family there, I am not a criminal." […]

P: "Do you understand why you are here?" – M: "Yes, I am illegal on Swedish territory, but I came as a tourist."

Pelle asks him if he knows the other apprehended men; P: "What did they do during the day?" – M: "I do not know them, but they went somewhere, however I did not see any working clothes."

P: "Do you have any questions?" – M: "Not really."

It is decided that he will be detained until travel arrangements are made. The man asks if he will leave on his own. Pelle wonders why he all of a sudden wants to leave. – M: "I thought to leave within the next week."

P.: "This is hard to believe,…"

(Fieldnotes, Swedish Border Police Unit 2017)

The interest of the officer is twofold: First, he wants to find out if the men were employed and by whom, clearly believing that this was their sole purpose for residing on the industrial premises. The disbelief towards the interviewee claiming he came as a tourist is even openly voiced in the end, when Pelle expresses his surprise that he is interested in a quick return. Assuming that work is the only reason for the apprehended individuals being in Sweden, officers, often during the observations and later on in their exchange, voice their suspicion about attempts to leave independently and evoke emotions through their questions (see Marek feeling the need to underline that he is not 'a criminal'). Respective deportees stress that they will leave, asking to do so independently and much like Marek they also repeat that they are 'not criminals', voicing irritation at the treatment and astonishment about the harsh consequences.

On the officers' side, emotions are shaped by experiences and the organisational culture, which teaches them to group certain people together as suspicious cheats (Allsopp 2017). Since officers mostly encounter their 'clients' as opposites who have an assumed interest in hiding certain facts (e.g. working illegally), suspicion is directed towards all of them and shapes their treatment (Hall 2010, 881). Emotions thus materialise in their judgement directed towards the migrant other. This allows for '...spaces of circulation and mobility rights' to emerge, which 'are structured by aspects of age, race, gender and class' (Tesfahuney 1998, 501). Officers are not expected to restrain expressions, since their workplace is supportive of the expressed feelings. For example, Albanian young men are classed as those trying to continue their journeys to the UK via ferry in order to find work or arriving in Sweden only as alleged tourists. They are scrutinised regarding their knowledge about cities and sights, and are generally portrayed 'fake' tourists, searching for illicit employment. Since personal feelings of distrust align with, and reflect, what is learned within the organisation, there is not even the need for a realignment of feelings for deep acting, neither do they need to use display rules.

Second, the man has transgressed migration law, enabling the officers to deport him back to Ukraine. While officers mention that 'unfortunately' the direct consequences of arresting 'illegal workers' mostly affects those soon-to-be deported, the officers' mandate is to focus on the detection, detention and deportation of individuals, rather than on criminal offenses committed by employers (fieldnotes 2017). Nevertheless, this leaves them at times caught between criminal and migration law. Several officers mention that they always try to file against the employer, and the decision can be made to not file case against the person employed. Yet for border police officers working under time pressure the easiest and shortest procedure is simply to file a case against the employee (fieldnotes 2016). It is recognised that employers are at fault, but officers remain unable to prosecute them, creating a misalignment between what they believe is right and their actual practices, thus causing emotional distress and thus challenging the successful deep acting. Their practices have a direct effect – deportation – but also cause anger or feelings of annoyance for the officers. This is initially directed towards the exploiting party, but the system in which they operate also encourages them to pay more attention to reducing the number of irregular migrants. This sometimes results in them focusing solely on the latter of the two groups (interview with Jim, Swedish Border Police 2016). At the same time, those voiced and, at times, supporting emotions 'comprise action tendencies' (Beatty 2014, 558), although they might be hindered by many 'illegal' workers, much like M., who do not want to disclose too much information. The officers rarely have enough evidence to make a case against a particular employer, causing an emotional dissonance between what is expected (punish the employer) and felt (anger or irritation that they should focus on the employee) and thus creating dilemmas for the street-level bureaucrat (Hochschild 2012; Introduction Chapter).

Sex work – moralising emotions and feelings

Ylva, a Swedish border police officer, interrogates Lina, a sex worker apprehended during her shift, with similar complex emotional discourses:

Ylva (Y): "Can you report a bit about the man in the hotel room? [...] You are not being the suspect of a crime here, but the witness. How did you get in contact?" – Lina (L): "Via the homepage."

Y: "Which one?" - L: "Sex-tjejer [Sex-girls]." [...]

Y: "What was it you arranged, like a Quicky,..." – L: "He was supposed to come over. Quicky." The interview continues, asking Lina about the price and the exact things they did before the police arrived.

Y: "What did happen then?" – Lina laughs a bit.

Y: "I have worked with this for many years, there is nothing you need to be ashamed of." – Lina explains that not much happened, because the police arrived quickly.

Y: "He says something entirely different. He says you had oral sex before the police came." – L: "No, that we did not. Truth spoken, I would have reported that. Why should I lie?" [...]

The interrogation now switches to the 'migration' part, in which the woman will no longer be the witness, but becomes the suspect of an administrative offence within migration law (illegal work without a working permit, being a third-country national without any residence status).

Y: "What is the purpose of you being here in Sweden?" – L: "Tourist." Ylva enquires when and where Lina entered the country, how long she intended to stay and whether she has been in Sweden before. She asks about a return ticket and how much money Lina earned.

Y: "How come you have a sex ad as a tourist?" – L: "I was here as a tourist, but then I thought I could earn a little bit of money."

Y: "How many customers did you have?" – W: "3 maybe." [...]

Y: "Do you work in Ukraine?" – W: "I work for an online enterprise."

Y: "Can you describe this a bit?" – L: "I sell products online." [...]

Y: "I have your visa application. On the application you did write 'manager'." – L: "That is correct, this job counts as a manager." [..]

Y: "What is your position in terms of returning back to Ukraine?" – L: "I thought about continuing to work for this enterprise. I understand that it does not work this way [referring to sex work]."

Y: "Do you want us to contact your government?" – L: "No."

Y: "Do you want us to contact the Ukrainian embassy, do you wish us to do that?" – L: "Why? What will happen now?"

Y: "We are just obliged to ask you that." – L: "No."

[...]

Y: "If you would be able to leave this office, what would you do?" – L: "I thought about buying a return ticket to go home. I do not want to do this [work] any longer."

Y: "You have a child?" – L: "Yes."

Ylva explains that it is now up to the decision maker to decide whether she will be freed or detained according to the Foreigners Act (2005).

Y: "In case you will have to go to detention, we will take your documents and you will receive them when you are on your way back." – L: "Ok."

Ylva adds that she does understand her situation and assumes she does not do it on her free will. L starts crying and says: "I just do it for my child."

Y: "We are here, if you want to talk to us. We do not do this to be bad to you, to do this against you. It is the opposite. The goal is to take you out of prostitution."

Finally, the decision is taken. The woman will be detained, a decision legitimated by arguing the woman provided for herself dishonestly ('oärlig försörjning'). Further, they suspect she would continue her work, if not detained.

(Fieldnote extract of the Swedish border police 2017, used in Borrelli 2019)

Similar to the dichotomy of offenses above, when a sex worker is apprehended by the border police, especially when the client is too, the sex worker will face two different interviews. The first section treats Lina as a victim and witness (or informant), whilst in the second she becomes the perpetrator. The client, who buys sex and is thus – in accordance with Swedish law – committing a crime, is not the person in whom the border guards are most interested. Most of the time women are found without clients and so the punishment of the 'buyer' does not occur. Again, we find a situation which causes emotional irritation on both sides. For Lina the transgression from first be the victim, asked to disclose private information, to being questioned in regard to her intentions to work and reside illegally might seem bewildering. Indeed, being perceived as suspicious and untrustworthy causes irritation ('why should I lie?'). Ylva here tries to establish a personal connection, performs emotional labour and presents emotional displays, which try to smooth the juxtaposition through her attentive questions, accommodating Lina. While this can be tough for the officer, the role Ylva takes on is clearly about eliciting information that will be useful for the case. At the same time, she sympathises with Lina, stating they are doing this to help her. Indeed, the presented emotions bring forward a double purpose: Ylva's practiced (and learned) emotional sensitivity supports bureaucrats to accommodate their own feelings with their expected organisational actions. It allows Ylva to side with Lina, by telling her they want to help and is even able to deceive her that the actions taken (deportation) serve a good purpose. Besides a strategic use of display rules, here showing emotional support, which enables officer to sympathise with the migrant individual, whilst trying to keep the situation calm, the presented extract also shows how a deception of their (officers) own feelings is used to realign institutional expectations. At the same time, the observed situation is highly emotional and challenges deep acting, since officers start to recognise patterns, which they deem morally wrong:

'They (sex workers) say that they are tourists [...] but we can see that this is not true.' Once apprehended, 'we have hours to do the preparations for all the forms and papers and they see that it is going to detention and say "well, if you are going to take me in, lock me in, then I say asylum." That is misuse.'

(Anton, Swedish Border Police 2017)

This example depicts gendered discrimination (since all apprehended sex workers were either women or transgender), though embedded in a structure, that allows for such emotions to come up. Within the organisation, officers share common experiences and thus some emotional overlap, clearly depicting how structures can shape emotional responses, but also how 'emotional attitudes to one another are part of the continual redefinition of ongoing relationships' (Parkinson 1995, 170) – for example in the interaction between Ylva and Lina, but also between officers. There are plenty of emotional attachments (Svašek 2010, 866), which play out in discourses, practices and experiences. Thus, we find 'job-specific requirements [which] often construct migrants in specific ways that push particular modes of emotional interaction' (Svašek 2010, 872). Irregular migrants might be depicted as illegal workers (first case), or moral wrong-doers (second case). Not only does Anton show frustration towards the alleged misuse of asylum, but also Ylva displays a moment where her moral view impacts on her way of questioning, causing Lina to cry. She asks if Lina has a child, something which seems highly irrelevant in the context and is otherwise not followed up on. During another incident where sex workers were apprehended, Ylva's colleague Bengt makes the hidden accusation more explicit: 'What would your child think of you?' (fieldnotes 2017). Emotions, such as voicing frustration, either expressed by those apprehended, or by the officers, can thus disclose moral values, which otherwise remain hidden behind legal and administrative procedures.

Much like Hochschild (2012) describes, there are several drivers of emotional labour, such as societal, organisational or occupational display rules. Sex work is clearly stigmatised and so interactions are often highly morally charged. Sex workers are often deemed 'dishonest' – a term used by the officers in this specific context, although it is part of the legal text and encompasses 'illegal labour' in general. In conclusion, it is possible to trace ideas about how morality – enshrined in organisational structures, laws and policies – influence the way emotions are displayed and thus emotional labour is performed.

Conclusions – who to punish?

> Me going into a barn does not make me a cow. You going into a police station does not make you a criminal.
>
> (Victor, Swedish Border Police Officer 2017)

In their everyday work, street-level bureaucrats, as with many others in public administration, are expected to manage feelings (Hochschild 2012). They evoke emotions in order to gain information, while also following certain rules on how emotions should be displayed. At the same time, officers act on different emotional levels in order to navigate their own and others' emotions. Since they encounter migrants with precarious legal status, who fear detention and deportation, it is not surprising that emotion management is a daily and essential part of their work. Officers face irritation (see Pelle), fear, crying (see Ylva), apathy, but also themselves express a broad range of emotions (see Bengt and Anton). However, the management of feeling, expected to be done by them as part of their waged labour, produces, at times, a commodification of feelings, which are expected to be controlled and led into 'productive' ways to govern those deemed to be without a right to remain (see Hochschild 2012). This requires effort by officers, but also causes irritation, especially when migration and criminal law converge. The cases presented in this chapter show that a clear distinction between criminal and administrative offense is lacking which, in turn, causes conflict between the display rules which are at play. Both Jim and Anton describe how they are frustrated by the lack of 'right' punishment (Jim not wanting to punish illegal workers, Anton wanting to punish sex workers claiming asylum). Further, the officer's deep acting is challenged by the discrepancy between their own feeling and those they are expected to show.

Securitisation and the criminalisation of migrants often result in heated and often emotional debates in migration offices and border police units, who have to implement political expectations and deal with public sentiments and the reactions of their clients – migrants with precarious legal status. Startled by some cases, where personal beliefs and emotions do not match the legal or administrative expectations, the question remains open: Who is 'a criminal'? Simply being in detention (Hall 2010), working illegally or applying for asylum can suddenly be perceived as similar acts of 'doing the wrong thing' even if done for the 'right' reasons (see Ylva and her colleague).

Moral values are prevalent in policies and legal frameworks but they also shape policies and legal frameworks. They are dismantled by emotional outbursts (see Anton or Bengt) or seemingly unemotional questions, which trigger reactions by apprehended migrant individuals. At the same time, suffering is brought onto the ostracised subject without much concern, as these subjects are *beyond* the community (Gupta 2012). It is thus relevant to further study how emotions are actively manipulated and suppressed by officers because this sheds light on potential detachment between the work and the self (see Introduction, this volume). There is no doubt that these strategies affect practices and allow for a more detailed analysis of how emotions, laws and organisations are structured, in such a way as to reinforce categorisations of migrant's deservingness.

Note

1 This research has been funded by the Swiss National Science Foundation Project No. 153225 and was supported by the National Center of Competence in Research (NCCR) on the move funded by the Swiss National Science Foundation (51NF40-182897).

References

Allsopp, J. 2017. 'Agent, victim, soldier, son: Intersecting masculinities in the European "refugee crisis"'''. In *A Gendered Approach to the Syrian Refugee Crisis*, edited by J. Freedman, Z. Kivilcim, and N. Ö. Baklacıoğlu, 155–78. New York: Routledge.

Baudouin, Dupret. 2006. *Adjudication in Action. An Ethnomethodology of Law, Morality and Justice*. Farnham: Ashgate.

Beatty, Andrew. 2014. 'Anthropology and emotion'. *Journal of the Royal Anthropological Institute* 20 (3): 545–63. doi:10.1111/1467-9655.12114.

Bernstein, Anya, and Elizabeth Mertz. 2011. 'Introduction bureaucracy: Ethnography of the state in everyday life'. *PoLAR: Political and Legal Anthropology Review* 34 (1): 6–10. doi:10.1111/j.1555-2934.2011.01135.x.

Borrelli, Lisa Marie. forthcoming. 'Encounters of despair. Street-level bureaucrat - migrant interactions in Sweden and Switzerland'.

Borrelli, Lisa Marie, and Annika Lindberg. 2018. 'The creativity of coping: Alternative tales of moral dilemmas among migration control officers'. *International Journal of Migration and Border Studies* 4 (3): 163–78. doi:10.1504/IJMBS.2018.10013558.

Chauvin, Sébastien, and Blanca Garcés-Mascareñas. 2012. 'Beyond Informal citizenship: The new moral economy of migrant illegality'. *International Political Sociology* 6 (3): 241–259. doi:10.1111/j.1749-5687.2012.00162.x.

———. 2014. 'Becoming less illegal: Deservingness frames and undocumented migrant incorporation: Becoming less illegal'. *Sociology Compass* 8 (4): 422–32. doi:10.1111/soc4.12145.

Cheliotis, Leonidas K. 2006. 'How iron is the iron cage of new penology?: The role of human agency in the implementation of criminal justice policy'. *Punishment & Society* 8 (3): 313–40. doi:10.1177/1462474506064700.

Ekman, Paul, and Wallace V. Friesen. 2003. *Unmasking the Face. A Guide to Recognizing Emotions From Facial Expressions.* Los Altos: Malor Books.

Eule, Tobias G., Lisa Marie Borrelli, Annika Lindberg, and Anna Wyss. 2019. *Migrants Before the Law: Contested Migration Control in Europe.* Basingstoke: Palgrave Macmillan.

Furman, Rich, Douglas Epps, and Greg Lamphear, eds. 2016. *Detaining the Immigrant Other: Global and Transnational Issues.* 1st ed. New York: Oxford University Press.

Gupta, Akhil. 2012. *Red Tape : Bureaucracy, Structural Violence, and Poverty in India.* A John Hope Franklin Center Book. Durham: Duke University Press.

Hall, Alexandra. 2010. '"These people could be anyone": Fear, contempt (and empathy) in a british immigration removal centre'. *Journal of Ethnic and Migration Studies* 36 (6): 881–98. doi:10.1080/13691831003643330.

Halliday, Simon, Nicola Burns, Neil Hutton, Fergus Mcneill, and Cyrus Tata. 2009. 'Street-level bureaucracy, interprofessional relations, and coping mechanisms: A study of criminal justice social workers in the sentencing process'. *Law & Policy* 31 (4): 405–28.

Hochschild, Arlie Russell. 2012. *The Managed Heart. Commercialization of Human Feeling.* 3rd ed. Berkely and Los Angeles, CA: University of California Press. www.ucpress.edu/book/9780520272941/the-managed-heart.

Jilke, Sebastian, and Lars Tummers. 2018. 'Which clients are deserving of help? A theoretical model and experimental test'. *Journal of Public Administration Research and Theory* 28 (2): 226–38. doi:10.1093/jopart/muy002.

Kalir, Barak. 2019. 'Repressive compassion: Deportation caseworkers furnishing an emotional comfort zone in encounters with illegalized migrants'. *PoLAR: Political and Legal Anthropology Review* 42 (1): 68–84. doi:10.1111/plar.12281.

Lavanchy, Anne. 2013. 'Dissonant alignments: The ethics and politics of researching state institutions'. *Current Sociology* 61 (5–6): 677–92. doi:10.1177/0011392113486883.

Leerkes, Arjen, Mark Leach, and James Bachmeier. 2012. 'Borders behind the border: An exploration of state-level differences in migration control and their effects on US migration patterns'. *Journal of Ethnic and Migration Studies* 38 (1): 111–29. doi:10.1080/1369183X.2012.640023.

Lipsky, Michael. 2010. *Street-Level Bureaucracy: The Dilemmas of the Individual in Public Service.* New York: Russell Sage Foundation.

Parkinson, Brian. 1995. *Ideas and Realities of Emotion.* London and New York: Routledge. https://trove.nla.gov.au/version/45707675.

Stumpf, Juliet. 2006. 'The crimmigration crisis: Immigrants, crime, and sovereign power'. *American University Law Review* 56 (2). http://digitalcommons.wcl.american.edu/aulr/vol56/iss2/3.

Suarez-Krabbe, Julia, Annika Lindberg, and José Arce. 2018. *Stop killing us slowly: A Research Report on the Motivation Enhancement Measures and Criminalization of Rejected Asylum Seekers in Denmark*. Copenhagen: Marronage.

Svašek, Maruška. 2010. 'On the move: Emotions and human mobility'. *Journal of Ethnic and Migration Studies* 36 (6): 865–80. doi:10.1080/13691831003643322.

Tesfahuney, Mekonnen. 1998. 'Mobility, racism and geopolitics'. *Political Geography* 17 (5): 499–515. doi:10.1016/S0962-6298(97)00022-X.

Tummers, Lars L. G., Victor Bekkers, Evelien Vink, and Michael Musheno. 2015. 'Coping during public service delivery: A conceptualization and systematic review of the literature'. *JPART* 25: 1099–1126. doi:10.1093/jopart/muu056.

van der Woude, Maartje, and Joanne van der Leun. 2017. 'Crimmigration checks in the internal border areas of the EU: Finding the discretion that matters'. *European Journal of Criminology* 14 (1): 27–45. doi:10.1177/1477370816640139.

Chapter 15

The emotional labour of prison Listeners

Sarah Nixon

Introduction

The Listener scheme was created in response to the suicide in 1990 of 15-year-old Phillip Knight in HMP Swansea (an adult prison), and also in response to a general increase in suicidal and self-harming behaviours across the prison estate (Biggar and Neal 1996). The Listener scheme is a confidential peer-support service offered in prison, to help prisoners who are vulnerable or suicidal.

Prisoners are selected, trained and supported by volunteers from local Samaritans branches, which then provide regular contact for Listeners through weekly meetings that are confidential and private from prison staff. The majority of prisons in England and Wales have Listener schemes in place: in 2017 there were 1,540 active Listeners in post (Bromley Briefings 2018). Prison Listeners are trained to demonstrate appropriate emotional responses and discourses when interacting with vulnerable prisoners. They are also closely monitored by the Samaritans to ensure that they protect themselves from burnout and emotional difficulties. Not every prisoner selected for training proves suitable after an intensive training course. Listeners are taught the values of non-judgement and confidentiality as part of their training, because this is an integral part of the Samaritan's ethos. The Listener scheme plays a key role in the prison service's safer custody agenda and coincides with a move to a multidisciplinary approach towards self-harm and suicide, involving officers, professionals and prisoners (HMPS 1992, 1993, 1994).

'Emotional labour' is normally performed in return for a wage (Hochschild 1983). However, Steinberg and Figart (1999) state that this is not always the case, identifying that work which is not waged can still demand emotional labour. Listeners are expected to regulate their emotions in accordance with the demands of the role, work unsociable hours and exhibit appropriate decision-making strategies, despite the pressure of their own lives in custody and the wider prison environment. They receive no financial remuneration for their contributions but are rewarded on both a personal and institutional level. Perrin and Blagden (2014) found that being a Listener had a transformative effect, developing 'new me' narratives. Listeners are paid back in time; a commodity controlled by the prison regime and prison authorities (Matthews 2009). Listeners receive extra time out of their cell, freedom to access the wider prison environment when other prisoners are locked away, and they can also receive a six-month 'retainer' to perform Listener work, which can facilitate local family visits. However, Liebling et al. (2005) found that Listeners were sometimes used as a token response to distress in prisons with a high number of staff who hold traditional cultural attitudes. Officers with limited views of prisoner care use Listeners as a way of personally avoiding dealing with the emotional concerns of prisoners (Liebling et al. 2005; Tait 2012). Often informing staff about prisoners' vulnerabilities has led to them being deemed a 'nuisance' by a small number of healthcare staff (Foster 2011). All that said, Listeners provide a vital service to the safe and effective running of prisons. They work tirelessly alongside prison staff whilst simultaneously having to negotiate their own custodial lives with the demands of vulnerable prisoners.

Methods

This research formed part of a wider PhD study around peer work and desistance (Nixon 2018). Male prisoners, probationers and former probationers were interviewed, alongside criminal justice personnel to explore the relationship between peer work and desistance, both in prison and the community. The researcher had prior experience and knowledge of working with male offenders, so an all-male sample was selected to reflect this experience. This chapter draws on interviews with seven prison Listeners who were interviewed as well as interviews with the safer custody coordinator and a Samaritans volunteer. The prison was a category 'B' local holding approximately 380 prisoners. Semi-structured interviews were used, based around an appreciative approach to peer work and the impact upon self-transformation and desistance. As an ex-prison officer and current prison tutor in the same establishment, the number one prison governor granted access to the wider prison to collect data, so prisoners were recruited using a convenience sample. Data was collected over a 12-month period and was analysed using thematic analysis (Braun and Clarke 2006). The emotional labour of prison peer workers, particularly Listeners, was not a theme that was expected to emerge during data analysis. Peer work was explored initially from the researcher's assumptions that the role would only yield positive experiences for those involved. However, the emotional toil and role commitment expressed by Listeners emerged as a theme to be explored. As Listeners outlined the complexity of the role and the impact it had upon their custodial lives, it was evident that emotional labour in peer work was a sensitising concept in need of further exploration.

Discussion

Themes identified for discussion are 'doing emotional labour', 'dirty emotional labour' and emotional support for Listeners, which will be explored in turn.

Doing emotional labour

Listeners have to manage a tension that exists when adhering to their role as well as their status as 'prisoner', which is particularly burdensome for them. The confidential nature of Listener work can (temporarily) invert the power relationships in prison and gives Listeners a situated knowledge that prison officers do not possess. Listeners are required to uphold confidentiality at all times and breaching this would be a serious threat to the fundamental ethos of the Listener scheme (exceptions are made in extreme circumstances, for example a terrorist threat, where Listeners are expected to inform staff immediately if threat is posed to the establishment). Listeners can be put under pressure by staff to disclose details around vulnerable prisoners (see Jaffe 2012). For example, one prisoner interpreted confrontation by a prison officer as intrusive and a threat to the integrity of his role, but he stood his ground:

> If you want to know what's up with him, you go and ask him!
> (Andrew,[1] Listener)

Prison Listeners are trained to not intervene with a prisoner's desire to take their own life or commit an act of self-harm. This however may conflict with their humanitarian concerns towards others. Andrew states that he uses strategies to help prisoners to find their own solutions, through asking them if they have put a canteen sheet request in; his logic behind this is that if they have, then they show signs of wanting to stay alive. Listeners must display appropriate body language to remain calm and in control, even when faced with the certainty that another prisoner is going to take their own life. Emotional dissonance is the conflict between emotions felt and the emotions expressed to conform to display rules (Abraham 1999). Steve expresses the emotional dissonance (Abraham 1999; Hochschild 1983) that he feels about this, despite the ethos of the programme:

> …if someone said to me that as soon as I leave I am going to kill myself, I would want to do something about it. If…. I got up in the morning and he was dead, I would feel terrible, like I should have been able to stop it.
> (Steve, Listener)

---

1 Names have been changed to protect the anonymity of participants.

Repeat prisoners harden up to this reality, more so than first timers, often expressing a level of detachment. Dan has been in prison several times and has accepted this aspect of the Listener role more so than less 'prison wise' prisoners:

> I've been called away at some silly hours just to talk. It is nice walking away knowing that that person is going to survive another day…but you also have to be prepared if that person wants to end his life. You have to accept it and not take it personally.
>
> (Dan, Listener)

John, however, expressed conflict around hearing this particular narrative. He adopts a strategy to address this dissonance, by going to visit the prisoner the next day, in an unofficial and informal capacity. Through checking up on the prisoner (to see if he is still alive), he addresses his own concerns in a way that does not contradict the Samaritan's ethos of respecting a prisoner's intentions, and not trying to control or influence the choice of the individual.

At certain times of the day Listeners will be required to rescind their role, reverting back to 'prisoner', and they must be willing to make this transition instantly at the request of the staff. Part of the Listener role is managing their frustrations at an operational regime that has been hit hard during austere times (Ismail 2019). Staff are not there to open cell doors in a timely manner for Listeners, because of staff shortages. John explains that certain operational decisions make him feel disempowered and angry:

> Nine times out of ten you will get the screws (prison officers) cutting the call for roll count…you can't say "no". They may give you 5 minutes, but they will come back. That's the regime versus the prisoner's needs; they clash. They say "deal with him tomorrow" but by tomorrow he may have cut up or killed himself. It's too late and we feel bad because we spoke to him last night and didn't finish the call. The screws still go home and have a good nights' sleep; it's nothing to do with them.
>
> (John, Listener)

However, the custodial manager who runs the Listener scheme contradicts John, stating the official prison policy around Listener calls:

> We should never end their call (the Listeners). We have a secure care suite and the majority of calls are facilitated in there….so the calls can go on for as long as needed because it is in use 24 hours a day.
>
> (Dave, Custodial Manager)

The tensions between Listeners and prison officers are clear and John has to manage his emotions in accordance with the expectations of his dual role as prisoner and Listener. The operational regime at certain times of the day will take precedence over peer support. It is down to the good will of staff to relocate Listeners and their prisoners to the care suite, which is contingent on cooperation and resources. A HM Inspectorate of Prisons (2016) report found that there were periods of the prison regime, for example during periods of lock up, and particularly at night time, where staff were reluctant to get Listeners out, or were reported to say that they were 'too busy' to assist. Some Listeners had to talk to prisoners through locked doors, thus conversations were not confidential (2016: 23). Prison Service Instruction 64/2011 states that prisoners should have timely access to Listeners wherever they are located, and where there is a dedicated Listener support suite, a protocol must be in place for its use.

The Listener suite gives prisoners a safe space to open up emotionally – what Crewe et al. (2014) calls an 'emotional zone'. The Listener suite gives both prisoner and listener time out from the highly charged aggression on the landings and permits the expression of emotive displays from both parties. The Listener can use this space to display qualities that conflict with the hegemonic masculinity (Connell 1995) that prevails on the landings. Crewe (2014) describes the public culture of most men's prisons as characterised by a particular kind of emotionally taut masculine performance. However, there are a number of situations where care and affection can be seen (although they can be hidden). The backstage space of a Listener suite fosters a safe place for both Listener and prisoner to explore the prisoner's needs.

Dirty emotional labour

The focus of this section is the notion of the dark side of emotional labour, described by Hughes (1958) and Ward and McMurray (2016) as situations where individuals encounter social, physical and moral taint in their work. Listeners perform 'dirty emotional work' (McMurray and Ward 2014), often in place of prison officers who deflect 'dirty' tasks to Listeners, for example difficult and challenging prisoners with complex mental health issues, rather than correct referrals being made to qualified healthcare professionals (Liebling and Arnold 2005). Paul, an experienced Listener, identifies the difficult scenarios that he has found himself in:

> …I had a couple of people and they start talking about the voices they are hearing in their head…I thought I'm not kind of equipped with these people…you know serious mental health issues…pacing up and down explaining all the different voices in their head.
>
> (Paul, Listener)

Paul has to manage his emotions in situations like these and using a limited skillset to work with prisoners with severe mental health issues, he has to conceal any vulnerability or fear that he might be experiencing in close proximity to delusional prisoners.

Listeners have to endure negative labelling from other prisoners, thus finding themselves in a liminal state (Van Gennep 1909), caught between the role expectations of being a trusted prisoner, from both prison staff and Samaritans, and also managing the expectations of their peers, with whom they share a landing. This illustrates the dirty side of emotional labour, where Listeners are perceived as 'tainted' for the role that they perform. The proximity they have to prison officers can be misinterpreted as defying aspects of the 'inmate code' (Sykes 1958) (for example contravening perceived acceptable boundaries of 'prisoner' and providing information to staff):

> Yes they call us 'screw boys'.…. but as a Listener it is your job to help others. That is our role. If somebody comes in and says they are being bullied and they don't want to tell the staff themselves, then it is our role to do that and keep people safe so that they don't self-harm or commit suicide.
>
> (Neil, Listener)

The trust placed upon prison Listeners creates difficulty with other prisoners who do not share the same level of privilege and respect from staff. Listeners have to maintain appropriate discourses to uphold the authenticity of their prisoner identity, and they are often seen as a 'soft touch' by other prisoners. Steve elaborated on how he manages this tension and puts his survival in the prison ahead of the expectations of being a Listener:

> …I think people see kindness as a weakness. I try not to let that bug me. There have been a couple of times when I have been in here and people have said they are going to knock me out. I've said to them 'just because I'm a Listener and a nice guy, doesn't mean I won't kick the shit out of you'. They will be quiet then and see a different side of me that I don't normally let out. I don't like being like that but if I need to I will.
>
> (Steve, Listener)

Prisoners can exploit Listeners for behaving like 'screw boys' and working closely with 'undesirable' prisoners like sex offenders, which renders them 'dirty' and 'tainted' in the eyes of other prisoners. They are often bullied to bend prison rules and bring contraband into the prison. This creates problems of personal safety for Listeners, making them targets:

> I don't mind helping people.… however about two months ago some prisoners tried to bully me, thinking I've got it good and they wanted what I have got. They tried to bully me to get drugs in. I had people in my cell punching me.…. If you are a listener you are a trusted person. I can't be seen to be behaving in that way.
>
> (Andrew, Listener)

Prison Listeners expressed concern that their authenticity was questioned by staff, and their status was inconsistently validated by prison officers. In the following example, one Listener was trying to access a prisoner who had urgently requested to see him, and he needed a prison officer to open the gate for him. It was the Listener's day off, so he was going over and above expectations of the role, and was subsequently challenged in an aggressive manner by a prison officer:

> Yeah but you are not on the rota today. Don't try and bullshit me and pull the wool over my eyes.
>
> (Gary, prison officer)

The Listener stated that his role was operational 24 hours a day and that he can speak to anyone at any time as a Listener, to which he was told:

> No, you can't. You can go in there now, but don't try and take the piss out of me again.
>
> (Gary, prison officer)

The Listener succeeded in his task of accessing the prisoner but felt obliged to show deference to the rudeness of the prison officer, so that he did not get in to trouble and lose his Listener post. He expressed his frustrations:

> I seem to get it a lot from the staff. They think being a Listener is a way to stay longer or make your time easier.
>
> (Paul, Listener)

Prison Listeners have greater access to the prison than other prisoners. This is something that gives a sense of personal agency but can also lead to cynicism and mistrust amongst prison officers, further highlighting the taint associated with the Listener role. Simon and Neil's cell was also a Listener suite (as they are located on the Vulnerable Prisoner Unit) and Simon identified how he was placed under greater surveillance from prison staff, who he felt did not trust and validate his Listener status. This further consolidates the liminal status of Listeners:

> I've had spells within a month where I have had 3 drug tests and had my cell turned over twice…they say it is all done on a random basis, but what's random about that? Compared to before I was a Listener, when I only had it once…. but I can understand why because you are given more opportunities to be out of your cell, you are given that little bit more freedom, so in return they are going to want to see you are squeaky clean and not abusing it.
>
> (Simon, Listener)

Listeners expressed emotional dissonance around working with sex offenders. Working alongside this demographic further highlights the concept of 'dirty emotional work' (McMurray and Ward 2014). In this particular prison, sex offenders are trained to be Listeners alongside non-sex offenders and these two groups interact during weekly meetings with the Samaritans. During their 'back stage' interview several non-sex offenders acknowledged that whilst they find sex offences and sex offenders distasteful, they are required to behave in non-judgemental ways and conform to display rules associated with the role, because otherwise they will have the role and status removed from them. Many prisoners are rejected for Listener work because they do not demonstrate correct display rules to work safely alongside sex offenders. Andrew describes the emotional suppression and surface acting involved in this type of work:

> I have to sit here and not judge that person. To me they have done wrong and I detest what they have done...but we have done wrong...so I just sit here. I don't give them any indication that I know what they have done. I just do my job and don't think about it.
>
> (Andrew, Listener)

The level of performance management that Andrew adopts as a Listener has convinced the sex offender prisoner that there will be no threat made towards them, which is the correct set of display and feeling rules to keep his job as Head Listener. One of the sex offender Listeners commented:

> I was a bit nervous at first.... I know we are looked upon badly.... there is still that stigma....it was amazing actually.... Listeners have to be coming from that frame of mind...of being non-judgemental.
>
> (Steve, Listener)

The convict code of not 'grassing' on others is paramount within a prison environment (see Clemmer 1940; Sykes 1958). Neil and Simon (both serving life sentences and waiting for appeal) did defy the inmate code of not 'grassing' on others, when it became apparent the extent of the bullying on their landing from one individual. They put their Listener obligations ahead of the convict code, risking potential ostracism as a result of their decision:

> I used to see what he was doing and I thought 'how can he do that to other people?' We are all human beings. He can't be like that. I removed myself; I didn't want to be around him. Something had to be done. All 3 Listeners sat down.... we had a little meeting. Someone came in and said they were going to slash up (self-harm) because of him. We spoke to staff on his behalf. After that another 8–10 people came forward and said that he was bullying them...he is now in the block (segregation).

You still have his little followers who keep doing things for him. They walk up and down the landings making smarmy comments. They know it was us Listeners. But our role, we have to do that. We are not part of this violence; we have to do the right thing.

(Neil, Listener)

The concept of the 'dark side of emotional labour' (Ward and McMurray 2016) is clearly useful in terms of understanding Listeners' interactions with other prisoners. However, these interactions with vulnerable individuals can also have a positive outcome on prison Listeners. From their ethnographic study of Samaritans, McMurray and Ward (2014: 1) found that these volunteers act as 'society's agents in the containment of emotional dirt' and that the management of difficult, negative or out of place emotions of others can be framed as a positive experience, generating satisfying emotions. Listener work can be a stark reminder of who or what they do not want to become, as they deal with prisoners who are experiencing prison in ways that generate suicidal ideations. Listeners use social comparison (Festinger 1954) as a strategy to distance themselves from vulnerable prisoners, and an opportunity to remind themselves of the relative advantage that they have over those in crisis:

I looked into his cell and there were no personal touches....no cards to suggest that anybody cares for him ... it reminded me of how lucky I am to have my family.

(Steve, Listener)

This section illustrates the complexities involved in the Listener role, where prisoners have to engage in emotion and identity work to interact with a variety of demographics in the prison, which can place them in positions of uncertainty and liminality. Engaging in tasks that are perceived as 'tainted' puts an enormous amount of pressure upon the Listeners' coping resources.

Emotional support for Listeners

This final section examines the way Listeners are protected by staff in terms of self-care, avoiding burnout and dealing with difficult emotional circumstances. Listeners perform a complex series of interactions with both prisoners and staff and they have to negotiate the boundaries of the role within the wider prison environment, which can affect them both physically and emotionally. South et al. (2014) suggest that prisons and prison staff have a responsibility to provide support for peer workers, to help them to cope and avoid burnout. Chinelo (2010) argues that prison officers fail to support Listener schemes by making the operational functioning of the scheme more difficult for Listeners. There are, however, prison staff who place great emphasis upon protecting the Listeners from emotional burnout. One prisoner stated that he needed to be reprieved of listener work to deal with a significant emotional event:

> Christmas was the anniversary of my mum's death and I thought at the moment that I shouldn't do any listening work because I can't spend any time on people with these things going through my mind. I was a bit gutted and a bit relieved … I knew I wouldn't be there for the people who are having problems … they wouldn't have my full attention. I would be letting them down, not listening to them.
>
> (Neil, Listener)

Neil recognises that he could not adhere to the correct set of 'feeling rules' and in spite of the training he had received as a Listener, he recognised that his judgement and emotional display may be impaired by the anniversary of his mum's death. Hochschild (1983) identifies the control that employers have over the emotional displays of their workers and in recognition of Neil's emotional state; the safer custody coordinator removed him from further duties:

> …we just take them off until they are ready to work again. They have got their own custodial lives and sentences to deal with…. you could have callers that are high intensity…we don't want them to burn out.
>
> (Dave, Custodial Manager)

Front stage performances (Goffman 1959) are hard to keep up in the prison environment because of the visibility and transparency of their lives, particularly in a small prison, where they are recognisable because of their Listener t-shirts. Giving emotional support to others means that the Listeners have to manage their own emotions very carefully. The prison regime controls the pace, timing and flow of emotions and there is very little private space for Listeners to express their own emotion (Crewe 2014). Deprivation of privacy (Schwartz 1972) is expressed as one of the pains experienced by prisoners (see Sykes 1958):

> I found out my grandma has cancer. I love her. I feel a bit of a let-down. I was in the shower yesterday; everyone was banged up. I must have been in there for about half an hour. I was just crying my eyes out. That's one of the hardest things about being in prison; you don't get any time alone. As a Listener, I rang for another Listener. It took the screws an hour to come and my next-door neighbour came in. When you are outside you can find a solution…in here there is nothing I can fucking do about that and that is really hard to deal with.
>
> (Steve, Listener)

The Listeners have a weekly meeting with the Samaritans, which is strictly off limits to prison staff. This gives Listeners a backstage opportunity to express emotions that they are feeling in their role and provides a collective support network for offloading. Voluntary workers like the Samaritans facilitate authentic emotional expressions amongst prisoners and provide non-judgemental working styles that are distinctly different from the authoritative approach taken by prison officers (Tomczak and Albertson 2016). Weekly meetings allow for honesty and openness, creating a safe space where Listeners can display vulnerability in front of other prisoners, thus providing a space where they can distance themselves from their prisoner self. Crewe et al. (2014) allude to spaces within the prison that are as "uncarceral as possible" and the weekly meeting allows prisoners to transcend their 'master status' (Becker 1963) for a finite period. Justin, one of the Samaritans, explains the utility of the Listener meetings:

> ...they offload to each other...I think that is the most important thing... if they are not getting the listening conditions they would like....eg calls cut short, brisk treatment, nowhere to go that is private, or staff don't know the rules of which we operate, they don't work the rota properly.... they offload...they have to exercise a huge amount of patience in the prison...
>
> (Justin, Samaritan volunteer)

Conclusion

This chapter has explored the emotional labour required by prison Listeners in carrying out their role. It is evident that Listeners perform an extremely complex role. Listeners have to negotiate many different aspects of prison life in order to survive the role, avoid burnout and placate both prison officers and their peers. Prison Listeners form an integral part of providing a safe prison and without their contributions, prison staff would struggle to cope with the increasingly challenging circumstances they face.

Further research could explore the extent to which Listeners are aware of the emotional labour involved and the 'taint' they may experience when performing the role. This may reduce the tensions experienced between prison Listeners and prison officers and improve current professional working relationships. It may also improve the relationship between Listeners and Samaritan's volunteers, though providing more insight into the 'dirty emotional work' that Listeners perform. The contrast between Listeners and prison officers in the performance of emotional labour is an interesting point with which to conclude; prison officers themselves engage in emotional labour during their work, engaging in culturally accepted feeling rules around emotional detachment from prisoners and an affinity for the punitive rather than the rehabilitative (see Chapter 5, this volume). An understanding of the consequences and costs of emotional labour may assist criminal justice workers, to understand the demands made upon Listeners, and assist them fully in their work.

References

Abraham, R (1999) The impact of emotional dissonance on organizational commitment and intention to turnover. *The Journal of Psychology*, 133, 4.

Becker, H (1963) *Outsiders; Studies in the Sociology of Deviance.* London: Free Press of Glencoe.

Biggar, K and Neal, D (1996) Caring for the suicidal in custody. *Omega*, 33, 207–213.

Braun, V and Clarke, V (2006) Using thematic analysis in psychology. *Qualitative Research in Psychology*, 3(2), 77–101.Chinelo, A (2010) *Listening in Prison.* Prisoner Education Trust, available online: http://pet.netefficiency.co.uk/index.php. Accessed 1 June 2016.

Clemmer, D (1940) *The Prison Community.* New York: Holt, Rinehart and Winston.

Connell, RW (1995) *Masculinities.* Cambridge: Polity Press; Sydney: Allen & Unwin; Berkeley: University of California Press.

Crewe, B et al. (2014) The emotional geography of prison life. *Theoretical Criminology*, 18(1), 56–74.

Festinger, L (1954) A theory of social comparison processes. *Human Relations*, 7(2), 117–140.

Foster, J (2011) *Peer Support in Prison Health Care. An Investigation into the Listening Scheme in One Adult Male Prison.* London: University of Greenwich.

Goffman, E (1959) *The Presentation of Self in Everyday Life.* Garden City, NY: Doubleday Anchor.

HM Inspectorate of Prisons (2016) *Life in Prison: Peer Support.*

HMPS (1992) *Caring for Prisoners at Risk of Suicide and Self-Injury: The Way Forward.* London: S.A.S. Unit.

HMPS (1993) *New Suicide Awareness Training Pack.* AG3/1993. London: HMPS.

HMPS (1994) *Caring for the Suicidal in Custody.* IG 1/1994. London: HMPS.

Hochschild, A (1983) *The Managed Heart: Commercialization of Human Feeling.* Berkeley: University of California Press.

Hughes, EC (1958) *Men and Their Work.* Toronto: Greenwood Press.

Ismail, N (2019) Rolling back the prison estate: the pervasive impact of macroeconomic austerity on prisoner health in England. *Journal of Public Health*, 19, 20143.

Jaffe, M (2012) Peer support and seeking help in a prison: a study of the Listeners scheme in four prisons in England, unpublished PhD, Keele University.

Liebling, A and Arnold, H (2005) *Prisons and Their Moral Performance: A Study of Values, Quality, and Prison Life.* Oxford: Oxford University Press.

McMurray, R and Ward, J (2014) 'Why would you want to do that?': defining emotional dirty work. *Human Relations*, 67(9), 1123–1143.

Matthews, R (2009) *Doing Time: An Introduction to the Sociology of Imprisonment.* Basingstoke: Palgrave.

Nixon, S (2018) "I just want to give something back" peer work and desistance, unpublished PhD thesis, De Montfort University, Leicester.

Perrin, C and Blagden, N (2014) Accumulating meaning, purpose and opportunities to change 'drip by drip': the impact of being a listener in prison. *Psychology, Crime and Law*, 20(9), 902–930.

Prison Reform Trust (2018) *Bromley Briefings Prison Factfile* (Autumn 2018). London: Prison Reform Trust.

Schwartz, B (1972) Deprivation of privacy as a functional prerequisite: the case of the prison. *The Journal of Criminal Law, Criminology, and Police Science*, 63, 272.

South, J, Bagnall, A, Hulme, C, Woodall, J, Longo, R, Dixey, R, Kinsella, K, Raine, G, Vinall, K and Wright, J (2014) A systematic review of the effectiveness and cost effectiveness of peer-based interventions to maintain and improve offender health in prison settings... *Health Services and Delivery Research*, 2(35).

Steinberg, RJ and Figart, DM (1999) Emotional labor since: the managed heart. *The Annals of the American Academy of Political and Social Science*, 561(1), 8–26.

Sykes, G (1958) *The Society of Captives: A Study of a Maximum-Security Prison*. Princeton: Princeton University Press.

Tait, S (2012) A typology of prison officer approaches to care. *European Journal of Criminology*, 8(6), 440–454.

Tomczak, PJ and Albertson, K (2016) Prisoner relationships with voluntary sector practitioners. *The Howard Journal of Crime and Justice*, 55(1–2), 57–72.

Van Gennep, A (1909) *The Rites of Passage*. Chicago: The University of Chicago Press.

Ward, J and McMurray, J (2016) The dark side of emotional labour. Abingdon: Routledge.

Chapter 16

Perspectives on the emotional labour of Special Constables

Iain Britton and Laura Knight

Introduction

Special Constables are volunteers in the role of part-time police officers, in possession of all the warranted powers of a 'regular' police officer, and typically indistinguishable in terms of uniform from the perspective of members of the public. Despite decreases in numbers over recent years, the official national total for Special Constables (Specials) stood at the sizeable number of 11,029 in September 2018 across the 43 police forces of England and Wales (Britton *et al.*, 2018a; Home Office, 2018). Specials represent a unique and interesting group, distinct from 'regular' officers in that they are volunteers, and distinguished from other groups of volunteers given the uniqueness of role and powers as fully warranted police officers. Increasingly, much of the operational context for their voluntary roles as police officers closely mirrors that of their paid 'regular' police officer colleagues. Involving frontline engagement with the public in policing contexts that are often confrontational, challenging, stressful and requiring the management and projection of a variety of positive and negative emotional responses. Exposure to emotionally challenging, disturbing and traumatic experiences, such as violent confrontations, serious road collisions and suicides, can be regular experiences for those in frontline policing roles (McCafferty *et al.*, 1990). There are also growing numbers of Specials in specialist policing settings, with one in ten Specials now being situated in a policing specialism such as roads policing and public protection (Britton *et al.*, 2018a). By the nature of such roles being 'specialist', this may potentially increase exposure to emotionally challenging contexts and to elements of trauma. Alongside converging operational contexts for Special Constables and 'regulars', there also co-exist cultural and identity differences between volunteer and 'regular' officers, which create challenges for Specials, particularly for those new in role.

In addition to exposure to situations which create both positive and negative emotional responses, the cultures evident in policing and the command and control structure of policing, set formal and informal standards and norms for emotional expression. Whilst the use of standardised rankings and uniforms create clarity of roles and responsibilities in emergency response and crisis situations, it is suggested that this highly visible structure has led to those working in uniforms to adhere to professional 'norms' and cultures (Chapman, 2009; Campeau, 2015). Police cultures tend to value and reward the suppression of emotion and the presentation of strength, resilience, professionalism and appearing in control (Van Gelderen et al., 2017). This is in part driven by the high visibility of the police officer role and responsibility, through uniforms, which provides a signal of assistance to the public and requires officers to be ready to respond or reassure anyone, at any time – resulting over time in the 'embodiment' of the role (Rafaeli and Sutton, 1987, 1991). Emotional labour is therefore considered an 'indispensable skill' in street-level occupations such as policing, to provide the control and reassurance required by the public (Mastracci et al., 2015:4) and required by policing command (Diefendorff et al., 2005). Whilst this literature points to a growing interest amongst academics in emotional labour in policing and law enforcement, this body of work has primarily focused on emotional labour in the context of paid, 'regular', police officers, and in common with much of the emotional labour literature has tended to neglect aspects of unpaid, voluntary emotional labour.

Over recent years, there has been only limited empirical research undertaken with volunteer officers either in the UK or internationally, representing a relatively neglected area of academic research in policing (Whittle, 2014; Hieke, 2015; Pepper and Wolf, 2015; Wolf et al., 2015; Bullock and Leeney, 2016; Dobrin and Wolf, 2016; Callender et al., 2018b). This is now changing, with increased research activity undertaken over the past five years, in particular in the UK context (Pepper, 2014; Whittle, 2014; Hieke, 2015; Pepper and Wolf, 2015; Wolf et al., 2015, 2016; Britton et al., 2016; Bullock and Leeney, 2016; Britton, 2017; Hieke, 2017; Britton et al., 2018b; Callender et al., 2018a,b).

Methods

The chapter draws upon findings from two national surveys of Special Constables in England and Wales, conducted in 2017 ($n = 1,096$), and 2018 ($n = 1,830$). These surveys represent an ongoing national online surveying programme managed by the Institute for Public Safety, Crime and Justice (University of Northampton), on behalf of the National Citizens in Policing Board. In each case, the surveys were distributed online to Special Constables across each of the 43 police forces in England and Wales in the spring of 2017 and the spring of 2018. The chapter also draws upon semi-structured interviews conducted with Special Constables, exploring their experiences and perspectives of volunteering as a Special, engaging Specials across five English police forces ($n = 90$). The semi-structured interviews allowed flexibility to engage with the key issues and elements of experiences and perspectives of the Special Constable participants. The interview schedule covered aspects of experience and perspectives in respect of their career paths and experiences as a Special, including motivations, recruitment, training, practice induction, their initial policing activities, field-training, experience in role, relationships with 'regular' police officers and others they serve alongside, supervision and support, their morale, their perspectives on culture and on leadership and their plans for the future. The interviews with Special Constable participants lasted approximately one hour each and were transcribed verbatim. The data from the interviews was then analysed thematically, following Braun and Clarke (2006) six steps of 'familiarisation' through reading transcripts, 'code generation', 'theme identification', 'review' of themes and codes, 'labelling themes' and 'report writing'. The quotations in the chapter each represent a different, distinct participant in the research.

Frontline exposure for volunteer police officers

Police work, unlike the majority of occupations, entails periods of constant alertness, being exposed to emotionally demanding interpersonal interactions requiring highly controlled mood and demeanour management, for the benefit of both the organisation and the public (Bakker and Heuven, 2006; Hochschild, 2003; O'Neill and Cushing, 1991). Alongside organisational stressors, such as lack of resources, shortage of officers and staff, poor equipment and difficult to navigate processes, the role of resilience and stress management in policing has been studied extensively (Miller, 2008; Shane, 2013; Balmer et al., 2014; Violanti, 2014; Andersen et al., 2015; Conn, 2016; Lovallo, 2016; Burke, 2017; McCreary et al., 2017). However, references to volunteer police officers are very rarely made across this wide research field, in the UK or internationally, despite experiences of similar context, role, emotional demands and stressors.

Experiences of emotionally challenging, negative, stressful and sometimes traumatic events were described by many Special Constables during interviews:

> And it was the smell, it will never go away from me, never. When I smell burnt toast, I am straight back. Back in that moment. You are experiencing someone's death. It hasn't affected me, I think you couldn't do this, this work, if it did. You have to stay professional. You have to be able to cope. We all have our ways of coping. It isn't for everybody, it really isn't.
> [SC interview]

> It's suicides I find the hardest. You do the process, do the job, then you come home, sit down, and it's so quiet, in the early hours, just thinking about it, thinking about that person, that life, their world.
> [SC interview]

Despite the voluntary nature of the Special Constable role, many used the language 'it's the job', reflecting their integration in the wider 'regular' police workforce and culture. The immersive nature of the social, cultural and emotional aspects of policing that are learnt 'on the job' (Chan *et al.*, 2003; Heslop, 2009) are paralleled in the Special Constabulary:

> Very early in my policing experience I attended a really bad RTC where people had died, you know... and it's just like, that's part of your job, mate, its part of the job, see you next week...
>
> [SC interview]

The desire to develop positive relationships with the 'regulars', to be perceived to be a competent and valuable asset to the team (Britton *et al.*, 2018a; Callender *et al.*, 2018b), drives swift adoption of police cultures in the Special Constabulary. This reflects similar traits in Police Community Support Officers (PCSO), a paid uniformed role in British policing which does not have the full warranted powers of constables, where police officers are considered 'higher' in social and cultural ranks (Cosgrove, 2016; O'Neill, 2017). For some Special Constables this may reflect the theory that officers protect and endorse aspects of the traditional policing culture because of its role in constructing and maintaining their identities as police officers (Cosgrove, 2016) which has social, and many more, benefits. In particular, it feeds the continued 'masculinisation' of police work, which values 'hard' policing and 'catching offenders' (Loftus; 2010; Cosgrove and Ramshaw, 2015). It is widely argued that this culture severely limits both the ability to recognise the emotional impact of police work and the willingness to access support (Reiner, 2000; Cockcroft, 2013; Lumsden and Black, 2018).

In addition to these frontline experiences and organisational stressors, some Special Constables reflect on the emotional challenges of being limited in their roles, skills or authorities, when there is an evident need or issue:

> She's wrong side of the bridge, I have to do 70 miles per hour, I've got members of the public going faster than me, going 80, 90 miles an hour and I can't do a damn thing about it, yet I could get there a little bit quicker and maybe stop that person.
>
> [SC interview]

> If there's a report comes in of a drunk bloke staggering down the hard shoulder, I wouldn't want to be sat on the motorway junction, you know, waiting for the call to come in to say that someone's just hit a bloke on the motorway and I've been sat there not doing anything about it when I could have gone down the hard shoulder and picked him up...the force, by not equipping you with training, it places you into that moral

dilemma because actually if you were trained it would be a no brainer. The call would come in, you'd go straight down there...

[SC interview]

These types of 'moral dilemmas' create emotional labour for Special Constables in ways that may differ to 'regular' officers. The part-time nature of volunteering as a police officer also means that opportunities to 'debrief' with colleagues informally, to talk through the challenging incidents or moments of the day or week, are limited. Over the course of 40 hours of police work, relatively speaking, Special Constables may deliver more frontline, emergency response and interactions with victims, offenders and members of the public, than 'regular' officers do. The nature of the voluntary role means that much of the administration burden, 'downtime' and engagement in wider organisational activities or 'bureaucracies' undertaken by 'regular' officers, is avoided or missed. Whilst this can be positive for engaging volunteers in meaningful, impactful, interesting and exciting work, it also means that Special Constables may in some senses be more exposed to frontline challenges and trauma.

Gaps in provision of support

The different, part-time operating models for Special Constables compared to their 'regular' paid police officer colleagues also leads to reduced involvement and connectedness with key elements of police organisations, such as HR support, welfare support and wider communications and briefings (Britton, 2017). These services often tend to operate on a weekday 9–5 model, which poorly maps against the times that many Special Constables are present. This results sometimes in Specials being missed or forgotten in debriefs, welfare and support considerations:

When attending distressing incidents I have known and seen Specials that have 'slipped through the crack' whereas the force has supported the 'regular' officers more vigorously. Ultimately sometimes there is a lack of ownership over the welfare of Specials.

[SC national survey]

I was injured while on duty, besides medical attention received nothing else, no follow up.

[SC national survey]

Lack of support was found to be the second highest reason behind intentions to leave the Special Constabulary (Callender et al., 2018a:17), the only higher factor being leaving to join the paid, 'regular' police service. Missing the 'downtime' and informal debriefing appears to be significant for Specials dealing with the emotional labour of frontline policing and emergency response. The concept of the 'canteen culture' in policing (Holdaway, 1983; Fielding, 1988; Reiner, 2000) pulls together the experience of being at risk of serious violence in the job, with the camaraderie of police officers looking out for each other in this 'perceived shared adversity' (Hopkins Burke, 2014:152). Whilst many point to this culture as a factor in stereotyping, 'other-ing', institutional racism and wider issues in police-community relations (see Waddington, 2008; Cockcroft, 2013; Hopkins Burke, 2014), its role in creating an environment of peer-support is important in relation to dealing with emotional labour.

The emotional toll of experiencing horrific events second-hand, often experienced by police officers, can lead to 'vicarious trauma' or post-traumatic stress (Mastracci *et al.*, 2015:36). Whilst this is widely understood and researched (Hart and Cotton, 2003; Manzoni and Eisner, 2006; Vaughan *et al.*, 2016) and increasing research explores the impact and efficacy of provision of support and initiatives to improve emotional resilience (Robertson *et al.*, 2015), much of this work does not engage the Special Constabulary. Whilst there are many cultural barriers to accessing support in policing more broadly, Special Constables in particular express a desire for more support without a sense of fear of stigma for receiving support:

> You see terrible things on a shift, then you go home. There probably should be more to support us but it's not usually the case that there is. I'm not complaining, I love policing, I do this only because I love policing, wouldn't change a thing, but a bit more support, yes, that would sometimes be good.
>
> [SC interview]

> I was one of the first on scene for a fatal hit and run, and there was no support given to me or even a welfare check to see how I was after it.
>
> [SC national survey]

This is supported by findings from the national survey of perceptions and experiences of volunteers in policing, which found that: over one-quarter of Special Constables, 27%, disagreed that they receive emotional support within their role; 19% disagreed that they would be provided with appropriate support if they experienced a traumatic event whilst on duty; and 29% disagreed that they would be provided with appropriate support 'if there was a problem or something went wrong' (Callender *et al.*, 2018a:15–17). In addition to this, the 2017 national representation survey found that whilst the majority of Special Constables agreed with the statement 'adequate support is provided to Specials who have had distressing experiences', 35% disagreed (Britton, 2017:7). A larger proportion, 45%, disagreed with the statement 'adequate support is provided to Specials who are injured in the line of their duties' (Britton, 2017:7). Reflecting failings to systematically implement specific and improved support for volunteer officers, perceptions of disparity between Special Constables and paid, 'regular' police officers is evident: 89% of respondents feel that 'regular' officers are better supported than Specials if an issue arises (Britton, 2017:8).

> The most important thing is having the same rights as the 'regulars' and the same support - there is a massive gap between the two – 'regulars' seem to get support all the time and the Specials are sometimes, not all the time but sometimes, forgotten about.
>
> [SC national survey]

> There is a process that should be followed, it is to an extent but that's about it, it's a tick box exercise. They ['regular' colleagues] do this all the time, but at that point in my life I hadn't experienced anything remotely like that.
>
> [SC interview]

Support for volunteer police officers is sometimes seen to be 'tacked onto' support to 'regulars', with failings in communication about what is available, poor accessibility of support out of office-hours, and poor knowledge amongst Special Constable supervisors and line managers about incidents that have occurred (Britton, 2017). This experience by Specials of shortcomings in visible, accessible support for Special Constables may impact upon their development of coping mechanisms for dealing with the emotional labour of frontline policing.

Surface and deep acting: being a volunteer in police cultures

Police officers, and those in other occupations, will often reframe or refocus the nature of their work to minimise the emotional 'dirty work' and 'socially problematic' features of their roles (Ward and McMurray, 2015:68). Research shows that first responders use a variety of techniques to deal with the mental and emotional images that they encounter and that stay with them long after the incident, including using 'little closets' in their minds, adopting a calm countenance despite inner-feelings, or they push a 'pause-button' (Mastracci et al., 2015:39). Pausing feelings until 'later', or compartmentalising them, can be seen as dehumanising the self, to take control of the highly charged emotional situation. In reacting to verbal abuse from the public for example, the police officer cannot react in a 'normal' way, due to the 'overt or covert control of the police command over the officer's response' (Chapman, 2009). A similar notion has been described as the police 'working personality' (Skolnik, 1994:41) in response to the elements of danger, authority and efficiency within the role, which also serves to dehumanise the self whilst in uniform (and often beyond).

For Special Constables, there is often the added pressure of 'surface acting' in respect of actively seeking to quickly 'fit in' with 'regular', paid police officers, to gain respect, credibility and social networks in policing to support development of skills and opportunities. This can be the result of the Special Constabulary being viewed by the 'regular' service as a 'creche' for police officers, due to the age profile tending to be younger and because the cohort tends to be around one-third new recruits and those in early training, and it takes time to build operational competence and confidence when volunteering on a part-time basis (Britton *et al.*, 2018a). The challenges of 'fitting in' and making fast progress to 'get on' can also result in a 'deep acting' over-identification with the police officer role, cultures and display personalities in policing (Gill and Mawby, 1990; Leon, 1991). Our research highlights the pressure that Special Constables put upon themselves to quickly adopt the language and style of police officers in their teams or departments, to prove themselves and to 'survive':

> My advice to any new Special would be to watch the regs in your team and try to be them, as much like them as possible. I don't mean like mimic them, just see what they do, how they approach jobs, how they speak. That way they come to see you, to see you as being one of them, part of the team.
>
> [SC national survey]

> You kind of have to prove yourself to the 'regulars'. So you have to prove that you're capable, and you can deal with things... Whenever you're out with someone, making sure that you're kind of pulling your weight, you're doing your bit. Putting the effort in and things... and then they respect you.
>
> [SC interview]

This additional emotional labour means the experience for those joining as new volunteer police officers appears to be mentally and emotionally exhausting, dealing with organisational cultures and expectations alongside frontline exposure to serious incidents and trauma, often with consequences of depersonalisation:

> My first shift? To be honest, terrifying. Everything went so fast. I hadn't done any of it before. The officer I was with, she was amazing, but didn't have much time to explain anything. We attended a nasty fight, a domestic and a serious collision. I'm used to it all now, but that first night was a major shock.
>
> [SC interview]

Turned up for the first shift not a clue who was who, what kit was needed etc. total lack of support… so in summary in my case there was no transition more like a blind leap. I had to learn to fit in, the language, know the team. I had to do the running to make all that happen myself.

[SC national survey]

Findings from the national survey reiterate this sense that Special Constables occupy a disempowered position in policing, where they are lacking in voice and influence to access the resources and support required to facilitate their ability and wellbeing in role. Twenty-four per cent of Special Constables disagreed that they were 'treated with respect' by 'regular' officers and 19% disagreed that they 'are treated fairly' (Callender, 2018a:12). Sixty-eight per cent of Special Constables felt that some of their time was wasted and for those having served two years or less; 29% do not think the police force understands the skills they bring to the role (Callender, 2018a:18–19). Supporting these findings, the national representation survey found that 23% disagreed that they felt they could voice concerns if they had them (Britton, 2017). This context appears to put the onus onto Special Constables to develop social networks, relationships and credibility to achieve a position where they are better supported by 'regulars':

They're a tight-knit group. I wouldn't say a matter of years but it certainly took a while to form relationships with 'regular' officers.

[SC interview]

In the end, yeah, it was fine. He kind of accepted me as part of the gang, I suppose. But it just took a while, which, fair enough, I suppose.

[SC interview]

However, this clearly creates challenges and issues for those working hard to achieve this goal, particularly in relation to the ambiguity of what it takes to 'fit in' to policing cultures and identities. Some of the comments made in interviews suggest there is a desirable, prototypical 'type', that displays confidence in taking control in unknown situations or speedily putting into practice what has been learned in theory. In addition, there appears to be a requirement for 'dealing' with banter and getting 'stuck in'. This reflects much literature regarding the values within policing cultures, for the perceived to be 'more masculine' traits of extrovert, commanding, controlling and forceful communication styles, as opposed to skills in calm and negotiating dialogue, for example (Loftus, 2010; Corsianos, 2011; Cosgrove and Ramshaw, 2015):

Learn from them ['regulars']. How to speak, to behave at scenes, talk to suspects, speak on the radio. Don't think you know it all. Be prepared to get stuck in. So many new Specials aren't the right sort and don't do that and they never fit in.

[SC interview]

It's about gaining credibility and trust. And unfortunately there are some Specials who, because of their manner the way they come across, 'cause they're the wrong sort, don't mean to sound horrible, the wrong sort of people, they don't get that, they can't deal with the banter or the humour, 'cause it is that type of environment, it's getting out in the van and going and doing your public order, you can't be a shrinking violet, you've got to have that level of confidence. And it's getting stuck in, what they hate is when people sit back.

[SC interview]

These themes in our findings and more broadly in police cultural studies align with concepts of 'display rules' in emotional labour literature, requiring the 'masking' of certain emotions to fit in or to survive in role long-term. This constant emotional labour requires effort, planning and control, particularly where the process of regulating negative emotions is taking place both in 'safe' contexts in policing, such as briefing rooms, and during unpredictable interactions with the public and when dealing with challenging and traumatic incidents. This discrepancy between feelings inside and displays leads to effortful emotion management and emotional dissonance (Rafaeli and Sutton, 1987; Bhomwick and Zubin, 2016). Special Constables describe learning how to hold it in:

Know your place. If you ruffle feathers all you do is get a target on your back, you're a troublemaker and an upstart acting above your station. No account whatsoever is taken of skills that are acquired outside the Police Service. You are regularly treated as an idiot and ignored as the culture is that any experience gained elsewhere doesn't count. I have built successful businesses from the ground up, recruited, employed and managed staff and large projects but the assumption is I know nothing. After a while you learn to hold it all in, there's just no point being the rebel.

[SC interview]

I hate that we're second-class police officers, but you learn to bottle it up.

[SC interview]

This results in both 'surface' and 'deep' acting, whereby Special Constables mask negative emotions and learn to display the emotions, characteristics and personality styles that are valued, respected and supporting in policing. However, these processes are linked to negative wellbeing outcomes (Trougakos *et al.*, 2011) and perhaps surface as perceptions of lack of support from 'regular' officers and contribute to the one-third of Special Constables who resign each year (Britton *et al.*, 2018).

Conclusions: the impacts of emotional labour for Special Constables

The context of emotional labour for volunteer police officers is highly significant. In operational respects, the emotional labour undertaken by Specials is consistent and resonant with that experienced by 'regular' police officers (Kwak *et al.*, 2018), reflecting a picture in which operational environment, and related aspects of emotion control and trauma exposure, are increasingly convergent for all police officers, voluntary and paid. In organisational and cultural respects, the position of Special Constable holds a distinction and distance to that of their 'regular' officer colleagues. Whilst Specials may experience less of the bureaucratic and organisational stressors that research reflects as significant for 'regular' officers (Brown and Campbell, 1990; Zhao *et al.*, 2002; Collins and Gibbs, 2003), they instead experience significant emotional work to manage challenges in respect of status, relating to connection and integration, and reflecting ambiguities of role, cultural positioning and professional identity. This emotional labour can lead to burnout for Special Constables (Hieke, 2015).

Early-in-career resignation of the majority of Specials, even those not intent on a career in the 'regular' service, alongside significant patterns of disengagement and dormancy within the Special Constabulary, are likely also to contribute to the emotional labour of the Special role (Britton *et al.*, 2018a). High turnover of volunteers and limited support and relationships with 'regular' officers provides a context in which Specials are learning and delivering frontline policing whilst continuously managing their presentation as credible and confident police officers.

To combat the potential impact of these different types of emotional labour, the experience of Specials needs to be much better understood and support needs to be tailored to the specific experience of volunteer officers. This support also needs to be better, and more consistently, organised, resourced and delivered. Alongside this, long-recognised challenges in respect of status, integration and role, cultural challenges and ambiguities of professional identity need to be recognised and tackled with a focus and urgency that has not been seen over recent decades. The example of Special Constables points to the importance of appreciating and engaging with aspects of emotional labour for volunteers in policing (and beyond) alongside a focus on the paid workforce, and for the emergent literature on emotional labour and the police to grow more convincingly from a 'regular'-centric orientation to engage across the police family as a whole.

References

Andersen, J., Papazoglou, K., Nyman, M., Koskelainen, M. and Gustafsberg, H. (2015) 'Fostering resilience among police', *The Journal of Law Enforcement*, 5(1), 1–13.

Bakker, A. and Heuven, E. (2006) 'Emotional dissonance, burnout, and in-role performance among nurses and police officers', *International Journal of Stress Management*, 13(4), 423–440.

Balmer, G., Pooley, J. and Cohen, L. (2014) 'Psychological resilience of western Australian police officers: Relationship between resilience, coping style, psychological functioning and demographics', *Police Practice and Research: An International Journal*, 15(4), 270–282.

Bhomwick, S. and Zubin, M. (2016) 'Emotional labour of policing: Does authenticity play a role?', *International Journal of Police Science and Management*, 18(1), 47–60.

Braun, V. and Clarke, V. (2006) 'Using thematic analysis in psychology', *Qualitative Research in Psychology*, 3(2), 77–101.

Britton, I. (2017) *The Representation of Special Constables: Headline Findings from the National Survey*. Northampton: Institute for Public Safety, Crime and Justice.

Britton, I., Callender, M. and Cole, S. (2016) *National Survey of Special Constables and Police Support Volunteers: Initial Findings Report*. Northampton: Institute for Public Safety, Crime and Justice.

Britton, I., Knight, L.J. and Lugli, V. (2018a) *Citizens in Policing 2018 Benchmarking Exercise*. Northampton: Institute for Public Safety, Crime and Justice.

Britton, I., Wolf, R. and Callender, M. (2018b) 'A comparative case study of Reserve Deputies in a Florida sheriff's office and Special Constables in an English police force', *International Journal of Police Science and Management*, 20(8), 259–271.

Brown, J. and Campbell, E. (1990) 'Sources of occupational stress in the police', *Work & Stress: An International Journal of Work, Health and Organisations*, 4(4), 305–318.

Bullock, K. and Leeney, D. (2016) 'On matters of balance: An examination of the deployment, motivation and management of the Special Constabulary', *Police and Society: An International Journal of Research and Policy*, 26(5), 483–502.

Burke, R. (2017) *Stress in Policing: Sources, Consequences and Interventions*. New York: Routledge.

Callender, M., Cahalin, K., Britton, I. and Knight, L.J. (2018a) *National Survey of Special Constables: September 2018*. Northampton: Institute for Public Safety, Crime and Justice.

Callender, M., Cahalin, K., Cole, S., Hubbard, L. and Britton, I. (2018b) 'Understanding the motivations, morale and retention of Special Constables: Findings from a national survey', *Policing: A Journal of Policy and Practice*.

Campeau, H. (2015) 'Police culture at work: Making sense of police oversight', *British Journal of Criminology*, 55(4), 669–687.

Chan, J., Devery, C. and Doran, S. (2003) *Fair Cop: Learning the Art of Policing*. Toronto: University of Toronto Press.

Chapman, D. (2009) 'Emotional labour in the context of policing in Victoria: A preliminary analysis', *International Journal of Police Science Management*, 11, 476–492.

Cockcroft, T. (2013) *Police Culture: Themes and Concepts*. New York: Routledge.

Collins, P. and Gibbs, A. (2003) 'Stress in police officers: A study of the origins, prevalence and severity of stress-related symptoms within a county police force', *Occupational Medicine*, 53, 256–264.

Conn, S. (2016) 'Stress in policing', In G. Fink (Ed.), *Stress: Concepts, Cognition, Emotion, and Behavior: Handbook in stress series* (Vol. 1). London: Academic Press, 393–400.

Corsianos, M. (2011) 'Responding to officers' gendered experiences through community policing and improving police accountability to citizens', *Contemporary Justice Review*, 14(1), 7–20.

Cosgrove, F. and Ramshaw, P. (2015) 'It is what you do as well as the way you do it: The value and deployment of PCSOs in achieving public engagement', *Policing and Society*, 25(1), 77–96.

Cosgrove, F. (2016) "I wannabe a copper': The engagement of Police Community Support Officers with the dominant police occupational culture', *Criminology and Criminal Justice*, 16(1), 119–138.

Diefendorff, J., Croyle, M. and Gosserand, R. (2005) 'The dimensionally and antecedents of emotional labour strategies', *Journal of Vocational Behaviour*, 66, 339–357.

Dobrin, A. and Wolf, R. (2016) 'What is known and not known about volunteer policing in the United States', *International Journal of Police Science & Management*, 18(3), 220–227.

Fielding, N. (1988) *Joining Forces*. London: Routledge.

Gill, M. and Mawby, R. (1990) *A Special Constable: A Study of the Police Reserve*. Aldershot: Avebury.

Hart, P. and Cotton, P. (2003) 'Conventional wisdom is often misleading: Police stress within an organisational health framework', In M. Dollard, A. Winefield and H. Winefield (Eds.), *Occupational Stress in the Service Professions*. London: Taylor & Francis, 103–142.

Heslop, R. (2009) Police recruit training and 'community engagement': Unintended consequences. EdD thesis. Leeds: University of Leeds.

Hieke, G. (2015) Burnout and connectedness within the Special Constabulary: An analysis of the factors associated with volunteer job satisfaction, organisational commitment and retention. PhD thesis. Warwick: University of Warwick.

Hieke, G. (2017) 'General perspectives on volunteer motivation within the Special Constabulary', In K. Bullock and A. Millie (Eds.), *The Special Constabulary: Historical Context, International Comparisons and Contemporary Themes*. Abingdon: Routledge, 80–93.

Hochschild, A. (2003) *The Managed Heart: Commercialization of Human Feeling* (20th ed.). Berkeley: University of California Press.

Holdaway, S. (1983) *Inside the British Police: A Force at Work*. Oxford: Blackwell.

Home Office (2018) *Police Workforce England and Wales: September 2018*. www.gov.uk/government/statistics/police-workforce-england-and-wales-30-september-2018 [accessed 20/4/2019].

Hopkins Burke, R. (2014) *An Introduction to Criminological Theory* (4th ed.). London: Routledge.

Kwak, H., McNeeley, S. and Kim, S. (2018) 'Emotional labor, role characteristics, and police officer burnout in South Korea: The mediating effect of emotional dissonance', *Police Quarterly*, 21(2), 223–249.

Leon, C. (1991) Special Constables: An historical and contemporary survey. PhD thesis. Bath: Bath University.

Loftus, B. (2010) 'Police occupational culture: Classic themes, altered times', *Policing and Society*, 20(1), 1–20.

Lovallo, W. (2016) *Stress and Health: Biological and Psychological Interactions* (3rd ed.). London: Sage publications.

Lumsden, K. and Black, A. (2018) 'Austerity policing, emotional labour and the boundaries of police work: An ethnography of a Police Force Control Room in England', *British Journal of Criminology*, 58, 606–623.

Manzoni, P. and Eisner, M. (2006) 'Violence between the police and the public: Influences of work-related stress, job satisfaction, burnout, and situational factors', *Criminal Justice and Behaviour*, 33(5), 613–645.

Mastracci, S., Guy, M. and Newman, M. (2015) *Emotional Labour and Crisis Response: Working on the Razor's Edge*. Oxford: Routledge.

McCafferty, F., Domingo, G. and McCafferty, E.A. (1990) 'Post-traumatic stress disorder in the police officer: paradigm of occupational stress', *Southern Medical Journal*, 83(5), 543–547.

McCreary, D., Fong, I. and Groll, D. (2017) 'Measuring police stress meaningfully: Establishing norms and cut-off values for the operational and organizational police stress questionnaires', *Police Practice and Research: An International Journal*, 18(6), 612–623.

Miller, L. (2008) 'Stress and resilience in law enforcement training and practice', *International Journal of Emergency Mental Health*, 10(2), 109–124.

O'Neill, M. (2017) 'Police community support officers in England: A dramaturgical analysis', *Policing and Society*, 27(1), 21–39.

O'Neill, J. and Cushing, M. (1991) *The Impact of Shift Work on Police Officers*. Washington, D.C.: Police Executive Research Forum.

Pepper, I. (2014) 'Do part-time voluntary police officers aspire to be regular police officers?', *Police Journal*, 87(2), 105–113.

Pepper, I. and Wolf, R. (2015) 'Volunteering to serve: An international comparison of volunteer police officers in a UK North East Police Force and a US Florida Sheriff's Office', *The Police Journal: Theory, Practice and Principles*, 88(3), 209–219.

Rafaeli, A. and Sutton, R.I. (1987) 'Expression of emotion as part of the work role', *The Academy of Management Review*, 12(1), 23–37.

Rafaeli, A. and Sutton, R.I. (1991) 'Emotional contrast strategies as means of social influence: Lessons from criminal interrogators and bill collectors', *Academy of Management Journal*, 34(4), 749–775.

Reiner, R. (2000) 'Crime and control in Britain', *Sociology*, 34(1), 71–94.

Robertson, I.T., Cooper, C.L., Sarkar, M. and Curran, T. (2015) 'Resilience training in the workplace from 2003 to 2014: A systematic review', *Journal of Occupational and Organisational Psychology*, 88(3), 533–562.

Shane, J. (2013) 'Daily work experiences and police performance', *Police Practice and Research: An International Journal*, 14(1), 17–34.

Skolnik, J.H. (1994) *Justice without Trial: Law Enforcement in Democratic Society* (3rd ed.). London: Wiley.

Trougakos, J., Jackson, C. and Beal, D. (2011) 'Service without a smile: Comparing the consequences of neutral and positive display rules', *Journal of Applied Psychology*, 96(2), 350–362.

Van Gelderen, B., Konijn, E. and Bakker, A. (2017) 'Emotional labor among police officers: A diary study relating strain, emotional labor, and service performance', *The International Journal of Human Resource Management*, 28(6), 852–879.

Vaughan, A., Moran, C., Pearce, L. and Hearty, L. (2016) 'The influence of organisational support on the life course of trauma in emergency responders from British Columbia', *Journal of Workplace Behavioral Health*, 31(3), 125–143.

Violanti, J.M. (2014) 'Police resiliency: An integration of individual and organization', *International Journal of Emergency Mental Health*, 16(2), 270–271.

Waddington, P. (2008) 'Police culture', In T. Newburn and P. Neyroud (Eds.), *Dictionary of Policing*. Collumpton: Willan.

Ward, J. and McMurray, R. (2015) *The Dark Side of Emotional Labour*. Oxford: Routledge.

Whittle, J. (2014) 'The rise of the Special Constabulary: Are forces getting value for money from their voluntary officers? An empirical study in Avon and Somerset Police', *The Police Journal*, 87(1), 29–40.

Wolf, R., Holmes, S. and Jones, C. (2015) 'Utilization and satisfaction of volunteer law enforcement officers in the office of the American sheriff: An exploratory nationwide survey', *Police Practice and Research*, 17(5), 448–462.

Wolf, R., Pepper, I. and Dobrin, A. (2016) 'An exploratory international comparison of professional confidence in volunteer policing', *The Police Journal: Theory, Practice and Principles*, 88(3), 209–219.

Zhao, J., He, N. and Lovrich, N. (2002) 'Predicting five dimensions of police officer stress: Looking more deeply into organizational setting for sources of police stress', *Police Quarterly*, 5(1), 43–62.

Chapter 17

Anger and the emotional culture of death penalty defense lawyers

Matthew John-William Greife, Mark Pogrebin and Sarah Goodrum

> We give a piece of ourselves to every client that we represent, and some-
> day there [are] not going to be any pieces left, but I still have a few.
> (CDL#2, Elliott Young, Death Penalty Defense
> Attorney with 31 Years of Experience)

Introduction

Despite the longstanding belief that the law should function in an unemotional manner and that lawyers should manage cases and clients with professional objectivity, emotions prove pervasive in the legal system in the United
States, particularly in *capital murder* cases (see also Chapter 3, this volume).
Emotions play a central role in jurors' deliberations about the guilt or innocence of the defendant, in prosecutors' characterizations of the defendant as
evil, in defense attorneys' depictions of the defendant's family background,
and in victims' grief-stricken accounts of who and what they lost (Bandes
1996; Goodrum 2013; Lynch and Haney 2014). The criminal justice system
creates a hostile setting for the death penalty defense attorneys representing
capital defendants (Sarat 1998) causing these attorneys to feel 'hammered' by
the public and frustrated with prosecutors and judges, while also feeling sad
for their client's troubled childhood and legal situation (Sarat 1998; see also
Sheffer 2013). Thus, death penalty defense lawyers develop what Sarat (1998)
calls a "bunker mentality" which is a self-righteous and defensive posture.
Yet, little systematic research explores the emotional dynamics experienced
within this mental bunker.

For more than 40 years, social scientists have studied the management of
emotions in the workplace, finding that employers expect employees to suppress certain negative emotions (Fineman 2005; Hochschild 1983; Lois 2005)
and maintain a stoic demeanor (Goodrum and Stafford 2003; Pogrebin and
Poole 1990; Smith and Kleinman 1989). Studies looking at criminal justice
employees largely find that workers like police officers and prosecutors are

expected to remain unemotional in encounters with volatile suspects, horrific tragedies and devastated victims (Goodrum 2011; Goodrum and Stafford 2003; Pogrebin and Poole 1991; Smith and Kleinman 1989). However, with defense attorneys, being emotionally detached from clients may lead to undesirable outcomes for those seeking legal assistance. For instance, legal aid lawyers that became detached and unemotional in their representation may leave their clients in worse situations than before they sought help from an attorney (Zaloznaya and Nielsen 2011: 940). Hence, for criminal defense lawyers emotion is an aspect of successfully defending their clients which suggests emotional labor is being performed.

That said, emotional labor is 'cultured' (Mesquita and Delvaux 2012: 252) and shaped within an organizational context (Pugh et al. 2012: 200–202). Within the criminal defense arena capital punishment defenders are highly unique because they work in a specialized practice area with its own cultural expectations and attitudes (Gould and Barak 2019: 44) where being emotional rather than emotionless are seemingly the best way to advocate for their clients (Mihai 2011). Virtually every death penalty defense lawyer has a deeply emotional moral opposition to the death penalty which is seemingly necessary to engage in capital defense work (Gould and Barak 2019; Sheffer 2013). The moral opposition to the death penalty exists within an emotional culture in death penalty defense work. However, it is unclear what emotions may be expressed within the death penalty defense lawyer's emotional culture that aids in supporting their moral opposition to capital punishment. This research relies on data from a larger qualitative study on death penalty defense attorneys and argues that attorneys largely embrace feelings of anger towards the death penalty, prosecutors and judges as part of their moral opposition to capital punishment. We argue the expression of anger is a significant part of the death penalty defense lawyer's emotional culture, and helps attorneys do the very difficult work of capital defense. By identifying the emotional culture of death penalty defense lawyers, future research can analyze when and how emotional labor is being performed.

Literature review

Emotional cultures are 'patterns of meanings embodied in symbols by which people communicate, perpetuate and develop their knowledge about attitudes towards emotions' (Gordon 1989: 115). Thus, emotional cultures not only dictate what emotions may result in certain situations but how emotions should be interpreted, acted on and expressed (Lois 2001: 382). To date, we are unaware of any research looking at the emotional culture of criminal defense lawyers generally and capital defense attorneys specifically.

Defense attorneys have been described as double agents working against their client's best interest in order to secure plea deals with minimal effort (Blumberg 1967) but recent work suggests this view may be inaccurate

(Uphoff 1992). For instance, Emmelman (1998) found that public defenders carefully evaluated the strength of the prosecution's case and prepare for a plea bargain similar to the processes used for trial preparation. Etienne (2005: 1196) argues that 'cause lawyering' represents a critical aspect of criminal defense work and finds that defense attorneys feel driven by deeply held moral belief which contradicts the 'hired gun' perspective of defense attorneys (see Blumberg 1967; Etienne 2005; Flower, 2018; Goodpaster 1983; Goodrum et al. 2015; Lefcourt 1996; Sheffer 2013; Skolnick 1967; Sudnow 1965).

In regard to death penalty defense lawyers, research suggests the attorneys have a deep moral opposition to capital punishment (Gould and Barak 2019: 66) that is expressed by empathetic connections with clients and feelings of sadness and melancholy when they are executed. Regarding empathy, death penalty defense lawyers discuss feeling empathetic for their clients and the lives they suffered through prior to committing serious crimes. In particular the lawyers discuss their emotional relationship with clients as 'the most important part of the work' (Sheffer 2013: 149). The empathy developed by death penalty defense lawyers for their clients through an emotional connection is how they personalize defendants to juries in order to secure a life sentence over death (Berman and Bibas 2008; Lynch and Haney 2014; Sheffer 2013). Empathy also reinforces a moral commitment against capital punishment (Gould and Barak 2019: 157–163).

Lawyers also indicate that death penalty defense work is sad and depressing because they are also advisors, confidants and therapists to their clients. Even in the hours before the execution, defense attorneys sit with and comfort their clients awaiting death. A California death penalty defense attorney, Charles Sevilla (1995: 96) wrote, 'One of my tasks, which I felt inadequate to handle, [was to monitor] Robert through the night [before his execution] to see if he was holding together'. In describing his client's last few hours and capturing the personal attorney-client connection, Sevilla (1995: 99) said:

> To members of his defense team, Robert reiterated his heartfelt thanks. He said he was proud of the people who worked for him, we had been good friends to him, and he appreciated the time he had been given to gain some insight as to how he could have perpetrated his crimes...we had our last hug. Then, they took him to the room behind the gas chamber...the feeling of powerlessness, failure and loss were overwhelming.

Despite the sadness, depression and melancholy experienced by the lawyers, they are largely able to move forward and begin working on the next case with vigor (Gould and Barak 2019: 201–240). This progression suggests feelings of sadness, depression and melancholy is an integral part of emotional culture.

Interestingly, most accounts of death penalty defense work do not look at negative emotions such as anger and hatred. Recently, Gould and Barak (2019) noted that death penalty defense lawyers do feel a significant amount of anger towards capital punishment but did not state whether or not expressing anger is appropriate in the specific emotional culture of capital defense lawyers. In this chapter, we analyze the negative emotion of anger and argue that it is an acceptable emotion to embrace within the death penalty defense lawyer's emotional culture because it helps in their moral quest of exposing the arbitrary and unfair nature of the death penalty through strong and passionate advocacy (Mello 1989) while reinforcing their moral opposition to capital punishment.

Data collection and analysis

The data for the study come from a larger project on death penalty defense attorneys conducted in 2012 and 2013 in a mid-sized Western state in the United States. The state's Public Defenders' Office is nationally recognized for its high-quality training of death penalty defense attorneys. As a result, the state and these defenders provide an excellent opportunity for a study on the development of death penalty defense attorneys.

We conducted in-depth interviews with 15 death penalty defense attorneys practicing in the state (3% of the population of death penalty defense attorneys in the United States). To recruit participants, we sent letters to the 15 attorneys that have defended capital cases through a snowballing technique requesting their involvement in the project, but not one of them responded to the letter. To follow up, we contacted each participant via phone, and in several cases, we called the participant multiple times before finally getting interviews with all 15 lawyers. All of the participants were talkative and candid about their backgrounds, law school training and work experience during the interviews.

Each interview relied on an active and unstructured approach (Holstein and Gubrium 1995), and took approximately one hour. Four of the participants (27%) are female. All participants are White. Nine participants (60%) worked as a private and public defense lawyer, and six participants (40%) worked in the public defender's office only. Fourteen of the fifteen participants had worked on death penalty trials; one of the participants worked specifically on death penalty appeals. Participants had between 18 and 41 years of experience in criminal defense work with an average of 29 years of experience. Fourteen of the fifteen participants are currently practicing defense attorneys. The high quality of criminal defense attorney training in the state and their lengthy experience may make these respondents more passionate about and personally invested in defense work than defense attorneys from other states.

Data analysis

All interview transcripts were read three times and the transcripts were manually coded using the principles of grounded theory (Charmaz 2006).

The questions and responses of focus addressed defense attorneys' motivations for their chosen specialty, feelings about the death penalty and their work, and relationship with their clients. All three broad themes capture the emotional experiences of our participants during death penalty defense work. Interview excerpts with awkward stalls and false starts (e.g., you know, um, well) were edited slightly to improve the flow and clarity of the quoted text (Wolcott 1994). To protect participants' identities, pseudonyms replace names, dates and places. The statements most clearly reflecting the recurrent themes in the data are reported in the findings. Participants' pseudo names and years of experience are listed at the end of their quotes.

Findings

After conducting our interviews, we found that the emotional culture of capital defense lawyers allows for an expression of anger to manifest in two distinct themes. The first theme was that death penalty defense attorneys expressed a deep moral opposition to capital punishment, and an intense anger for the state's continued use of the death penalty. The second theme was that our participants expressed anger towards individuals (e.g., prosecutors, judges and citizens), institutions (e.g., courts and government), and our culture which allows for the continued use of capital punishment. Admittedly, the presence of anger in this type of cause lawyering is not surprising; however, the intensity of the anger is. In regard to the first theme of moral opposition the following accounts were expressed by Elliott Young and Tina Carter, two attorneys with more than 20 years of experience in death penalty defense litigation.

> I hate the death penalty. I feel a moral obligation...to fight...And my moral outrage at [the] twenty [or more judges] in this state who are getting to make decisions about who lives and who dies, I just can't stomach it...And that's what it comes down to.
> (Elliott Young, 31 Years of Experience)

> I am philosophically, morally, emotionally, physically opposed to the death penalty so it angers me every time I have a case.
> (Tina Carter, CDL#4, 23 Years of Experience)

The moral outrage towards the death penalty (and the legal officials who sought it) provoked anger, and even physical discomfort, among participants. Elizabeth Horberg and colleagues' (2011) explanation for the role of emotions in moral judgement sheds light on the significance of anger and disgust in prioritizing political causes and social concerns. Injustices evoke feelings of anger; while concerns about impure behavior – what Durkheim might call profane behavior – evoke feelings of disgust (Horberg et al. 2011).

Participants' physical, stomach-turning rage, illustrates the depth of their anger for the injustice of capital punishment and their disgust towards the officials pursuing it. This anger and disgust motivated their work and is demonstrated by Evan Leeman's description of his visceral reaction to the death penalty process:

> I never thought the system was fair and equitable; in fact, I've always thought it to be an atrocity...For me, it is visceral. I cannot get past the fact that they are gonna drag a guy down the hall and stick a needle in his arm and kill him like a fucking dog. That is just morally wrong... fundamentally, it is an argument of decency and morality.
> (CDL#10, Evan Leeman, 18 Years of Experience)

Regarding our second theme of anger towards judges and prosecutors, we found that our participants' responses reveal an underlying sentiment of: How could we, *the American people*, an advanced, modern democratic society allow this injustice to continue? While participants' felt disgusted by the government's continued use of the death penalty, this negative response may have the added benefit for self-identity by boosting the virtue of their defense work (Horberg et al. 2011).

> I have a very difficult time sitting across the table from someone that wants to kill another human being and have a nice discussion. What motivated them to have the contention? I think it's – right or wrong – they believe they're on the moral high ground. I think it's political. [And] I think they're extremely judgmental.
> (Eric Mason, CDL#9, 33 Years of Experience)

> The public at large who really doesn't understand the criminal justice system but is so quick to pass judgment and takes sides in high profile cases. So, I get angry at that sometimes.
> (Gregory Matthews, CDL#8, 39 Years of Experience)

The continuing emotion of anger felt by the death penalty defense lawyers provided the motivation needed to continue the uphill legal battle within an unfriendly criminal justice system. The idea is that without the anger, the work would prove more difficult to endure. The rage provides the energy and motivation to continue the battle.

> [What keeps me doing this work is] the anger. It is my opposition to it that motivates me to fight this hard and to sacrifice what I do to fight it. I mean, it is physically exhausting and unhealthy to do this work. It is not good for your family. It is not good for your friends. It is not good for anyone who comes in contact with me when I have a death penalty

case…So, it is detrimental to my life to do this work, but.. now, I feel obligated to fight it even if it's not good for me.

(Tina Carter, CDL#4, 23 Years of Experience)

I've always felt like it is God's work in a sense. You know, righteous work, important work.

(Frank Stephens, CDL#3, 33 Years of Experience)

The majority of our participants felt that in one way or another anger fueled their work (Harrington 2000, cited in Schildkraut 2012). The feeling that the fight represents a higher calling may mean the personal sacrifices are worth it. Thus, the anger needed for this type of litigation serves to boost the moral value of the individual conducting the work (Goffman 1959). While emotional anger can push people towards action we found limited examples of these feelings caused some participants to feel uncomfortable. Mary Vinson explained:

I became a hater, and that's not who I wanted to be…I hate the fact that I hate.

Mary felt uncomfortable with the amount of anger she felt, and she found a way to remind herself to forgive and feel less hate for prosecutors, judges, and other death penalty supporters. She got a dog and named her Amnesty. She explained:

Everyone says, "Why did you name your dog Amnesty?" And I say, "Because I have got to remember to forgive everybody in the world. I have to have that sense of forgiveness." And I'm really struggling with that right now. So, I got this Chihuahua to remind me, and [I] named her [Amnesty] to remind me to be more forgiving and not to hate.

(Mary Vinson, CDL#1, 26 Years of Experience)

Conclusion

Death penalty defense attorneys navigate several paradoxes in their work, including upholding sacred society values of innocent until proven guilty and right to legal representation, while representing defendants who had committed profane or heinous criminal acts. What is the emotional toll of managing this irony? Sarat writes (1998: 318) "because lawyers use their professional skills to move law away from the daily reality of violence and toward a particular vision of the Good". These attorneys work for their individual clients, but also towards a larger calling for a good society.

As seen through the interviews of our participants the anger felt towards the death penalty comes from a personal view of what is 'moral' and 'right' in society. It is this anger that motivates the work but also serves to make the death penalty defense attorneys successful. All of our participants have secured life sentences for their clients even in the most highly publicized murder trials where commentators believed a death sentence was guaranteed.

Thus anger, along with empathy and sadness, is a part of the emotional culture of death penalty defense lawyers. It is unclear from our interviews if the anger is ever overtly expressed to anybody other than fellow death penalty defense lawyers. Furthermore, it is not clear if attorneys overtly expose empathy and sadness. It seems clear to us capital defense litigation is highly emotional and has a unique emotional culture. Therefore more work is needed in order to determine how emotional labor is being performed within the emotional culture practice of capital punishment defense.

References

Bandes, S. (1996). Empathy, narrative, and victim impact statements. *University of Chicago Law Review*, 63(2): 361–412.

Berman, D & Bibas, S. (2008). The heart has its value: The death penalty's justifiable persistence. *Faculty Scholarship at Penn Law*, 229. Https://scholarship.law.upenn.edu/faculty_scholarship/229

Blumberg, A. S. (1967). The practice of law as confidence game: Organizational cooptation of a profession. *Law & Society Review*, 1: 15–40.

Charmaz, K. (2006). *Constructing Grounded Theory: A Practical Guide Through Qualitative Analysis*. Thousand Oaks, CA: Sage.

Emmelman, D. S. (1998). Gauging the strength of evidence prior to plea bargaining: The interpretive procedures of court-appointed defense attorneys. *Law and Social Inquiry*, 22: 927–955.

Etienne, M. (2005). Criminal law: The ethics of cause lawyering: An empirical examination of criminal defense lawyers as cause lawyers. *Journal of Criminal Law and Criminology*, 95: 1195–1260.

Fineman, M. (2005). Feminist theory in law: The difference it makes. *Columbia Journal of Gender and Law*, 2(1): 1–24.

Flower, L. (2018). Doing loyalty: Defense lawyers' subtle dramas in the courtroom. *Journal of Contemporary Ethnography*, 47(2): 226–254.

Goffman, E. (1961). *Asylums: Essays on the Social Situation of Mental Patients and Other Inmates*. Chicago: Aldine Publishing.

Goodrum, S. & Stafford, M. C. (2003). The management of emotions in the criminal justice system. *Sociological Focus*, 36(3): 179–196.

Goodrum, S. (2011). Expecting an ally and getting a prosecutor. In: *Voices from Criminal Justice: Thinking and Reflecting on the System*, Eds. Copes, H. & Pogrebin, M. New York: Routledge Press, 198–218.

Goodrum, S. (2013). Bridging the gap between prosecutors' cases and victims' biographies in the criminal justice system through shared emotions. *Law & Social Inquiry*, 38(2): 257–287.

Goodpaster, G. (1983). The trial for life: Effective assistance of counsel in death penalty cases. *New York University Law Review*, 58: 299–362.

Gordon, S. (1989). Institutional and impulsive orientations in selectively appropriat-ing emotions to self. In: *The Sociology of Emotions: Essays and Research Papers*, Eds. Franks, D. D. & Doyle McCarthy, E. Greenwich, CT: JAI, 115–135.

Gould, J. & Barak, M. P. (2019). *Capital Defense: Inside the Lives of America's Death Penalty Lawyers*. New York: New York University Press.

Harrington, C. L. (2000). A community divided: Defense attorneys and the ethics of death row volunteering. *Law & Social Inquiry*, 25: 849–881.

Hochschild, A. R. (1983). *The Managed Heart: Commercialization of Human Feeling*. Berkley, CA: University of California Press.

Holstein, J. & Gubrium, J. (1995). *The Active Interview*. Thousand Oaks, CA: Sage Publications.

Horberg, E., Oveis, C., & Keltner, D. (2011). Emotions as moral amplifiers: An appraisal tendency approach to the influences of distinct emotions upon moral judgment. *Emotion Review*, 3(3): 237–244.

Lefcourt, G. B. (1996–1997). Responsibilities of a criminal defense attorney. *Loyola of Law Angeles Law Review*, 30: 59–68.

Lois, J. (2001). Peaks and valleys: The gendered emotional culture of edgewwork. *Gender and Society*, 15(3): 381–406.

Lois, J. (2005). *Heroic Efforts: The Emotional Culture of Search and Rescue Volunteers*. New York: New York University Press.

Lynch, M. & Haney C. (2014). Emotion, authority, and death: (Raced) Negotiations in capital jury deliberations. *Law & Social Inquiry*, 40(2): 377–405.

Mello, M. (1989). Another attorney for life. In: *Facing the Death Penalty: Essays on a Cruel and Unusual Punishment*, Ed. Radelet, M. (pp. 81–91). Philadelphia, PA: Temple University Press.

Mesquita, B. & Delvaux, E. (2012). A cultural perspective on emotional labor. In: *Emotional Labor in the 21st Century: Diverse Perspectives on emotion Regulation at Work*, Eds. Grandey, A., Diefendorff, J., & Rupp, D. New York: Routledge Publishing, 251–272.

Mihai, M. (2011). Emotions and the criminal law. *Philosophy Compass*, 6(9): 599–610.

Pogrebin, M. & Poole, E. (1990). Culture conflict and crime in the Korean-American community. *Criminal Justice Policy Review*, 4(1): 69–78.

Pogrebin, M. & Poole, E. (1991). Police and tragic events: The management of emo-tions. *Journal of Criminal Justice*, 19(4): 395–403.

Pugh, D., Diefendorff, J., & Moran, C. (2012). Organizational-level influences, strat-egies, and outcomes. In: *Emotional Labor in the 21st Century: Diverse Perspectives on emotion Regulation at Work*, Eds. Grandey, A., Diefendorff, J., & Rupp, D. New York: Routledge Publishing, 199–221.

Sarat, A. (1998). Between (the presence of) violence and (the possibility) of justice: Lawyering against capital punishment. In: *Cause Lawyering: Political Commitments and Professional Responsibilities*, Eds. Sarat, A. & Scheingold, S. New York: Oxford University Press.

Schildkraut, J. (2012). An inmate's right to die: Legal and ethical considerations in death row volunteering. *Criminal Justice Studies: A Critical Journal of Crime, Law and Society*, 26(2): 139–150.

Sevilla, C. (1995). April 20, 1992: A Day in the Life. https://paperity.org/p/83034551/april-20-1992-a-day-in-the-life.

Sheffer, S. (2013). *Fighting for Their Lives: Inside the Experience of Capital Defense Attorneys*. Nashville, TN: Vanderbilt University Press.

Skolnick, J. H. (1967). Social control in the adversary system. *The Journal of Conflict Resolution*, 11(1): 52–70.

Smith, A. & Kleinman, S. (1989). Managing emotions in medical school: Students' contacts with the living and the dead. *Psychology Quarterly*, 52(1): 56–69.

Sudnow, D. (1965). Normal crimes: Sociological features of the penal code in a public defender office. *Social Problems*, 12: 255–274.

Uphoff, R. J. (1992). Criminal defense lawyer: Zealous advocate, double agent, or beleaguered dealer? *Criminal Law Bulletin*, 28(5): 419–456.

Wolcott, H. F. (1994). *Transforming Qualitative Data: Description, Analysis, and Interpretation*. Thousand Oaks, CA: Sage.

Zaloznaya, M. & Nielsen, L. B. (2011). Mechanisms and consequences of professional marginality: The case of poverty lawyers revisited. *Law & Social Inquiry*, 36(4): 919–944.

Chapter 18

Conclusion

What do we now know about emotional labour in criminal justice? Culture, context and conflict

Jake Phillips, Chalen Westaby,
Andrew Fowler and Jaime Waters

Introduction

In the introduction to this volume we noted that emotional labour has been used as a lens with which to examine penal practice in most areas of criminal justice and criminology, but to varying degrees. We also argued that there had – thus far – been little attempt to bring this knowledge into a coherent publication/volume which we considered a real gap in the literature. Emotional labour is a powerful analytic lens which can shed light on how institutions function, their aims, how staff and service users will experience them and – more broadly – what criminal justice is 'all about'. Our aims for this collection, therefore, were to learn about where emotional labour has and has not been used in the field of criminal justice and criminology; to synthesise what literature there is; and to extend our knowledge. We gave our contributors some guidance in terms of what we wanted them to do: in Part One, the brief was to do a review of extant research, with a view to bringing out the main ways in which workers perform emotional in their allotted institution. In Part Two, the task was to extend what we already know through short empirical chapters which bring hitherto unexplored areas of criminal justice and criminology to the fore. Without exception, all contributors have risen to the challenge we set and for that we are grateful.

Rather than go over each chapter, in turn, we use this concluding chapter to identify and highlight some of the themes which cut across some – and indeed, in some cases, all – of the chapters.

The importance of culture

A constant theme throughout all chapters is the importance of culture. This is, perhaps, unsurprising considering culture – in many ways – shapes the occupational display rules which, in turn, govern the performance of emotional labour. The importance of having to understand display rules and the difficulty in doing so comes out in most of the chapters in Part Two. It seems that organisational and occupational display rules can be aligned but can also be in conflict. We see this most clearly in Borelli's chapter on immigration officers where they have to fulfil dual roles which have different aims. This, we would argue, makes it difficult for staff to know which rules to conform to, resulting in both inter- and intra-display rule conflict – see Chapter 3 for a particularly good example of this in the context of family lawyers. This also comes out clearly when we look to the hierarchical nature of many criminal justice organisations. Thus, we see different emotional labour expectations being placed upon people doing similar jobs with similar aims, but with differing statuses such as Special Constables in England and Wales (Chapter 16), and non-sworn officers in the US (Chapter 13).

There are deeply engrained cultural expectations (e.g. in the key criminal justice institutions of the police, prison and probation) which inform the emotional labour of workers. On the one hand, this can be beneficial for staff who are embarking on a new job in the sector because it allows them to learn – on the job – the occupational display rules which are at play. However, it raises potential detrimental effects for those who do not 'fit in' with these highly prescriptive display rules. We can see this particularly in relation to the chapter on Special Constables in England and Wales (Chapter 16). Special constables learn that they must quickly integrate into the 'regular' police workforce, which means conforming to police culture and the emotional labour expectations that come with it. Police culture is highly masculinised and limits recognition of its emotional demands and the need to access support.

Furthermore, in Chapter 5 where the focus is prisons, we see the importance of formal and informal feeling rules, again, in the perpetuation of a masculinised image (albeit at times an altered image of masculinity which does not conform to the tough, hardened masculinity) of prison officers. This has been seen to impact upon the type of emotional labour regarded as appropriate for male and female prison officers and the expectation to conform to those gender stereotypes.

Gender and emotional labour?

In her studies of air stewardesses and bill collectors, Hochschild (1983) highlighted the gendered nature of the concept, and the chapters in this book show that criminal justice is no exception. Masculinised working practices dominate certain criminal justice institutions and the emotional displays within. Furthermore, we see men and women doing gender in their work with men's emotional labour being more aligned with, while women perform work in more nurturing roles. However, there is little evidence that the gendered nature of emotional labour in criminal justice and criminology has been adequately nor comprehensively analysed and we urge researchers to focus on this area.

The importance of context

Related to the concept of culture, is the importance of context. What stands out throughout this book is the way in which contexts in criminal justice are changing and having a resultant impact on criminal justice sectors. Chapter 5 on the emotional labour of prison work brings this out particularly clearly. Moreover, there has – over recent years – been a steady move towards commercialisation and managerialism in almost all areas of criminal justice and this has put particular pressure on staff when it comes to the performance of emotional labour. In many cases, the display rules associated with heavily managerialised and commercialised institutions are at odds with the occupational display rules that emanate from work cultures, which are often the result of many years of shared practice. Thus, in Chapter 2, we saw evidence of police officers having to resist managerialism through the use of humour; in Chapter 4, the managerialisation of probation was considered crucial in the marginalisation of emotion in probation policy; and in Chapter 7, prison officers experienced and had to manage the conflict between their own emotions and the way in which the organisation's aims required them to manage their emotions. By ignoring the emotion work inherent to much criminal justice practice means workers conform to particular emotional labour expectations but with little guidance in how to do so. Ultimately, this also means that workers' emotions in the field of criminal justice are being increasingly appropriated in order to maximise profit for the organisations for whom they work: quite how this sits with those embedded cultures and values discussed above is in need for further exploration.

The omnipresence of conflict

It is evident from all chapters in this volume that criminal justice work requires the performance of emotional labour. But it is also the case that most criminal justice work requires some element of boundary spanning. Boundary spanning (Mastracci et al., 2012; Needham et al., 2017) requires practitioners who engage in collaborative work to adhere to a different set of display rules across organisational and professional boundaries at the same time and this can present particular issues for staff having to manage their emotions (Needham et al., 2017). A particularly good example of this can be seen in Chapter 6, by Quinn and Tomczak, on practitioners in the penal voluntary sector (PVS). They highlight the emotionally labourful working environment of PVS practitioners who are required to negotiate their way through different, and often dissimilar, display rules emanating from a variety of organisations. Furthermore, emotional labour is performed in such a way as to ensure that PVS practitioners are able to access criminal justice institutions such as prisons and other correctional facilities in order to enable them to work with service users. There is a need for organisations to explicitly recognise the boundary spanning nature of the work they demand from their staff, and support is undoubtedly required for staff working in settings where boundary spanning forms a part of their day-to-day work.

Criminal justice personnel work across institutional boundaries, but they also work across the boundary between the criminal justice system and the general public. Crime and punishment and criminalised people are emotive topics amongst the general public, and the political rhetoric around crime and justice is often designed to invoke strong emotions. Moreover, the rhetoric – especially in recent months in the English and Welsh context – has served to stigmatise those who have broken the law in particularly negative ways. In turn, this means that criminal justice work can increasingly be understood as a form of dirty work. Importantly, some of the chapters in this volume have highlighted the burden that this can place on people in terms of emotional labour, particularly in relation to societal display rules (although more research needs to be done in here in terms of teasing out this particular relationship), but also the ways in which they reframe or deflect their work in order to minimise it.

Emotional labour and the aims of criminal justice

The lens of emotional labour requires us to think about the aims of the organisation and the way in which staff members' emotions are being managed to achieve those aims. Whilst chapters in this book highlight the ways in which organisations appropriate emotions in order to achieve the formal aims of the organisation they also uncover the ways in which staff resist and even subvert those structures by managing their emotions in a way which sheds light on what else the criminal justice system is doing over and above what organisations want them to do. Thus, probation officers (Chapter 4) manage their emotions to achieve the goals of the organisation such as risk assessment but they also do so in order to convey empathy to offenders; immigration officers in Sweden (Chapter 14) display emotions to the 'irregular workers' in order to both decide whether they should be detained for breaches of immigration rules as well as to convey sympathy for the plight in which they find themselves in; and defence lawyers in Sweden (Chapter 12) convey neutrality to their clients in order to secure a successful outcome to the case but also in order to manage the expectations of their clients. It is here that the chapters in this book really get to the crux of the 'civic heart' which lies at the centre of much of this type of work (Guy et al., 2019).

Values and performing emotional labour

Many people in criminal justice – especially those working in prison, probation and the penal voluntary sector – adhere to the occupational and cultural values of believing in the ability of people to change. A key component of this cultural outlook is the belief that honesty and transparency are key to good work as that enables the creation of constructive professional relationships. Yet they also describe having to manage and conceal emotions from the people with whom they are working. Thus, work in criminal justice appears to be inherently distrustful and deceptive. In many respects this is the result of the contexts in which people work and comes from the need to manage the tensions and conflicts that exist between the different display rules which are at play (see, in particular the case study at the end of Chapter 3 on the Legal Professions). But that does not make it okay. There is an ethical dimension to this; there is the need for a debate about whether it is acceptable for staff who expect clients to be open and honest to be, at the same, dishonest by concealing emotions. Putting the ethics to one side, and looking at this through the lens of emotional labour serves to emphasise the complex emotional labour needed to conform to these competing display rules.

People engaged in the criminal justice system are there under duress and this makes truly genuine, open relationships difficult – some may say, impossible without the use of deep acting or genuine emotional displays. Yet, the question – is it possible to create policies and modes of practice that enable more genuine use of emotion possible? – is, in our view, worth asking because it requires workers to hold two different values at the same time. The chapters in this book shed light on the encounters which drive public service in a way which other modes of analysis do not but there is more work to be done in this particularly difficult area.

Next steps for emotional labour in criminal justice and criminology

It may seem trite to say that more research in this area is needed but, in this case, we genuinely believe that to be the case. This volume has highlighted some of the different ways in which performing emotional labour has had positive and negative effects on workers. However, the vast majority of studies cited in the chapters have been relatively small in scope. The book has shone a light on some under-researched groups of people such as special constables, defence lawyers and prison officers working with people at the end of their lives. Yet there are still important gaps and we would argue that future research needs to concentrate on identifying and filling those gaps in knowledge. Not only is most of the research in this book small in scale, but is also qualitative in approach (the only real exception is those data presented in Chapter 13). This is not the place to go over the pros and cons of different approaches to research (in any case, we would argue that qualitative and quantitative approaches result in different forms of knowledge and different levels of insights). However, we would argue that future research on emotional labour needs to adopt a dualistic or mixed methods approach to generating data. In terms of what the focus of this research should be, we would suggest beginning with the following: people doing different roles in organisations; comparative work between privatised and public sector providers (e.g. private versus public prisons); and studies which take explicit gendered and racialised perspectives.

And finally

All of the workers discussed in this book are affected – to varying degrees – by the demands placed upon them in terms of performing emotional labour as part of their work. As outlined in the introduction this type of work can have real – and potentially serious – consequences. Moreover, staff whose wellbeing is affected by their emotional labour are less likely to work as effectively as they could. They are more likely to become burnt out, are more likely to go off sick and, ultimately, are more likely to leave their jobs. Thus, the emotional labour demands of these jobs are important to understand as it enables organisations to better support their workforce which, in turn, will mean service users receive a 'better' service.

Policy makers can make emotional labour less burdensome in a range of ways – through more explicit recognition of the demands of the job, through support networks or with better training. Organisations should also look at reducing caseloads and limiting time spent at work, high rates of which are linked to burnout and compassion fatigue. Emotional labour is a lens which enables us to look critically at the way in which organisations appropriate workers' emotions for their own ends: it is a critical exercise which should serve to highlight the structures in which people work, rather than the strengths of the individuals within them. Thus, the burden for improving the situation should not be down to individuals. Some organisations are increasingly reliant on resilience building amongst their staff. While resilience is a useful skill to have, especially in the criminal justice system, we would instead argue that if organisations really want to improve the wellbeing of their staff then they need to address the cultures, contexts and conflicts (covered in this book) to make the performance of emotional labour in the criminal justice system and discipline of criminology less damaging. Once organisations commit to this then we should begin to see the emergence of a more humane, relational and effective system. Of course, it should go without saying that the primary – and ultimate – beneficiaries of such work will, and should, be victims and those who find themselves in conflict with the law. We hope that this volume goes some way to achieving this.

References

Guy, M.E., Mastracci, S.H. and Yang, S.B., eds. (2019). *The Palgrave Handbook of Global Perspectives on Emotional Labor in Public Service.* Cham: Springer Nature.

Hochschild, A.R. (1983). *The Managed Heart. Commercialization of Human Feeling.* Berkeley: University of California Press.

Mastracci. S.H., Guy, M.E. and Newman, M.N. (2012). *Emotional Labour and Crisis Response: Working on the Razor's Edge.* Armonk, NY: M.E. Sharpe.

Needham, C., Mastracci, S.H. and Mangan, C. (2017). The emotional labour of boundary spanning. *Journal of Integrated Care*, 25(4), 288–300.

Index

Note: Page numbers followed by "n" denote endnotes.